791.45
C436f

The Format Age
Television's Entertainment Revolution

JEAN K. CHALABY

D0556668

polity

Copyright © Jean K. Chalaby 2016

The right of Jean K. Chalaby to be identified as Author of this Work has been asserted in accordance with the UK Copyright, Designs and Patents Act 1988.

First published in 2016 by Polity Press

Polity Press
65 Bridge Street
Cambridge CB2 1UR, UK

Polity Press
350 Main Street
Malden, MA 02148, USA

All rights reserved. Except for the quotation of short passages for the purpose of criticism and review, no part of this publication may be reproduced, stored in a retrieval system, or transmitted, in any form or by any means, electronic, mechanical, photocopying, recording or otherwise, without the prior permission of the publisher.

ISBN-13: 978-1-5095-0258-5
ISBN-13: 978-1-5095-0259-2(pb)

A catalogue record for this book is available from the British Library.

Library of Congress Cataloging-in-Publication Data

Chalaby, Jean K.
  The format age : television's entertainment revolution / Jean K. Chalaby.
    pages cm. -- (Global media and communication)
  Includes bibliographical references and index.
  ISBN 978-1-5095-0258-5 (hardcover : alk. paper) -- ISBN 1-5095-0258-0 (hardcover : alk. paper) -- ISBN 978-1-5095-0259-2 (pbk. : alk. paper) -- ISBN 1-5095-0259-9 (pbk. : alk. paper)
  1. Television program genres. 2. Television programs--Social aspects. 3. Television and globalization. I. Title.
  PN1992.55C47 2015
  791.45'09--dc23
                              2015018308

Typeset in 11 on 13pt Adobe Garamond Pro by
Servis Filmsetting Ltd, Stockport, Cheshire
Printed and bound by Clays Ltd, St Ives plc

The publisher has used its best endeavours to ensure that the URLs for external websites referred to in this book are correct and active at the time of going to press. However, the publisher has no responsibility for the websites and can make no guarantee that a site will remain live or that the content is or will remain appropriate.

Every effort has been made to trace all copyright holders, but if any have been inadvertently overlooked the publisher will be pleased to include any necessary credits in any subsequent reprint or edition.

For further information on Polity, visit our website: politybooks.com

San Diego Christian College
Library
Santee, CA

The Format Age

Global Media and Communication

For Jane, my wife

Contents

Acknowledgements

In the process of researching this book, I was fortunate to receive support from many people. First, I would like to express my deep gratitude to all the interviewees for their time and cooperation (see full list of interviewees before the references at the end of the book). Their insights into the format business have been invaluable and my endeavour would not have been possible without their contributions, in particular those of the industry leaders that have opened doors for me and supported my work. I am also grateful to Dr Andrea Esser and Dr Gerd Hallenberger for help on Germany and Northern Europe, Professors Michele Hilmes and Tom O'Malley for insightful suggestions on early sound broadcasting adaptations, and Professor Gary Gerrefi for his expert comments on my global value chain analysis. Jane, my wife, expertly edited the manuscript and acted as a sounding board for my ideas, and I am indebted to her. I gratefully acknowledge Polity's anonymous readers for their constructive comments on the manuscript, and would like to thank Polity's editorial team, notably Andrea Drugan, who commissioned the work, Elen Griffiths and India Darsley, for their help throughout the publishing process, and Fiona Sewell for her wonderful support in the preparation of the manuscript. I am also grateful to Sheila Munton, City University London Library, Jeff Walden, BBC Written Archives Centre, the librarians at Radio France's Service Archives écrites et Musée, and my colleagues at City University London for the research leave that enabled me to finish this project. Last but not least, I would like to thank our three beautiful daughters, Felicity, Lucy and Jemima, for bearing with my absences during the final stages of this project.

Tables and Figures

Introduction

There are many reasons why TV formats – shows that are adapted to local audiences – deserve our full attention. Following a quiet fifty-year period, the format revolution that came with the new millennium suddenly transformed a small commerce that was lying at the fringe of the TV industry into a global business. Today, hundreds of shows are adapted across the world at any one time, reaching a cumulative value (in terms of distribution and production fees) of several billion dollars per year. In Europe alone, the income that broadcasters have generated from the top 100 formats reached US$2.9 billion in 2013 (*TBI Formats*, 2014a: 23). From a handful of companies in the 1990s, hundreds create, produce, distribute or acquire TV formats, with one firm alone, ITV Studios Global Entertainment, selling more than 4,300 hours' worth of format in 2013 (*TBI Formats*, 2014a: 23).

The impact of formats on television is manifold, starting with TV schedules. In Europe, eighty-four channels aired 28,386 hours of formats in 2013 (the equivalent of 338 hours per channel) (*TBI Formats*, 2014a: 23). It is estimated that around a third of primetime programmes scheduled by American and German commercial broadcasters has been bought or sold for adaptation (Esser, 2013). In many a market, the top-rating shows and innovative cross-platform programmes, from game shows to talent competitions, are often formats. And gone are the times when trade was limited to reality and light entertainment: fiction has caught up. Telenovelas, dramas, crime series and comedies have joined the format revolution and are being remade across borders.

The TV format business is deepening media globalization on several counts. It has added volume and complexity to international TV flows. Finished programming still travels well but the format business has spawned a new market for the intellectual property (IP) that lies within TV shows. It is furthering the transnational interdependence of TV firms across the world by leading to the formation of a trading system that is global in scope (chapter 4). The system has not only enabled the emergence of the first TV production majors (chapter 6), but connected local broadcasters to a global value chain. These broadcasters used to be entirely nation-bound: their market was heavily protected against foreign competition, they aimed at self-sufficiency (producing much of what they aired) and their few suppliers were domestic (apart from the Hollywood studios). Today, even though they may still operate in a national market, they act as buyers in a global value chain and have many more international suppliers than in the past. They also make programming and scheduling decisions based on the ratings performance of shows in other territories.

Finally, the study of the TV format trade gives us an opportunity to shed light on the complex interaction between culture, globalization and capitalism. This book will argue that the TV format business can only be understood if economic history is taken into consideration, because the core engine of media globalization is the expansion of the capitalist world-system into IP trading. History partly explains why TV formats tend to travel on particular routes and why the format trading system reproduces features and patterns of earlier trades. History can also enlighten us on the likely cultural impact of TV formats, as their relationship with local cultures seems to follow patterns established by commodities made global by earlier trade routes.

Global media studies present many theoretical and methodological challenges. For several decades, the international communication field was suffused with methodological nationalism and its operating concepts were shaped by the politics of the nation-state. It was not so long ago that the exponents of the cultural imperialism thesis asserted that 'powerful forces have been trespassing over national boundaries on an unprecedented scale' and that 'the preservation of national sovereignty may be understood best as a step in the still larger struggle to break the domination of the world business system' (Nordenstreng and Schiller, 1979: ix and xii). Others pondered whether nations could retain control over television 'in the face of foreign broadcasting' (Negrine, 1988: 1). The institutions that commissioned international communication studies, such as UNESCO, were themselves a theatre of conflicting national interests and saw the world through the prism of the nation-state (Chalaby, 2007).

The discipline of international communication had to disentangle itself progressively from a nation-centric discourse. Once the myths of the cultural imperialism thesis were dispelled (e.g. Ang, 1985; Fejes, 1981; Liebes and Katz, 1993; Sinclair et al., 1996; Stevenson, 1984; Tomlinson, 1991; Tracey, 1985; Tunstall, 1977) a new paradigm could emerge, one less fearful of change and better equipped to face the complexities of global media. Attention began to be given to regional and transnational media flows (including those from the Global South to the West), the formation of hybrid cultures drawn from different locales, the phenomena of transnationalization and deterritorialization, and migrant media and transnational audiences (e.g. Chalaby, 2009; García Canclini, 1995; Gillespie, 1995; Thussu, 2007; Tomlinson, 1999).

Despite considerable progress, some international communication scholars felt that the new globalization paradigm needed to be rooted in a firm theoretical basis. It is in this context that Ulrich Beck's cosmopolitan outlook began to be discussed, as illustrated by Robins and Aksoy:

> We are interested in developments and possibilities that move us beyond the national frame. We would situate our research agenda in the context of the cosmopolitan project addressed by Ulrich Beck. . . .Like Beck, we recognize that, in social research, the shift away from methodological nationalism will require us to radically scrutinize the naturalized categories of modern social science, which has been very much *national* social science – categories that now exist as 'zombie categories' [Beck, 2002: 24]. For if one sees and thinks through a national grid, then one is always likely to see national things – and we will argue that a great deal of research on transnational phenomena does precisely this. (Robins and Aksoy, 2005: 15–16)

According to the late German sociologist, methodological nationalism fails to grasp the ramifications of the process of globalization, which 'not only alters the interconnectedness of nation-states and national societies but the internal quality of the social' (Beck, 2000: 87). 'Political, economic and cultural action and their (intended and unintended) consequences know no border' and thus the 'challenge is to devise a new syntax, the syntax of cosmopolitan reality' (Beck, 2006: 18). This syntax is a perspective – a 'vision' – that does not take for granted the congruence between national societies and economic, social and political realities that have acquired a transnational dimension and which transform these societies from within.

However, despite Beck's growing influence in international communication (e.g. Chalaby, 2009: 3; McCabe, 2013: 3), issues with the cosmopolitan outlook made it unsuitable for this study. Beck adopted a theoretical position that is normative in character and seeks to influence Europe's political future as much as to analyse globalizing processes. As noted by Victor Roudometof, the notion of cosmopolitanism and related concepts are 'prescriptive terms' that 'engage in the process of simultaneously assessing a pervasive feature of modern life and proposing ways policy-makers should deal with this reality' (Roudometof, 2005: 116). The problem with this discursive strategy is both epistemological and methodological, as it affects the objectivity of the interpretative perspective and the instruments with which the social is measured. Too often with Beck, the line is blurred between the social reality that is claimed to be interpreted and the reality that normative concepts imagine into being. Second, apart from wishing for a 'pacifist and cosmopolitan capitalism', Beck has remarkably little to say about the economic dimension of globalization (Beck, 2005: 59–64).

An alternative theoretical framework was selected for this research that has to deliver on three objectives: to help us understand the historical evolution of the format trade, to explain the dynamic of the globalizing processes and to give insight into the commercial and industrial strategies of economic agents. This theoretical framework also needed to have the potential to make further contributions in international communication.

Whilst some of these objectives could be shared by political economists, deficiencies that lie at the core of their approach make it wholly unsuitable for the study of global media. As Nicholas Garnham, a pioneer of the political economy school, states: 'much current PE [political economy] is underpinned by a crude and unexamined romantic Marxist rejection of the market per se, which has blocked analysis of how actual markets work and with what effects' (Garnham, 2011: 42). A contribution was unlikely from an approach that 'has become a euphemism for a vague, crude, and unself-questioning form of Marxism, linked to a gestural and self-satisfied, if often paranoid, radicalism' (Garnham, 2011: 42).

This study, however, resides within a research tradition Garnham terms the 'historical materialist analysis of the cultural sphere' (Garnham, 2011: 41), and its theoretical underpinning is provided by a body of literature initially labelled global commodity chain (GCC) analysis, later evolving into global value chain (GVC) theory (Bair, 2009; Gereffi et al., 1994; Sturgeon, 2009). The benefits of the GVC approach will soon become apparent, but in short it gives us the possibility of understanding how the TV format trading system is organized at a global level and how the interplay between economic agents continuously reshapes it. It gives us an insight into the role of places and institutions, production patterns and trade routes, the power distribution within the TV format chain and the impact of regulation, national or otherwise. Above all, the GVC framework enables us to unfold the inner logic of media globalization and unveil one of its key engines. As the World Trade Organization (WTO) notes, as 'companies divide their operations across the world, from the design of the product and manufacturing of components to assembly and marketing', 'international production networks or global value chains' have become a mark of our times (WTO, 2013: 181). Today, trade within these chains is worth more than half the total value of non-fuel global exports: the WTO estimates that trade in intermediate goods was worth US$7,723 billion in 2011, or 55 per cent of world non-fuel exports (WTO, 2013: 182–3). This book tells the story of the formation of a new trade and the creation of a new global value chain.

The GVC approach was developed by Gary Gereffi and colleagues but was initiated by Hopkins and Wallerstein (Hopkins and Wallerstein, 1986). As is well known, the father of world-systems theory was inspired by Fernand Braudel, who was also called upon to theorize the TV format trade as a transnational singular space (chapter 4). A fundamental methodological principle laid down by Braudel and the Annales School as a whole was also selected for this study: *l'observation concrète*, as he called it, comes before theory and ideology. While Braudel acknowledged the contribution of theoretical models, only a thorough empirical analysis of the observable reality, he argued, can reveal trends and patterns previously unnoticed. He contended that it is only after carefully studying the economic data and statistics of pre-industrial Europe that he noticed how little connection there was between this period and the grand theories that claimed to understand it (Braudel, [1967] 1992: 23). This basic principle is rarely observed in contemporary media studies, a discipline where academics too often appoint themselves judges of good taste and guardians of democracy.

The benefits of following this approach are extensive yet counter-intuitive. Lucien Febvre, the co-founder of the Annales School with Braudel, applied this method with spectacular success in his seminal *The Coming of the Book*. Febvre and co-author Martin (who carried out the project following Febvre's death) were among the first to understand how the advent of the printed book transformed the Western world and helped bring about modernity by augmenting available material and creating *un système perspectif nouveau* (Febvre, 1997: 10). But they also knew that printing was a fledgling industry and the printed book a commodity, and meticulously described how printers, authors, tradesmen and booksellers went about their business and how the whole industry developed across Europe, from printing workshops to book fairs.

As will be seen, TV formats are complex and multi-faceted products whose study benefits from a multi-disciplinary approach. Thus, this book complements the GVC framework with concepts borrowed from anthropology, sociology, management studies and narrative studies. It also draws from the body of literature on the creative industries (including texts from the earlier 'cultural industries' label), as this research aims to analyse the globalization of television in the wider context of rapid industrial and technological change that is happening across these industries (e.g. Flew, 2012, 2013; Garnham, 2005; Hesmondhalgh, 2013; Holt and Perren, 2009; Lacroix and Tremblay, 1997b; Kunz, 2007; Lotz, 2007; Miller, 2011; Winseck, 2012).

The book is organized in three parts: the first is devoted to the history of trade, the second to the format business in a global context, and the third to

TV formats themselves. Chapter 1 traces back the origins of the TV format trade, uncovering the world's first deals and identifying the first TV formats. Gathering evidence from previously unseen BBC written archives, this chapter shows how the key principles of the format business were established as early as the 1950s. It also contends that the TV format industry can be labelled an Anglo-American invention because the first format licences were exchanged between British and American broadcasters. Then, this chapter examines the next stage in the history of the trade and analyses how the 1978 Goodson Worldwide Agreement opened up the US game-show era.

The foundations of today's multi-billion-dollar industry that comes with trade bodies, awards ceremonies in Cannes, and formats that travel around the world at blazing speed and top ratings in fifty-plus territories were laid down in the 1990s. Chapter 2 examines the factors behind the TV format revolution that unfolded with the new millennium. How did the first super-formats sweep the world, and why did a fifty-year-old fringe activity become so central to the TV industry in the space of a few years? As always, profound changes were triggered by a powerful congruence of factors.

Although formats were crossing borders in growing numbers by the end of the 1990s, many TV executives needed the rise of the super-formats in order to take notice. Supported by exclusive interviews with their creators, chapter 3 tells the story of four exceptional formats that changed the face of television: *Who Wants to Be a Millionaire?*, *Survivor*, *Big Brother* and *Idols*.

Part II begins with chapter 4, which offers an in-depth study of the formation of the *TV format trading system*. The chapter opens with an examination of the globalization of the trade in the 2000s, analysing the format traffic figures that reveal a complex trade flow. It also looks at the arrival of new firms in the business and the organizations, including market fairs, the trade press and trade associations, which support that system.

The chapter then focuses on the *global value chain* that lies at the system's core and which is the outcome of the process of *disintegration of production* that took place in the TV industry. The chapter determines the chain's input–output structure and scrutinizes its governance, examining the balance of power between buyers and suppliers. It then establishes the chain's geographical configuration, identifying three tiers of format exporters and the trade routes along which many formats travel. Then, considering the chain's institutional framework, this chapter argues that the format trade has begun to be protected by an embryonic international regulatory regime and that it stands on firmer legal ground than ever before. The viability of this trade rests almost entirely on the recognition of IP rights that are increasingly acknowledged by courts of law around the world.

A startling aspect of the TV format revolution has been the emergence of a new trade leader: the UK. In a short timeframe, a country used to relying heavily on US imports has turned itself into the world's leading format exporter. Chapter 5 argues that the UK should be considered as the international benchmark for upgrading strategies in the TV content sector and posits the following question: can this process be duplicated elsewhere? This chapter assesses the upgrading strategies of those nations that have embarked on the journey from the local production of imports to the local creation of formats.

Chapter 6 analyses the modern *production* of TV formats, arguing that a new business model has emerged in recent years. In the early decades of the TV format trade, rights holders simply sold a show's licence to a local production company or broadcaster who would then adapt and produce it for a local audience. Many formats are still produced under licence but firms increasingly favour a new production model: wherever possible, rights holders prefer to adapt and produce their shows themselves in as many markets as possible, a strategy that has in turn led to the international expansion of TV production companies.

First, this chapter offers an overview of the international production model, tracing back its origins and exploring its development in recent years. It shows how it was pioneered by game-show producers before being adopted by British independent production companies and European broadcasters, and eventually by Hollywood studios. The chapter argues that this model is a key factor in the two recent waves of sector consolidation that led to the emergence of the first *international TV production majors*. The second part contextualizes it, arguing that TV production companies have had to adapt to the *globalization of the IP market* created by the format trading system. Using interviews with TV executives and creative leaders, this section reviews the risks and benefits associated with this model in terms of IP generation, exploitation and protection.

The final part of the book explores key contemporary trends in the TV format trade. Chapter 7 opens up with a brief analysis of the relationship between the format industry and TV genres, examining how the trade has progressed from game shows to reality to fiction. It then provides an overview of key formats in the game-show genre and across three reality strands: observational documentaries, factual entertainment and reality competitions. Close attention is paid to the narrative structure of these shows and, illustrating the argument with material gathered in interviews, this chapter explains how the TV industry has learnt to tell a story without a script.

Chapter 8 focuses on a key reality strand for the format trade: talent competitions. It analyses their narrative structure and, in order to understand their essence, it compares and contrasts them with hero myths from other civilizations. This chapter also explores the emergence of the TV franchise, that is, a format that no longer merely crosses borders but also platforms.

Chapter 9 focuses on the format trade in the scripted space, which covers the full spectrum of serials (soaps, series and telenovelas) and scripted genres from drama and comedy to constructed reality programming. The binarism between scripted and unscripted programmes may appear blunt as shows labelled by the industry as 'unscripted' may in fact be partially scripted; however, I use these labels to align with the trade.[1] The industry grew on the back of unscripted (or partly scripted) shows, and while the TV format revolution initially bypassed scripted formats, their number has risen sharply of late. Analysing both the reasons for this late rise and the factors behind it, this chapter shows that the adaptation of scripted formats is more complex and risks remain higher than for other genres. The underlying economics of their production and distribution also differs from non-scripted formats. When demand for drama increased worldwide, Hollywood studios began to mine their catalogues, new exporters and scripted genres emerged, and knowledge transfer techniques improved.

The conclusion connects this study with theories of international communication and makes an intervention in the debate between proponents of media imperialism and cosmopolitan globalization. It also assesses the cultural impact of the TV format trade.

What Is a TV Format?

Formats are notoriously difficult to fathom. Cynics say that a format is any show that anyone is willing to pay for, and some lawyers claim there is no such thing as a format since ideas cannot be copyrighted. Formats are indeed complex and multi-faceted cultural commodities that can be defined in four dimensions.

The TV format as a licensed remake

First and foremost, a TV format is a show based on the format rights of an existing show, that is, a *remake produced under licence.* This aspect is revealed clearly in the following two definitions by Christoph Fey, former managing director of the Format Recognition and Protection Association (FRAPA): a format is 'a recipe for "making remakes"' and format trading is 'the selling of *remake rights* which enable buyers to produce a local remake of the original programme tailored to suit their domestic television market' (EBU, 2005: 3).

Format rights emerged in the 1950s (chapter 1) and while their legal foundations have progressed they are not always respected and protected (chapter 4). A leading UK-based distributor (the company has asked not to be mentioned) defines format rights, for their own purpose, as follows:

> 'Format Rights' means (a) the right to license third parties outside the territory of the Primary Broadcaster the right to develop and produce one or more New Programmes based on the Format; (b) the right to authorize such third parties to distribute, exhibit, perform, broadcast or otherwise exploit such New Programmes in the territory where the New Programmes are produced in perpetuity; and (c) the right for Distributor to exploit the New Programmes in any media worldwide and/or license such right to a third party. (2012)

These rights exist alongside others, which include:

1. *Ancillary rights* are all the rights to exploit a programme (or any elements thereof in whole or in part) in any media, and comprise merchandising rights, interactive and multimedia rights, music publishing rights, online rights, publishing rights, radio rights, record rights, stage rights and theatric rights.
2. *Clip sales rights* (the right to sell or license extracts from the programme for inclusion in other programmes or other media).
3. *Television rights* cover broadcaster new media rights, collecting society rights, interactive television rights, non-theatric rights and video-on-demand rights.
4. *Video rights* (meaning the right to manufacture, duplicate, promote, distribute and sell or rent the programme on or in a videogram such as videocassette, DVD, UMD, CD ROM and any other similar device).

When a legal issue arises, not all TV formats are equal before the law. Scripted formats are the most easily protectable because ideas are expressed in simply identifiable storylines and characters, whilst the rules and structure of a reality show can be difficult to safeguard against copyright infringement. The point was made by Fey when commenting on a 2003 judgement by the German Supreme Court which stipulated that copyright laws cannot be applied to TV formats:

> We hope to use the analogy of the novel [in future legal cases] to prove that formats are copyrightable. Intellectual properties like novels go beyond words on the page but are about the characters and their relationships. Similarly, TV formats should be seen as a narrative of televisual events arranged in a time sequence. (in Waller, 2005)

It explains why FRAPA's own definition places the emphasis on storytelling: 'In the making of a television program, an ordering of television elements such that a distinctive narrative progression is created' (Gilbert, interview 2008). Indeed, as will be detailed in chapters 7 and 8, unscripted formats create and organize a narrative similarly to fiction:

> *Supernanny, Faking It, Wife Swap, The Apprentice, Secret Millionaire* and *Grand Designs* – all giants of the reality genre. All have very clear first and last acts – a call to action and a final judgment – but between them too, within the constraints of reality they're derived from, the same structure as Shakespeare, as Terence and as Horace. In all you can see the pattern – initial enthusiasm, goals achieved, things falling apart, catastrophe faced and victory snatched from the jaws of defeat. The king of them all, *The X Factor*, works by following a very clear – if elongated – act structure; in fact all reality television is built on classic Shakespearean shape. (Yorke, 2013: 195)

Among the differences is the way the story is engineered. Unscripted formats replace the script with an *engine* (Keane and Moran, 2008). The engine is essentially the set of rules and format points designed to create *dramatic arcs* and *storylines*. Format points are the distinctive elements (which may or may not be entirely original) that support the storytelling. They can be an object (e.g. the piles of cash in *Money Drop*), a particular task or challenge in a factual entertainment show, or a special feature such as the swivel chairs in *The Voice*. The classic reality engine is the elimination process, which can be structured in countless ways and organized around a variety of format points to suit different competitions. Drama is also created with *trigger moments* (also known as 'jeopardy' moments), the equivalent of cliffhangers in fiction. In reality programming, such moments are produced by unexpected twists or nomination nights; in quiz shows, jeopardy is generated with questions worth a large sum of money; in talent competitions, such moments occur when the presenter announces the outcome of the public vote. Finally, reality shows also build a dramatic arc around the protagonist's transformation (Yorke, 2013: 196), whether it is a process of self-discovery (e.g. *Wife Swap*), the opening up of a new career (e.g. *MasterChef*) or the journey to fame (e.g. *Got Talent*). Using different techniques, both scripted and unscripted formats tell stories (chapters 7 and 8).

The TV format as a recipe

The TV format as a *recipe* covers two ideas. First, it points to the fact that a format combines a kernel of rules and principles that are immutable and elements that are adaptable as it travels. This is the most common definition. For instance, Albert Moran, an Australian scholar who pioneered format studies, equates a format to a 'cooking recipe', that is, a 'set of invariable elements in a programme out of which the variable elements of an individual episode are produced' (Moran, 2006: 20). Michel Rodrigue, a 1990s industry pioneer, explains that:

> A format is a recipe. A format is not a product, it is a vehicle, and thus the only *raison d'être* of formats is the international market. [. . .] the format is a vehicle which enables an idea to cross boundaries, cultures, and so on, and to be localized in every place where it stops. (Rodrigue, interview 2008, my translation)

These elements are succinctly echoed by Nadine Nohr, chief executive officer of Shine International: 'you have a recipe and you can migrate it around the world and ad lib the sensibilities' (Nohr, interview 2013). These quotes hint at the transnational nature of format trading. Since the licence of a programme cannot be bought twice in the same territory (in the same period of time), a show becomes a format only once adapted outside its country of origin. But formats do not merely fly across borders: they change as they do so and always involve an interplay between the local and the global. Format rules might be global but their adaptation is local. Formats acknowledge both the universality of great ideas and the perennial nature of local cultures and languages.

As a recipe, a TV format is also a formula, an idea which is best illustrated with the analogy of sport. A football game is played according to rules established by an international association. These rules – the engine – set how the game is played, where it is played (the size of the pitch) and for how long. Let's now take a football game played in a local competition. Supporters pay for their season ticket beforehand, journalists put the game in their diaries and the TV rights are sold years in advance. Everything is set: the date, the place, the duration and even the promise of a resolution. What is a football game? A stage set for a specific outcome, an arena for *managed* and *reliable unpredictability*, as is a TV format. In the words of David Liddiment, former director of programmes at ITV, co-founder of All3Media and BBC trustee:

> Stephen Lambert [creator of some of the world's leading formats in factual entertainment] worked out that what broadcasters want is they want to know the outcome, they don't want to commission a film with an outcome they don't know. So what a format does is it creates an outcome, it creates an arc, a story and it does it week in week out, so you can manufacture it like a production line. So what starts as a form, which is a singular individual voice, the documentary becomes part of factory television. (Liddiment, interview 2011)

This applies to all (good) TV formats. For instance, talent competitions do not need to concoct a winner. For the broadcaster, it is enough to know that the format rules will generate drama during the process and an outcome at the end. A TV format is 'about creating moments with absolute certainty that something interesting will happen and having the camera in the right place to capture it' (Liddiment, interview 2011). Like a football game!

The TV format as a proof of concept

Outcome management is one good reason that has made the TV format trade a multi-billion-dollar business, and another is *risk management*. The format industry rests on a compelling premise: *the willingness of broadcasters to pay for the privilege of outsourcing risk.* Formats do not travel alone and are preceded by ratings data that TV buyers browse before committing themselves. This data details the show's performance in a large array of territories, scheduling scenarios, channels and audiences. Performance in some countries matters more than in others and TV executives look for ratings on channels similar to theirs (public service, youth-skewed, etc.) (chapter 4). If the show's ratings performance is internationally consistent, it indicates that the structure of the programme is solid – the proof of concept – and buyers like to think that an adaptation will perform equally well in their territory. A track record does not offer them a guarantee of success but will at least enable them to manage risk.

The TV format as a method of production

Acquiring a format licence is a way of getting hold of a show that has been in development for several years and produced in several other countries. This accumulated knowledge is part of the format package and a licensing agreement leads to a significant transfer of expertise. Licensees obtain a document that is known as the 'production bible' which teaches local teams everything they need to know in order to produce the show. These can run to hundreds of pages and contain information about run-throughs, budgets, scripts, set designs, graphics, casting procedures, host profile, the selection of contestants, and every other possible aspect associated with the show's production.

Bibles also lay out the format rules, determining the elements that can be altered and those which must remain intact. As already seen, formats are geared up to hit specific points throughout the narrative and are constructed to take viewers through a succession of emotional states. As with civil engineering, miscalculating a pressure point can lead to the collapse of the entire edifice. Thus, a bible is intended to protect the show's mechanics and guard against ill-thought-out modifications.

Production bibles contain a certain amount of local knowledge. These documents can be updated with information accumulated in the territories where the show is produced. If an idea that is tried in a market works, it is passed on; if it fails, licensees are warned against it. As Sue Green, an industry veteran, explains, a format is a show that has been 'debugged' to remove 'the mistakes that have been made that won't be made again' (Green, interview 2010). Therein lies the third reason behind the extraordinary growth of the format business: as production is being refined from one territory to another – and from one year to the next – costs are gradually driven down. The refinement of the production model, which is consigned to the bible, constitutes one of the key economic benefits of format licensing.

Information is also passed on by consultant producers (sometimes known as 'flying' producers), whose role it is to help local teams set up the show. They will stay on site as long as necessary, as their remit is governed by the complexity of the show. If the show is still produced in its country of origin, local teams can be invited to visit the original set. Leading brands such as *The Bachelor*, *Come Dine with Me* and *Dancing with the Stars* organize international conferences for local licensees and share knowledge (interviews with producers, clips of local episodes, videos of the set layout, etc.) on intranet websites.

A successful transfer of expertise is in the interest of all parties. Formats are bought with the hope of ratings success and licensees need to understand the show's principles as well as they can. Getting a local hit is equally important for the vendor because a ratings failure in a major territory can damage a format's prospects. The heads of acquisitions and programming that scan the world TV market can lose interest in a show if they sense any sign of weakness (Clark, interview 2008). I would define the formatting process thus: *a TV format is the structure of a show that can generate a distinctive narrative and is licensed outside its country of origin in order to be adapted to local audiences.*

Discovering the 'Material Life' of the TV Format Trade (Methodological Note)

Without neglecting the academic literature, this study privileges primary sources in order to uncover new practices and processes, reveal current trends and enrich the theoretical debate with new findings. It relies on two ranges of sources: trade press and trade reports, and in excess of sixty interviews that were conducted over a six-year period. Many were conducted in London but my interviewees cover a wide range of countries and industry roles from creative leaders to high-ranking executives. There are many benefits to interviews, apart from the fact that they are exclusive to this research. First, they are the only way of gathering information about facts and occurrences that so far are not in the public space. Hypotheses can be checked, theories can be tested and anecdotes can be collected. Seemingly minute details and trivial episodes can turn out to be important pieces of the puzzle and be invaluable in the reconstruction of the chain of events. Interviews also offer an insight into personal impressions and experiences that are also part of the industry. Only format creatives know how they stumbled upon an idea, who helped them develop it and what commissioners told them behind closed doors. Industry leaders with decades of experience are often reflective about their trade, and those who were kind enough to share their wisdom made a great contribution to this research. Interviews made it possible to discover the 'material life', to follow Febvre and Braudel, of the TV format trade and depict an altogether intimate and accurate picture of this industry.

In any study of the creative industries, there will be a tension between the 'model of the creative genius' that leans on 'atomistic concepts of human nature and human action' and structural approaches that lay emphasis on 'social and market structures and regulation that shape innovations, and creativity, and their success and failure' (Pratt and Jeffcutt, 2009: 267). Although 'individuals are a primary source of creativity' (Jeffcutt and Pratt, 2002: 226), interviews can exacerbate the danger of attributing too much weight to agency and couch history in terms of the choices and opportunities available to creators and industry leaders. This risk, however, is countered by the global value chain framework, which is both historical and structuralist in scope.

Finally, some material in this book is based on previously published articles, notably in the *European Journal of Communication*, the *International Communication Gazette*, the *Journal of Media Business Studies*, *Media, Culture & Society* and *Television & New Media*. However, a great deal of research has taken place since these publications and this text completes, and sometimes corrects, these articles.

Part I

Birth of a New Trade

1   TV Formats as an Anglo-American Invention

This chapter traces back to the origins of the TV format trade, uncovering those first deals and identifying the first formats to be aired across Europe. It shows how the key principles of the format industry were established by the early 1950s and contends that it is an Anglo-American invention, because the first format licences were adaptations of US shows acquired by British broadcasters. This chapter surveys the evolution of the trade up until the US game-show era, which started with the 1978 Goodson Worldwide Agreement.

The World's First TV Format Agreements

Cross-border adaptations began in the sound broadcasting era and versions of US shows appeared on the BBC in the late 1920s. Adaptations also travelled to several Commonwealth countries, particularly Australia and Canada. *Major Bowes' Original Amateur Hour* was an early favourite. A talent show that first aired in New York in 1934, it was adapted by the BBC in 1936 and four years later by a commercial station in Australia (Camporesi, 2000: 92, 119–20; Griffen-Foley, 2009: 212, 260). In March 1937, the BBC showed a version of an NBC contest called *Spelling Bees* and then, two years later, its first quiz show, *Information, Please* (also from NBC), which became *The Brains Trust* on the Corporation's Home Service (Camporesi, 2000: 121–4). For the British broadcaster, the United States was a steady source of inspiration despite an overall ambivalent attitude towards American entertainment. The programmes selected by the BBC were popular, hence the rather acerbic comments published in *Radio Pictorial* in March 1938:

> Why is it that the B.B.C. has been so slow to appreciate the appeal of this form of entertainment, and so loath to follow where America leads the way? The B.B.C. has its own representative in New York whose job is to pick up new ideas for transportation over here, and famous variety chiefs such as Eric Maschwitz have been in constant touch with the American studios. Yet the Spelling Bee was a radio feature for many years in the States before it was given its tardy radio debut in this island. It is the same story of the 'Amateur Hour' all over again. (cited in Camporesi, 2000: 122)

While it is unlikely that licences were acquired for these unscripted shows, scripts legally changed hands in the sound broadcasting era, and the Australian radio stations purchased scripts of the American dramas they were adapting in the 1930s (Griffen-Foley, 2009: 212–16). In the next two decades, when Havana was Latin America's broadcasting hub, Cuban scripts for radionovelas travelled across the region. This trade was started by US advertising agencies, such as J. Walter Thompson and McCann-Erickson, interested in generating audiences in which to advertise the products of their clients (which included General Motors and Procter & Gamble) (Rivero, 2009). It was Richard Penn, an American radio specialist who worked on the marketing of Colgate-Palmolive, who brought the first Cuban script to Brazil. *Em busca da felicidade* [*In Search of Happiness*] aired in 1941 on Ràdio Nacional, establishing a model for future local adaptations in the region based on international formats (McCann, 2004: 217–18).

After the Second World War, the BBC returned to America for ideas, and the world's first format to air on television (albeit only once) was a comedy panel radio show called *It Pays to Be Ignorant*, which premiered on WOR New York in June 1942 and made its US TV debut on CBS in June 1949 (Schwartz et al., 1999: 103–4). The show had come to the attention of Michael Standing, the BBC Light Programme's head of variety, who insisted colleagues listen to a recording. They agreed that it was 'hilariously funny' and decided to purchase the UK rights from Maurice Winnick, a Manchester-born bandleader who represented in the UK the interests of some American radio and TV producers.[1]

The BBC retitled the show *Ignorance Is Bliss* and paid Sid Colin 40 guineas per episode to adapt the American scripts. It debuted on 22 July 1946 on the Light Programme and went on to be a notable success. Several series were recommissioned and the programme stayed on air until 1953.[2] A one-off television broadcast took place on 24 April 1947 that came live from the Paris Cinema in central London.[3] Before the performance went ahead, however, the BBC's programme contracts director had to assuage the fears of panellists by promising them to 'adhere to the undertaking that they will not be asked to take any notice of the television cameras or modify their normal performance in any way whatsoever.'[4]

This was followed by *Twenty Questions*: a quiz show based on the parlour game, it required a five-strong panel to guess the identity of an object in up to twenty questions. It premiered on the Mutual radio network in February 1946 and on American television (NBC) in November 1949 (Buxton and Owen, 1972: 314–15; Schwartz et al., 1999: 239). It crossed the Atlantic as a radio show airing on the BBC on 26 February 1947, with Winnick holding the UK rights again. The show proved very popular, attracting up to 9 million listeners, and was recommissioned for several series.[5] In 1950 it was translated and broadcast on the Polish and Pakistani services. However, despite approaches from the BBC's Television Service in 1951 and 1954, *Twenty Questions* never made it to the small screen because of a dispute with Winnick over rights (see next section).[6]

What's My Line? was the first format to cross borders as a TV show. It began on 2 February 1950 on the CBS network and required four panellists to solve the problem of a guest's occupation, with the guest's replies to their questions limited to yes or no. *What's My Line?*, created by Bob Bach and produced by Mark Goodson, became exceptionally popular and ran for no less than seventeen years in the USA (Schwartz et al., 1999: 246). The show reached the BBC via Maurice Winnick, and debuted there on 16 July 1951.[7] *What's My Line?* proved to be equally popular with a British audience and the BBC recommissioned on average two thirteen-episode series per year until 1963.[8] It got another run on BBC Two between August 1973 and May 1974, and was revived by Thames Television for ITV between March 1984 and August 1990.[9]

The fourth American show adapted by the BBC was *This Is Your Life*, which launched on the NBC radio network in 1948. Two ingredients helped to make it a hit: the guest was kept in the dark until the actual show, and his or her former colleagues, close friends and relatives were invited along for the surprise (Buxton and Owen, 1972: 306–7). In 1955, within two months of the idea being floated by Ronald Waldman, a licence agreement was signed between the BBC and MCA, the rights holder. The show debuted in August, beginning a nine-year first run.[10]

Inventing Format Rights

The BBC archives reveal diverging views and some sharp exchanges between the Corporation's executives, Maurice Winnick and the American rights holders. The sticking point was much less about fees than rights. For the BBC, the idea that something as intangible as the concept of a show could be copyrighted and thus legitimate a fee for duplication was hard to grasp at first.

The issue arose with *Ignorance Is Bliss*. The American original was heavily scripted and even though Sid Colin scantily referred to these scripts the BBC was comfortable with the idea of paying for them. However, the Corporation was opposed to paying a licence fee for the programme itself, which would have been paramount to admitting that it was broadcasting the show under licence. In December 1948, Michael Standing wrote to Winnick in order to remove any ambiguity about the nature of the payments the latter was receiving: 'We should continue to look to you to provide the basic American script for each programme, and it would be for that specific purpose that the fee would be paid.'[11] Winnick did not pursue the matter because he was unsure about the issue himself, and his preoccupation lay primarily with securing bookings for his band to play on the radio programme and subsequent road show.[12]

The issue became more pressing with *Twenty Questions*. As before, the BBC was willing to pay a fee as long as it was not akin to a royalty payment. Since no script was involved with this particular show, G. D. G. Perkins, the BBC's assistant director of the legal department, wrote to Winnick in March 1947 to say that his fee would be 'for his enterprise and labour in obtaining the American recording and bringing it to the Corporation'.[13] Eight months later, Perkins stated that he was 'quite certain that there is no copyright recognised either by English or American law in the title, idea, plan, or form of this programme', and enclosed a £150 cheque 'for [. . .] services in bringing us the idea of this programme in a form suitable for broadcasting'.[14]

This time round, however, the BBC met with fierce opposition. First, as reported by L. Wellington, the Home Service controller, the American rights holder was unhappy about not receiving a fee. In his note, Wellington elaborated: 'the owner considers that his copyright does exist – not in the idea, but in the <u>format</u>, i.e. the ghost voice, quickies, etc.'[15] The BBC's New York attorney, Bernard Smith, agreed with him and advised the Corporation to proceed with caution because the format owner could build a lawsuit on four grounds, including unfair competition and copyright infringement. He warned the BBC:

> In several recent cases where negotiations took place in New York, the Courts of this State have recognized the right to recover compensation for the submission of a 'combination of ideas expressed in a concrete formula original' with the author and entrusted to a third party for sale. [. . .]
>
> Mere ideas also cannot be the subject of copyright. However, a person's particular method or expression of portrayal is the subject of copyright, and cannot be copied or plagiarized. Thus, it has been held that there may be literary piracy without actual use of the dialogue.[16]

However, the BBC chose to maintain the Perkins line whilst settling its dispute with Winnick in January 1949. The agreement made no mention of copyright but included a £1,000 payment in order to settle all claims related to the 'sound broadcasts' of *Twenty Questions* in the UK.[17] The unresolved issue of rights prevented the show's transfer to television, and when Ronald Waldman began planning a weekly TV version, he was told that this would be impossible because the BBC refused to recognize that TV rights were attached to the programme.[18]

It was with the third programme, *What's My Line?*, that the BBC and Winnick broke new ground. The Corporation signed a licensing deal with Winnick soon after it had expressed interest in the show. The contract was signed on 29 June 1951 and its opening clause stipulated the purpose of the fee:

> I [Maurice Winnick] grant the B.B.C. the right for 26 single performances on television in the British Isles only for a fee of £300.0.0. (Three Hundred pounds). Television performances are scheduled to commence on or about the third or fourth week of July 1951.[19]

The UK TV rights having been established, the fifth clause listed the other rights attached to the property:

> It is agreed that all other rights in the feature entitled 'What's My Line' in the form supplied by me [Maurice Winnick] including, but not limiting them, film rights [. . .], stage rights, sound broadcasting rights, foreign rights, and translation rights and the rights of publication are reserved to me.[20]

This contract establishes the legal foundations of the TV format industry and must be considered its birth certificate. For the first time, a broadcaster agreed to pay for the idea and package of a show – its format – as opposed to something tangible such as scripts. The document pins down the notion of the format as the right to remake a programme for a given territory that exists alongside other rights that are attached to a given IP.[21] As these rights can be traded, this led to the formation of a rights market, on the back of which the international TV format trade grew.

Those early deals also reveal the commercial engine that propels the TV format business. BBC executives had no blueprint to work with and at times showed their frustration at having to wrangle for rights that they were not certain existed in the first place. But they stuck with negotiations on the basis that these shows had been ratings hits in their home market. They even agreed to pay inflated fees once they knew that *What's My Line?* was a 'winner' with the audience.[22] More than sixty years on, the principle remains the same. The format trade has become a multi-billion-dollar industry because broadcasters feel reassured by buying shows that come with a proof of concept and established track record.

ITV: An Early Boon for the Nascent Format Trade

The launch of ITV, the UK's first commercial network, on Thursday 22 September 1955 presented the fledgling format trade with a boon. Within its first week on air, ITV broadcast five formats. Three were game shows: *Take Your Pick*, *Double Your Money* and *Beat the Clock*. The first two were brought by their respective presenters, Michael Miles and Hughie Green, from Radio Luxembourg (although both programmes were clearly based on US game shows), and the third was a Goodson-Todman quiz show that had debuted five years earlier on CBS. The fourth format, *People Are Funny*, was a comedy stunt programme based on audience participation. Rapidly 'condemned as cruel, tasteless and pointless' (Sendall, 1982: 321), it also came from America, where it started out on the radio network NBC in April 1942 before beginning a television run in September 1954 (Buxton and Owen, 1972: 238; McNeil, 1997: 649; Schwartz et al., 1999: 14–17; Sendall, 1982: 319–23).

The fifth show was a talent-spotting competition called *Chance of a Lifetime*. Winnick had offered the format to the BBC four years earlier, before it premiered on ABC in May 1952, but Ronald Waldman, the BBC's head of Light Entertainment, turned it down.[23] He professed to liking for another show but in truth the BBC was already well served in the genre with *Opportunity Knocks*, a talent discovery show that began on the Light Programme on 18 February 1949.[24]

The commercial network transmitted at least seven other formats before the decade was out, four of them in 1956. *The 64,000 Question*, in May 1956, was based on the popular *The $64,000 Question*. The show had been going out on CBS for eleven months and was the first American 'big-money' quiz show, with the British version substituting sixpences, and then shillings, for dollars. *Do You Trust Your Wife?*, which involved married couples, was derived from a CBS show of the same name, and *Spot the Tune* came from *Name That Tune*, a phenomenally popular musical quiz show devised by Ralph Edwards that started a long career on US TV in July 1953. *Two for the Money* was produced by Associated-Rediffusion and had its first screening in August 1956. It was a Godson-Todman creation that premiered on NBC in September 1952 (Schwartz et al., 1999: 57, 148–9, 201–2, 239; Sendall, 1982: 348–9).

The following year, *Criss Cross Quiz*, which was produced by Granada, debuted in June for a ten-year run. It was adapted from a hugely successful Barry & Enright Productions show called *Tic Tac Dough* which first came on air on NBC in July 1956. Then, in July 1958, *Twenty-One* started a six-month run. The US version of the same name, also devised by Barry

& Enright, had debuted on NBC in September 1956, but the US network abruptly took it off air two years later amid fixing allegations that led to a congressional investigation (and, much later, a Robert Redford movie) (Boddy, 1993: 218–21; Graham, 1988: 23–34; Schwartz et al., 1999: 237–9). Granada's British version was not above suspicion and allegations were made that some participants were given 'advance knowledge of the questions' (Paulu, 1961: 138). Finally, *Dotto* began a nineteen-month run in September 1958. It was based on an American show of the same name that premiered in January 1958 on CBS and had also been caught up in the scandals (Graham, 1988: 29–31; Paulu, 1961: 138; Schwartz et al., 1999: 59).

ITV did not acquire another format for four years, despite the immense popularity of quiz shows (Black, 1972: 111–13). Not only was the network cautious following the whiff of scandal, it was also accused of 'exploiting the indolence of popular taste' (Black, 1972: 164). It had no alternative but to appease the Independent Television Authority and all those who were planning to 'improv[e] public taste by legislation' (Black, 1972: 168) (see section on '"High culture" fights back: Broadcasting policy versus TV formats').

The TV Format Trade as an Anglo-American Invention

Considering trade practices in markets beyond America and Britain, it can be established that the TV format was an Anglo-American invention. As already seen, the BBC, Maurice Winnick and the US rights holders established that for a TV show to become a format, a licence needs to be purchased. And ITV also acquired the UK rights of their formats. For instance, Denis Forman, the former chairman and managing director of Granada Television, remembered Cecil Bernstein buying the rights of *Tic Tac Dough* (Forman, 1997: 91).

There is evidence that this was not common practice elsewhere until the 1980s. American television may have been influential in Europe in the 1950s (e.g. Bettetini, 1980; Bourdon, 2001), but when broadcasters turned to US TV networks for inspiration they simply stole their shows. The few producers who were involved in light entertainment, such as Louis Merlin for Radio Luxembourg or Peter Frankenfeld in Germany, had travelled to the United States, watched plenty of television in their hotel rooms and came back to Europe with a notebook full of observations (Hallenberger, email correspondence 2011; Merlin, 1966).

For instance, in 1957, a few months after its TV channel began transmissions, the Swedish public service broadcaster adapted *Double or Nothing* (*10.000 kronor – kvitt eller dubbelt*). Following its great success, Sveriges Radio, as it was then called, sent a representative to the USA with the task of monitoring the networks there. He 'referred to his activities as "spy work"' and when he wrote to draw attention to a popular programme, he was told that 'it was better to "steal the idea and do a show of that kind ourselves"' (Bjork, 2009: 221).

Similar practices were common in other territories. In France, early sound broadcasting adaptations include local versions of *Double or Nothing*, *Queen for a Day* and *Twenty-One* that aired either on Radiodiffusion et Télévision Française (RTF) or Radio Luxembourg in the 1950s (Schmitt, 2005: 108). The first TV remakes were *Jouons le jeu* (RTF, 1951–2) (*What's My Line?*) and *Oui ou non* (RTF, 1955–6), Radio Luxembourg's sound broadcast version of *Twenty-One* (Leveneur, 2009: 37). The only show for which a French licence was acquired was Radio Luxembourg's *Reine d'un jour* (*Queen for a Day*) – being the exception that proves the rule (Merlin, 1966: 213–25).

A few years later RTF adapted an Italian game show called *Campanile Sera*, which consisted of two village teams competing in various outdoor games of dexterity and endurance. *Intervilles*, which debuted in 1962, became one of RTF's most iconic programmes; it remained intermittently on air in France until 2013 and was the inspiration behind the pan-European version, *Jeux sans frontières*. It became *It's a Knockout* in the UK, where it broadcast on BBC One between 1966 and 1982 (Bourdon, 2012: 116; Leveneur, 2009: 37, 39, 59).

In Italy, Radiotelevisione Italiana (RAI) adapted four game shows in the 1950s. The first was *Duecento al secondo*, which premiered in June 1955 and stayed on TV for the summer (Grasso, 2004: 34–6). Although it appears that RAI versioned *Dollar a Second*, it was the local version of a French quiz show, Radio Luxembourg's *Cent francs par seconde*. This was followed by *Lascia o raddoppia?*, a quiz show based on *The $64,000 Question* that was recommissioned for many years and became a cultural phenomenon (Grasso, 2004: 43–50). *Telematch*, based on a French game show of the same name, premiered in January 1957, and by the end of the year RAI got another hit with *Il musichiere*, an adaptation of *Name That Tune*, which ran for ninety episodes over three years (Grasso, 2004: 5, 59–60).

US shows also proved popular in Germany, where nine were adapted for home audiences in the 1950s and early 1960s. This started with *1:0 für Sie* (*People Are Funny*, 1954–5), followed by *Was bin ich?* (*What's My Line?*, 1955–8, 1961–89), *Alles oder Nichts* (*The $64,000 Question*, 1956–9, 1963, 1966–88), *Hatten Sie's gewußt?* (*Twenty-One*, 1958–66, 1968–88), *Tick-Tack-Quiz* (*Tic Tac Dough*, 1958–61, 1964–7), *Dotto* (1959–61), *Gewußt wo . . .* (*Concentration*, 1959–61), *Sag die Wahreit* (*To Tell the Truth*, 1959–71) and *Nur nicht nervös warden* (*Beat the Clock*, 1960–1) (Hallenberger, 1992: 91–2).

According to Hallenberger, the German versions bore little resemblance to the American originals and no transfer of expertise ever took place. German television was in its infancy with fewer than one million potential viewers and TV stations did not have the resources to send producers to the USA. Rights were never acquired, with the exception of *What's My Line?*, when the presenter, Robert Lembke, purchased them from Winnick on a visit to London (Hallenberger, email correspondence 2011).

In Spain, Televisión Española (TVE) began transmitting in 1956 and aired its first quiz shows the following year, most of them 'inspired' by US TV programmes (Lacalle, 2001: 53–4, my translation). *Adivine su vida* (*What's My Line?*) in 1957 was followed by *X-O da dinero* (*Tic Tac Dough*) in 1959, *Esta es su vida* (*This Is Your Life*) in 1962, *La unión hace la fuerza* (combining RAI's *Campanile Sera* and RTF's *La Tête et les jambes*) in 1964, and *Reina por un día* (*Queen for a Day*) the same year (Baget Herms, 1993: 48–61).

From this rapid *tour d'horizon*, it emerges that aside from two exceptions, none of these adaptations were licensed. Table 1.1 shows that *What's My Line?* and *Campanile Sera* were the most widely travelled formats in Europe, while four others were adapted in three territories.

Outside Europe, the first TV formats reached Australia in the late 1950s, where a commercial TV system had developed (Moran, 1998). However, as elsewhere, borrowings were rarely acknowledged. Jeremy Fox, a British TV producer with personal experience of the Australian market, confirmed that local producers did not purchase licences until the 1980s (Fox, interview 2010). The problem was identical in Latin America, where Mark Goodson complained that he 'has had trouble with [. . .] stations pirating ideas under slight disguise' (see also Moran, 1998: 18).[25]

'High Culture' Fights Back: Broadcasting Policy versus TV Formats

After its promising start, the TV format trade remained dormant throughout the 1960s and 1970s. As television emerged as a medium for the millions, European governments sought to harness it for educational and cultural purposes. France provides the strongest case in point. When Charles de Gaulle came to power in 1958, television fell firmly into the hands of the state. A monopoly was created and de Gaulle referred to the RTF as the 'voice of the state in France and the voice of France in the world' (Peyrefitte, 1994: 98, my translation). The national broadcaster was given a mission to promote national culture, strengthen national identity and reinforce the emotional and ideological foundations of the nation. Since the monopoly

Table 1.1 Leading TV formats/adapted shows in top five European markets, 1950s (in alphabetical order of original version)

USA	UK	France	Italy	Germany	Spain
Beat the Clock	*Beat the Clock*			*Nur nicht nervös warden*	
	It's a Knockout	*Intervilles*	*Campanile Sera*	*Spiel ohne Grenzen*	*La unión hace la fuerza*
Concentration				*Gewußt wo . . .*	
Dollar a Second		*Cent francs par seconde* (radio and TV)	*Duecento al secondo* (US version)		
Dotto	*Dotto*			*Dotto*	
Name That Tune	*Spot the Tune*		*Il musichiere*		
People Are Funny	*People Are Funny*			*1:0 für Sie*	
Queen for a Day		*Reine d'un jour* (radio only)			*Reina por un día*
The $64,000 Question	*The 64,000 Question*		*Lascia o raddoppia?*	*Alles oder Nichts*	
Tic Tac Dough	*Criss Cross Quiz*			*Tick-Tack-Quiz*	*X-O da dinero*
This Is Your Life	*This Is Your Life*				*Esta es su vida*
To Tell the Truth				*Sag die Wahreit*	
Twenty-One	*Twenty-One*	*Oui ou non*		*Hatten Sie's gewußt?*	
Twenty Questions	*Twenty Questions*				
What's My Line?	*What's My Line?*	*Jouons le jeu*		*Was bin ich?*	*Adivine su vida*

protected RTF from any competition, it did not need to take risks or bow to popular taste. Up to 1976, the two RTF TV channels broadcast in the evening only, nullifying any need for daytime programming (Jost, 2005: 15–16). In truth, there was a space for light entertainment but one with strings attached: it had to be homegrown (Chalaby, 2002: 177–88). Since it was part of RTF's remit to develop the country's TV production capacity, it developed its own game shows. All in all, it explains why there was only one imported format, a sport celebrity contest called *Superstars*, among the ninety-one game shows on TV in France between 1970 and 1979.[26]

It was during this period that French television invented *Des Chiffres et des lettres*, a programme that showcased contestants' mental skills, reflecting the policy priorities of the age (Bourdon, 2001: 220). Debuting in January 1972, *Des Chiffres et des lettres* was to become France's most illustrious format export (alongside *Fort Boyard*); it started its international career as *Countdown* on Channel 4 ten years later.

France's regulations were statist in the extreme, but similar policies were in place across Europe where governments attempted to 'raise' the standards of television and harness the power of the medium for political purposes (see also Bourdon, 2012: 114–15). Even in the UK, voices were raised expressing dissatisfaction with commercial television. Following growing anxiety surrounding ITV among the cultural elite, the Committee on Broadcasting was appointed in July 1960; chaired by Sir Harry Pilkington, it published its report two years later. Submitted representations expressed concern about the low standards of TV programming. 'There was', the report stated, 'a preoccupation in many programmes with the superficial, the cheaply sensational'; 'many mass appeal programmes were vapid and puerile', it continued, 'their content often derivative, repetitious and lacking in real substance' (Committee on Broadcasting, 1962: 33). These were views shared by Richard Hoggart, a prominent member of the Committee who had lamented, in his oeuvre, the displacement of a community-based, working-class culture by one that was commercial, manufactured and alien (American) in character (Hoggart, [1957] 2009). On these premises, the Committee levelled its sharpest criticism against quiz programmes offering large prizes:

> It is not that an intellectual minority finds the programmes trivial. Rather, it is that as quiz programmes some of them do not stand on their merits – whatever the educational standards of the audiences. In relying upon the appeal to greed and fear, and to the pleasure of watching these emotions roused in others because valuable prizes are at stake, and in relying on an atmosphere of artificial good fellowship, these programmes abandon the objective – light entertainment which amuses because it is good – for light entertainment which is poor in invention and needs the support of extraneous appeals. (Committee on Broadcasting, 1962: 58)

Thus, the Committee recommended that 'where programmes or games call for no skill, prizes should be of nominal value only' (Committee on Broadcasting, 1962: 292). Such a climate slowed down the number of

American imports into the UK. After a gap of a few years, the ITV network played it safe and went upmarket for its next quiz show. It resumed international acquisitions with *College Bowl*, which Granada renamed *University Challenge* and which premiered in September 1962 (Black, 1972: 206). It still airs on BBC Two.

These were adverse conditions for the TV format trade and not many formats crossed borders in the 1960s and 1970s. The most influential was *Candid Camera*: hidden filming and practical jokes formed the series, created by Allen Funt, that started as *Candid Microphone* on ABC radio in June 1947, before moving to television in August the following year. It crossed the Atlantic in 1960 and was adapted and produced by ABC Television, an ITV franchise holder, for sixteen years. Adaptations came from France (*La Caméra invisible*, RTF/ORTF, 1964), followed by Italy (*Specchio segreto*, RAI, 1965) and Spain (*Objectivo indiscreto*, TVE, 1965) (Bourdon, 2012: 115; Kavka, 2012: 15–19).

The one country seemingly less affected by these policies was Germany, which adapted several US game shows during those years, notably *Twenty Questions* (*Gut gefragt ist halb gewonnen*, 1964–70), *Password* (*Passwort*, 1964–6), *The Newlywed Game* (*Sie und Er im Kreuzverhör*, 1971–2) and *The Match Game* (*Schnickschnack*, 1975–7) (Hallenberger, 1992: 2).

The US Game-Show Era

The TV format trade revived in the 1980s. The configuration of national broadcasting markets began to change as public monopolies were broken up and commercial broadcasters emerged (the decade started with only two private TV channels of note in Europe – ITV and RTL) (Brants and De Bens, 2000: 10). As deregulation opened up markets and fostered more competition, broadcasters began to shop around for popular programmes. The expansion of broadcasting hours to daytime also increased demand for content. This swelled cross-border TV trade and new shows appeared on European TV screens: US soaps (e.g. *Dallas* and *Dynasty*), telenovelas and formatted US game shows.

Format Pioneers and the 1978 Goodson Worldwide Agreement

Until the late 1970s, only a few distributors were involved in the format trade. Paul Talbot established Fremantle Corporation in 1952 and his company pioneered the international sale of US TV series. While this remained his business staple he also helped to develop franchising by selling locally adapted shows. The first such franchise was *Romper Room*, a programme for preschoolers that was adapted in various US local TV markets before Talbot acquired the international rights. By the end of the 1960s, twenty-five local versions were in production around the world (Guider, 2005; Moran, 2006: 22–3, 2013a: 7).

The breakthrough – both for Fremantle and for the international format trade – came later in 1978, when Talbot obtained the representation of the complete Goodson-Todman catalogue, first for the UK and then for Europe and the Middle East (Usdan, interview 2010). This agreement helped transform the format trade into a business by sparking a wider and *lawful* international distribution (Moran, 2013a: 8–10). Mark Goodson was America's most prolific game-show creator and, as seen earlier, several of his creations had already travelled to Europe, including *What's My Line?*, *Beat the Clock* and *Two for the Money*. In addition, *Play Your Hunch* started a six-month run on the BBC in April 1961, and *Call My Bluff* began a twenty-three-year run on BBC Two in October 1965. However, the 1978 deal brought in many more Goodson shows and soon there were forty on air across Europe. Some markets took a few (the most popular was *The Price is Right*) and the UK took the most. They include *I've Got a Secret* (first aired in the USA in 1952), *The Price is Right* (1956), *To Tell the Truth* (1956), *Concentration* (1958), *Password* (1961), *The Match Game* (1962), *Now You See It* (1974), *Showoffs* (1975), *Family Feud* (1976), *The Better Sex* (1977), *Card Sharks* (1978), *Blockbusters* (1980) and *Child's Play* (1982) (Usdan, email correspondence 2010). Many of these games were among Europe's most watched shows. In the UK, for instance, *The Match Game* (*Blankety Blank*, January 1979, BBC One) and *Card Sharks* (*Play Your Cards Right*, February 1980, ITV) were big hits, *Blockbusters* acquired a cult following, *The Price is Right* aired off and on until 2007, and a celebrity version of *Family Feud* was still on the ITV schedule in 2015, airing as *All Star Family Fortunes*.

Talbot Television – as Fremantle's international division was called – took on the representation of several other American game-show producers, notably Chuck Barris (*The Dating Game*, *The Newlywed Game*), Bob Stewart (*The $10,000 Pyramid*) and Monty Hall (*Let's Make a Deal*) (Hearsey, interview 2010). Talbot Television also produced two Merv Griffin creations (*Jeopardy!* and *The Wheel of Fortune*) in some territories, alongside King World International, which by 1983 held the biggest number of licences worldwide (Moran, 1998: 31–2, 2006: 97–8). This made Fremantle the world's largest producer of game shows, and it was estimated that in the 1980s the company produced or distributed around half the game shows on air worldwide. Early in the next decade, it had ninety-three game shows in production in twenty-seven countries (Gibson, 1997; Miller, 2005).

Reg Grundy first adapted American game shows for Australian television in the late 1950s, then signed an agreement to produce Goodson shows in Australia, and eventually came back to the American producer to negotiate a deal for the rest of the world in the late 1970s. Goodson did not want one person representing all his formats and took this opportunity to split his world-wide rights, giving the Australian businessman the rights to his shows outside Europe and the Middle East. Grundy Worldwide developed internationally on the back of this deal, progressively building its own catalogue. It specialized in high-volume genres, and key properties included game shows such as *Hot Streak*, *Going for Gold*, *Man O Man* and *Sale of the Century*, and two Australian soaps (*The Restless Years* and *Sons and Daughters*; see chapter 9). All were adapted in various markets but Grundy was especially successful in Europe (Moran, 1998: 55–71; Usdan, email correspondence, 2010).

In Europe, Action Time was among the first European companies to get involved in the format business. It was established in 1979 by Jeremy Fox, who left Granada to set up as an independent game-show producer. Fox created his own shows but also imported American formats in large numbers, including *Catchphrase* and *Truth or Consequences*, the latter being one of the key sources of *Game for a Laugh*, a popular 1980s light entertainment show. Fox only adapted US formats to the UK, but his successors Stephen Leahy and Trish Kinane (who took over in 1988) extended sales to Europe, and international hits included *The Alphabet Game* and *You've Been Framed!* They also launched Action Group, a loose European association of producers for preferential trading in formats (Fox, interview 2010; Kinane and Leahy, interview 2010; see also chapter 9).

Finally, two Dutch production companies, Joop van den Ende's JE Entertainment and John de Mol Productions, were early exponents of the format strategy for reasons related to the size of their home market. Both sold formats to develop overseas sales (the scope for growth being limited in Holland) and both bought foreign scripts to adapt in their domestic market because of a dearth of writing talent at home (Bell, 1994: 23). Van den Ende, a TV producer with roots in theatre, began selling formats in the Netherlands, Germany and Southern Europe in the early 1980s. Later in the decade, JE Entertainment became a member of Action Group, giving it access to British formats. In addition to its own *The Honeymoon Quiz* and *The Soundmix Show*, the producer adapted several UK drama series (notably Thames Television's *The Bill* and London Weekend Television's sitcom *The Two of Us*) in various countries. John de Mol Productions was a younger company that was less active in the format market, although *Love Letters* and *All You Need Is Love* – two programmes that prefigured reality TV – were adapted in about five territories. The two companies merged in January 1994, creating Endemol Entertainment, a company that was soon to play a key role in the globalization of the format business (see chapters 2 and 6) (Moran, 1998: 33–5, 2006: 91–4; Smith and Life, 1993).

The First Global TV Formats

The 1978 Goodson Worldwide Agreement and subsequent deals between US game-show producers and Fremantle and Grundy galvanized the international format market. These agreements prompted a wave of US game shows travelling across the world. *The Wheel of Fortune* became the most widely adapted show of the 1980s, breaking a record with twenty-five local productions, followed by *The Price is Right* (approximately twelve), *The Dating Game, Family Feud* and *Jeopardy!* (Cooper-Chen, 1994: 146). Often successful where they aired, and sometimes still on air, these game shows made an immediate impact on TV schedules worldwide:

- In Italy, *The Price is Right* (*OK il prezzo è giusto!*) arrived in 1983, followed by *The Dating Game* (*Il gioco delle copie*) and *Blockbusters* (*Doppio slalom*) in 1985, *The Newlywed Game* (*Tra moglie e marito*) in 1987, *Hollywood Squares* (*Il gioco dei nove*) and *Family Feud* (*Cari genitori*) the following year, and *The Wheel of Fortune* (*La ruota della fortuna*) in 1989 (Grasso, 2004: 400, 430, 465–6, 486, 497–9).
- France adapted *The Dating Game* (*Tournez manège*) in 1985, *The Price is Right* (*Le Juste prix*), *The Wheel of Fortune* (*La Roue de la fortune*) and *The Newlywed Game* (*Les Mariés de l'A2*) in 1987, *Jeopardy!* in 1989 and *Family Feud* (*Une Famille en or*) in 1990. Grundy adapted *Going for Gold* (*Questions pour un champion*) in 1988. It has since become a classic access primetime game that still airs on a public channel in France and throughout the francophone world on TV5 Monde (Cooper-Chen, 1994: 272–3; Leveneur, 2009: 59).
- The American formats arrived later in Spain. Following *The Price is Right* (*El precio justo*) in 1988, four formats debuted in 1990: *The Wheel of Fortune* (*La ruleta de la fortuna*, later renamed *La ruleta de la suerte*), *The Newlywed Game* (*Su media naranja*), *Hollywood Squares* (*VIP*) and *Every Second Counts* (*Los segundos cuentan*) (Cooper-Chen, 1994: 274).
- The number of game shows steadily increased in Germany to reach fifty-five by the end of the 1980s. Many were homegrown and aired regionally

but a few imports were added to complement the popular *What's My Line?* (*Was bin ich?*) and *The $64,000 Question* (*Alles oder Nichts*). The *$10,000 Pyramid* (a game show that first aired on CBS in 1973) aired as *Die Pyramide* on ZDF between 1979 and 1990. *The Gong Show* (*Die Gong-Show*, Nord 3, 1981), *The Wheel of Fortune* (*Glücksrad*, SAT 1, 1988–9) and *The Price is Right* (*Der Preis is heiß*, RTL Plus, from 1989) were also adapted for the German market. One of the great successes of the decade, however, came from Italy. *Rischiatutto*, Italian television's second most successful quiz show behind *Lascia o raddopia?*, was adapted into *Der Groß Preis*, and aired between 1974 and 1990 on ZDF (Hallenberger and Kaps, 1991).

• In the UK, ITV and to a lesser extent the BBC made numerous adaptations throughout the 1980s (as already seen). By 1990, they were airing fourteen formats between them, including *The Dating Game* (*Blind Date*), *Blockbusters*, *Family Fortunes*, *What's My Line?*, *Concentration* and *The Pyramid Game*, all on ITV, and *Every Second Counts* and *The Match Game* (*Blankety Blank*) on the BBC (Cooper-Chen, 1994: 271).

At least three-quarters of formats originated in America but there were other exporting nations of note. Both Australia and the UK exported scripted formats (chapter 9). From France came *La Chasse au trésor* (*Treasure Hunt*) and *Des Chiffres et des lettres* (*Countdown*), which was in at least four countries by the late 1980s, and ITV sourced *Wetten Das* (*You Bet*) from Germany. Japan exported several formats. The most popular was *Waku Waku Dohbutsu Lando* (*Exciting Animal Land*), which was based on video clips of animals and was produced in fifteen territories by the end of the decade (Cooper-Chen, 1994: 146–7, 271).

End of an Era

The world TV format trade progressed by leaps and bounds in the 1980s and early 1990s: some shows travelled widely, a few international producers emerged with a dominant share of the trade, and format rights started to be recognized beyond the USA and the UK as broadcasters began to accept that paying a licence fee for a ratings winner was worth the expense. As Moran writes, 'the era also witnessed the increasing formalization of programme content exchange' (Moran, 2013a: 9); and Leveneur's observation about France can be applied to other European territories: 'Contrary to the 1960s and 1970s, from then on the [format] exchanges are regulated and subject to the acquisition of adaptation rights' (Leveneur, 2009: 59).

The USA's (late) ratification of the Berne Convention for the Protection of Literary and Artistic Works in 1989 reinforced the rights position of its TV producers (Moran, 2013a: 9). The first format practitioners emerged and the transfer of expertise became professionalized. The format business was born as a 'tape and handshake' trade. Against a handshake and a vague promise that rights would be paid for one day, the format owner handed over a tape to a visiting local producer who would have to work out how to put the show together once back in his or her country. US producers began to send 'flying producers' whose job was to help local teams set up their game shows. For instance, Mark Goodson was keen that broadcasters stick to his guidelines when adapting his shows, and Pamela Usdan and Gil Fates began to travel the world armed with scripts, set plans and sample questions (Usdan, interview 2010).

For all this progress, however, it would be erroneous to interpret this period as the dawn of a new age, and it is more accurate to see it as the crowning era of the industry's early period. The structure of the trade flow remained unchanged. Even though, as already noted, not all formats were American, it was still largely a one-way traffic. And while Australian and British scripts began to be adapted (chapter 9), game shows formed the backbone of the trade. The geographical scope of the format flow enlarged but, as table 1.2 suggests, it was yet to reach a global scale. The USA and Japan imported no game shows and only Australia and five Western European countries had a larger number of imported formats than home-grown programmes. Elsewhere, the majority of game shows were home-

Table 1.2 Number of homegrown versus imported game shows, 1990

	Total number of game shows	Homegrown	Imported format
USA	34	34	0
UK	24	9	15
France	11	4	7
Italy	10	2	8
Spain	7	0	7
Germany	16	3	13
Holland	9	5	4
Eastern Europe	9	6	3
Africa	15	13	2
Australia	7	0	7
Asia (incl. China)	30	23	7
Japan	30	30	0
Latin America	14	12	2

Source: adapted from Cooper-Chen (1994: 270–89).

grown (even though a large proportion may well have been inspired by US programmes). In 1990, just over one third of game shows aired worldwide were formatted, against two thirds in Northern and Western Europe (Cooper-Chen, 1994: 146). Formats travelled slowly and very few reached more than ten territories.

Finally, the TV format trade did not have the allure it has gained since. TV formats were confined to a minor daytime genre of which no one took much notice, and they lacked the glamour of drama and the prestige of primetime programming. Format producers and distributors operated at the fringes of the TV industry, in which they were barely known; they were 'door-to-door salesmen' visiting broadcasters with 'a bag of tapes' selling formats as one would sell 'brushes' (Hearsey, interview 2010). The TV format trade certainly came a long way between the 1950s and 1980s, starting with the only client for US fare reluctantly paying a fee for a show without a script, and developing to formats like *The Price is Right* and *The Wheel of Fortune*. There was still no inkling of things to come, however, as the TV format revolution would be set in motion by factors and circumstances that had yet to materialize.

2   The Making of an Entertainment Revolution

The foundations of today's multi-billion-dollar format business were laid down in the 1990s. This chapter analyses the circumstances that produced an industry-changing shift and its key features. Why did a decades-old trade situated at the fringes of the TV industry turn so fashionable within a few years? And why did the super-formats sweep the world in the late 1990s? As always, profound change was triggered by a powerful congruence of factors.

International Expansion and the Formation of two Format Powerhouses

The 1990s was a period of rapid expansion for a handful of format distributors and producers, and their growth and influence in the trade facilitated the international distribution of formats. Jeremy Fox, Action Time's founder, had never sold a format in Europe when his company was acquired by Zenith (itself owned by Carlton Communications) in 1988. The new joint directors, Trish Kinane and Stephen Leahy, realized that expansion could come from selling formats abroad, and within five years they had forty-one shows in production in Europe. By the time they left the company in 2001, Action Time was trading in thirty countries. It brought *Stars in Their Eyes* and *You've Been Framed!* to the UK, and the firm's own international hits included *The Alphabet Game*, *Catchphrase* and *Wipeout*, all three produced in more than ten territories (Aston, 2001; Fox, interview 2010; Kinane and Leahy, interview 2010).

The BBC was not especially active in the format trade, even though *Antiques Roadshow*, *Jim'll Fix It* and *That's Life!* were adapted abroad. Things changed in the 1990s when the Corporation realized that formats were a way of exploiting its expansive IP. The Corporation appointed Colin Jarvis to the new position of head of format licensing in February 1994, two months before launching BBC Worldwide, with eyes set firmly on international growth. *Ask the Family*, *Confessions* and *Noel's House Party* were some of the first formats the BBC pushed for export, and it met with success in *The Generation Game* and *Pets Win Prizes* (fifteen adaptations) (Carter, 1996; Jarvis, interview 2010).

Table 2.1 Endemol's key formats, 1994

Formats developed in-house	Formats acquired
The Honeymoon Quiz Germany, Greece, Italy, Spain, UK *The Soundmix Show* Australia, Belgium, Germany, Portugal, UK *Love Letters* Belgium, Germany, Greece, Sweden *All You Need Is Love* Germany, Italy, Portugal, Spain, Sweden	Game shows: *Surprise, Surprise* (origin: UK); *Love at First Sight* (UK) Dramas: *The Bill* (origin: UK); *Casualty* (UK) Sitcoms: *The Two of Us* (origin: UK); *Who's the Boss?* (USA); *Married with Children* (USA); *The Mary Tyler Moore Show* (USA) Soaps: *Ryan's Hope* (origin: USA); *The Restless Years* (Australia) Reality: *Rescue 911* (origin: USA)

Source: Bell (1994: 24).

It was also the time when two global format powerhouses formed. When Endemol was created in January 1994 (chapter 1), it became the world's largest independent production company, worth an estimated US$225 million (Smith and Life, 1993). The firm started life with a sizeable format catalogue (table 2.1) and RTL Germany rapidly became a volume buyer. Soon enough, the newly established conglomerate was delivering between 2,500 and 3,000 hours of programming a year, some of it produced in the firm's seven-studio complex at Hilversum. By the time *Big Brother* launched at the end of the decade, Endemol was selling formats in about twenty territories (see also chapter 6) (Bell, 1994; Endemol, 2007; Fuller, 1994a).

Pearson Television was formed at the same time. The company, best known for owning the *Financial Times* but essentially a hedge fund specializing in media assets, began investing in television in the early 1990s. It acquired Thames Television, the UK's largest independent producer, in April 1993 and appointed Greg Dyke, formerly LWT's managing director, to head its TV division in January 1995. Dyke immediately saw that growth was to be had from international expansion and thus acquired Reg Grundy's company for £175 million within four months of his appointment. It proved a very good deal as Grundy had an exceptionally large international footprint: by the mid-1990s, it had subsidiaries in Asia, Latin America, the USA and several European countries (Bateman, 1995; Dyke, interview 2010).

All American Communications was another significant acquisition which Dyke chased for two years before the board accepted his £233 million offer in October 1997. All American was a lucrative syndication business but much of its value resided in a company it had acquired three years earlier:

Fremantle. What Dyke was after was the Goodson-Todman formats that Fremantle licensed or produced in thirty territories, and of course the library's crown jewel: *The Price is Right* (Dyke, interview 2010; see also Dyke, 2005: 128–30).

Within a few years Dyke had made Pearson the world's leading format producer and by 2000 his company was selling formats in at least thirty-six territories. Its twelve formats totalled in excess of 150 local versions, and three of them (*Child's Play, Family Feud* and *The Price is Right*) were distributed in over twenty markets each (table 2.2).

Endemol's and Pearson's strategies were essentially similar: to use formats in high-volume genres (game shows and serial dramas) in order to control risk, manage uncertainties and of course expand internationally. So similar were they that they came close to a merger several times throughout the 1990s (Dyke, interview 2010).

The Rise of the British Independents

British producers played a prominent role in the TV format revolution as they became the world's leading source of IP (chapters 4 and 5). An embryonic independent TV production sector existed in the UK from the 1950s but it developed in earnest with the establishment of Channel 4. Britain's fourth TV channel was set up in 1982 as a 'publisher-broadcaster' that was required to *commission* its programming from independent producers. This set-up was innovative and unique in Europe – and still is – and necessitated years of skilful campaigning and lobbying from the production sector (Darlow, 2004; Potter, 2008). The independents grew but as Channel 4 was their sole client they initiated a campaign to force other public service broadcasters to commission them for content. Establishing its reputation for efficient lobbying, the independent TV production sector achieved success with the Broadcasting Act 1990. Coming into effect in 1993, the Act introduced 'the statutory independent quota' to other terrestrial broadcasters, stipulating that they must commission at least 25 per cent of their programming from independent producers. The Broadcasting Act 1996 expanded the principle to digital terrestrial television channels (Ofcom, 2006: 34).

By the mid-1990s, the sector had an annual turnover of £722 million, made 10,000 hours of TV and employed 12,000 staff. The sector was composed of hundreds of small and barely profitable firms with an annual turnover of less than £2 million,[1] but a few larger companies began to emerge (Jones, 1995: 5) (table 2.3).

Table 2.2 Pearson's formats worldwide, 2000

Countries	Card Sharks	Child's Play	The Dating Game	Family Feud	Forbidden Love	Good Times, Bad Times	Greed	Hot Streak	Let's Make a Deal	The Lyrics Board	Man O Man	The Price is Right
Argentina							Artear				Canal 13	AZUL
Australia				7 Network				7 Network	Network 10		7 Network	9 Network
Belgium		RTBF		VTM				VTM		TVI	VT4	VTM
Chile				TVN7								
Denmark		TV2	TV3	Scansat						TV2	TV3	TV3
Estonia		ETV		TV1						ETV		
Finland		YLE2	MTV3	Nelonen (TV4)			MTV3			MTV3		TV4
France		TF1	TF1	TF1				France 2	TF1	France 2	TF1	TF1
Georgia	GTV1	GTV1										
Germany	SAT1	SAT1/ARD	ARD	RTL	ARD	RTL	ZDF	TM3	SAT1			RTL
Greece	Antenna TV	Antenna TV	Mega	Mega				Mega	Sky TV			Antenna TV
Hungary			RTL KLUB						MTV			
India				Star TV								
Indonesia		Anteve		IVM	RCTI							
Ireland										RTE		
Israel				Golden Channel			Telad	Channel2	NCP			TV2 (Telad)
Italy		RETE	RE4	RTI (Canale 5)			RAI2		RTI (Canale 5)		Canale 5	RTI (Rete 4)

Country									
Lebanon				MTV					
Lithuania									TV3
Mexico				Televisa					Canal 2
Netherlands		NCRV	NED2	RTL4	RTL4			Veronica	RTL4
New Zealand									TV3
Norway		TV Norge		Scansat			TV Norge	TV3	TVN
Paraguay								SNT Canal 9	
Poland	Polsat	Polsat/TVP1	TVP1	TVP2		RTL7	Polsat	TVN	
Portugal	RTP1	RTP1/TVI	SIC	RTP		SIC	SIC	SIC	RTP1
Quebec		SRC		TQS					
Romania									PRO TV
Russia		RTR	RTR	RTR			RTR	RTR	
South Africa						SABC3	MNET		
Spain	Antenna 3	Antenna 3/TVE	TELE 5	TVE		TVE	Canal 9	Telecinco	TVE
Sweden	SVT	SVT	TV2	SVT			SVT2	TV3	
Turkey	ATV	ATV/Kanal 6	Show TV	Kanal D		ATV	Kanal D	Kanal D	Show TV
UK	ITV	ITV	ITV	ITV				ITV	ITV
Uruguay								Canal 10	
USA	CBS	CBS		Syndicated	Fox	ABC	Fox	UPN	CBS

Source: Elliott (2001), in *Broadcast.*

Table 2.3 Top fifteen independent production companies, UK, 1995

Company (Parent company)	Revenue, end of 1993 or 1994 (£m)	Number of staff
Thames Television (Pearson)	99.2	257
Reuters TV (Reuters)	75.1	488
ITC Entertainment	54.9	13
CSI	24.4	38
Broadcast Communications (Guardian Media)	17.8	99
Carnival (Film and Theatre)	14.7	10
Alomo Productions (SelecTV)	11.6	7
Planet 24	10.4	137
Action Time (UK)	8.5	31
Jim Henson Organisation	7.8	106
TalkBack Productions	7.4	16
Channel X	6.5	46
Witzend Productions (SelecTV)	6.1	9
Sunset + Vine	6.0	31
Reg Grundy Productions (UK) (Grundy Worldwide)	5.8	33

Source: Phillips (1995: 5).

McKeown's Alomo (chapter 9), Action Time and Grundy were dealing in formats by the mid-1990s and were soon joined by others. One of these companies was Bazal Productions, which was founded by Peter Bazalgette in 1987. He sold it to the Guardian Media Group's TV production concern (Broadcast Communications) three years later. Realizing that GMG could not develop the business any further, he urged them to sell it to Endemol, forming GMG Endemol Entertainment in 1998 (Bazalgette, interview 2009).

In 1994, Bazalgette devised and sold to the BBC a cookery programme with a competition element: *Ready Steady Cook* (see next section). It got big audiences in daytime and even bigger numbers when moved to primetime. On the strength of these ratings, the BBC asked Bazalgette to develop the concept around DIY, which became *Changing Rooms*, and then gardening: *Ground Force*. They were among the most successful formats of the 1990s, with *Ready Steady Cook* selling in about thirty countries, *Changing Rooms* in twenty and *Ground Force* in ten (Bazalgette, interview 2009).

Another producer was Mentorn, Barraclough and Carey (MBC), the result of a merger between Barraclough Carey and Mentorn in 1997. With offices in Holland, Germany, Spain and the USA, MBC went to market with three formats: *Whose House?*, *Claim to Fame* and *Robot Wars*. The last of these was a TV show developed by Steve Carsey based on an American 'sport' invented by Mark Thorpe. It proved particularly successful on the international TV market and developed a cult following in several territories (Carsey, interview 2010; Littlejohn, 1997).

RDF Television was founded in 1993 by David Frank and began to distribute its programmes internationally three years later. Its first formats were *Scrapheap Challenge*, a returning series on Channel 4, and *Wheeler Dealers*.

Hat Trick Productions, founded by Denise O'Donoghue and Jimmy Mulville, established a stand-alone international format sales company in November 1998 and soon had six local versions of its shows in production. Hat Trick produced several pilots for US networks, notably its BBC One comedy panel show *Have I Got News for You* and its BBC Two sitcom *Game On*, but found success with another panel show, *Whose Line Is It Anyway?*, which was eventually versioned in more than ten territories (Rouse, 1999; Whittock, 2011b).

Finally, NBD Entertainment had two formats on its books, *Endurance* and *The Cooler*, and Planet 24 managed to sell a few remake licences for *Big Breakfast* and *Hotel Babylon* (Handley, 1998).

There is a risk of post-rationalizing British producers' pioneering foray into the format trade, as with a few exceptions such as Action Time and Pearson, in general they did not set out to produce formats at the time. Bazalgette recalls that he 'didn't invent *Ready Steady Cook* with the aim of creating an international format, but it became an international format' (Bazalgette, interview 2009). At the BBC, David Morgenstern, who was working at the Features Department, 'can't remember us even discussing anything that could be sold internationally' (Morgenstern, interview 2009). Even Paul Smith, the creator of *Who Wants to Be a Millionaire?*, explained that he 'didn't really have international aspirations at all' (chapter 3) (Smith, interview 2009). John Silver, the creator of *MasterChef*, *Grand Designs* and *Property Ladder*, makes a similar point:

> That's a good example of a show [*How Clean is Your House?*], we didn't sit down and say let's make a format. We said let's make a show about cleaning dirty houses, how can we make that fun? And then, even in Channel 4 it became a model for other shows. Now the reason I don't like the format thing is because it very quickly goes to formula, and I don't think you can, you don't start out with a formula. What you do is you try and make something that you think is going to be a good piece of television, and now we understand that it has to have a structure, it has to have what we call a form, and it will find that form if you're lucky when you're making it, and then if it's a success, you might refine that form, and then you may have a format

at this point. But you didn't use to say I'm making a format. Now I say I'm making a format. (Silver, interview 2010)

It was only later, when British producers realized that formats were a passport to international growth and a means to financial stability, that they set out to make formats. Nonetheless, the growth of British IP represented a shift from the USA to Europe that was underscored by the growing presence of Dutch firms in the business. Aside from Endemol, one such company was Harry de Winter's IDTV, originally a producer of game shows and 'docusoaps' for the Dutch market. More quickly attuned to international demand than its British counterparts due to the small size of its domestic market, IDTV developed a whole range of game shows – many with a burgeoning reality element – that sold well internationally. These included *Grand Slam*, *Gossip*, *Karaoke TV*, *Lingo* (more than ten versions) and *Young Matchmakers* (Baker, 1996b).

The US Market Opens Up

It was in the late 1990s that the US networks began paying attention to overseas IP. The significance of this development lay in the size and stature of the world's largest media market. To a producer, selling a remake licence to a US broadcaster not only brings substantial revenue but also guarantees international sales, of the format and of the show's completed US version. Foreign broadcasters reason – usually rightly so – that if a show is good enough for the ultra-competitive US market it is good enough for them.

Until the late 1990s, foreign adaptations on US soil were few and far between. Although some scripted adaptations led to significant hits, not least *All in the Family* (chapter 9), adaptations in the unscripted space were rare. *Dollar a Second* was a version of Radio Luxembourg's *Cent francs par seconde* (chapter 1). It premiered on DuMont Television Network in September 1953, where it was set up with help from a French team, before moving to NBC and then ABC (Schmitt, 2005: 467; Schwartz et al., 1999: 58). Created by Jacques Antoine, a prolific French producer, this show is possibly the first format ever purchased by an American network and one of the very few French games adapted on US television.

The Krypton Factor came nearly twenty years later. The game show was devised by Jeremy Fox, then at ITV, and when the broadcaster went on strike he took the tape to America. The US version was picked by ABC, where it stayed on air very briefly in 1981 (Fox, interview 2010).

It was only towards the end of the century that US networks began to select a few unscripted formats for adaptation and independent British TV producers registered their first hits across the pond. It started with *Ready Steady Cook*, which Bazalgette sold to the Food Network in 1995. The channel relabelled it *Ready. . . Set. . . Cook!*, and the show embarked on a long syndicated career. It was followed by MBC's *Robot Wars* and Hat Trick's *Whose Line Is It Anyway?*, which ABC kept on air for ten seasons (Davies, 1998).

These shows seem innocuous but their presence on US TV screens denotes a slow shift in attitude from American broadcasters, and their success paved the way for the four European super-formats that were about to change American television (chapter 3).

The Rise of Unscripted Programming and Reality Television

The advent of reality television was another innovation that helped to bring about the TV format revolution. In terms of genre, TV schedules had not changed much in half a century: 1990s TV staples such as drama, comedy, news and current affairs, quiz shows, panel shows, and amateur and talent shows had all begun life in the sound broadcasting era. Thus, the rise of a new unscripted genre is an event of historical significance that both denotes profound changes and heralds new ones. TV genres are 'constructs created through social relationships between creators and audiences that delineate the similarities and differences among cultural objects', and they matter for several reasons (Bielby and Harrington, 2008: 67). From the production side, they enable broadcasters to manage risk, as they can roughly gauge the size and type of audience that exist for each category (Bielby and Harrington, 2008: 67). For viewers, it is about managing expectations. In the same way that a consumer purchasing a tin labelled 'tomato soup' would expect exactly that having opened the tin, a TV viewer selecting a romantic comedy looks forward to the story of a lead character overcoming misunderstandings and obstacles to find love, not being dismembered in a wood by a maniac with a chainsaw.

Reality television is a broad church, with many strands in constant evolution, and therefore does not lend itself easily to grand statements. The history of the genre, its boundaries and cultural significance, remain open to debate (e.g. Bignell, 2005; Holmes and Jermyn, 2004; Kavka, 2012; Kilborn, 2003; Ouellette, 2014). For my purposes, I will separate reality programming into the following categories:

- observational documentaries (e.g. *Benefits Street*)
- factual entertainment (e.g. *Wife Swap*)

- reality competitions (e.g. *Big Brother*)
- talent competitions (e.g. *Dancing with the Stars*)
- constructed reality (e.g. *Made in Chelsea*)

It is inevitable that some programmes will fall in between the shifting boundaries of these categories, but the purpose of this typology is to differentiate formats, not deliver a detailed genre analysis. The first three strands will be analysed in chapter 7, talent competitions in chapter 8 and constructed reality in chapter 9. Constructed reality is bundled with other scripted formats since its German variant has been the most widely adapted and tends to be fully scripted. Apart from these, all reality sub-genres consist, to a varying extent, of three basic elements: (1) unscripted storytelling, (2) contestants who play themselves and (3) claims to a connection with the real world. In reality shows, the narrative arc is not generated by a script but engineered by *rules* and *situations* that create drama (chapters 7 and 8). As ever in television, boundaries are fluid and some reality programmes are partially scripted (dating shows in particular), just as some constructed reality shows are fully scripted.

The distinction between scripted and reality genres is not about the casting of everyday people versus actors but about characters who play a scripted role versus characters who play themselves. A soap actor on *Celebrity Big Brother* or *I'm a Celebrity . . . Get Me Out of Here!* plays himself or herself, and viewers hope to get to know the person behind the persona. Finally, all reality shows lay claim to authenticity, which is stronger and more genuine in the case of observational documentaries than in that of talent competitions. Fixed-rig productions that use remotely controlled cameras unobtrusively reach areas that were previously out of bounds to film crews. Shows like *24 Hours in A&E*, *Educating Essex* or *Gogglebox* do well with viewers because they offer a depiction of life in schools, hospitals and living rooms that viewers feel is both honest and intimate. With more structured shows like talent competitions, an element of doubt over authenticity is inherent to the genre, and production teams know that establishing the degree of manipulation of such programmes is a game that audiences like to play (Carter, interview 2014).

The origins of reality TV are still being debated, and competing claims are made about its history. The long trail of entertainment shows starring 'real' people constitutes a source for at least the first two elements of reality formats. These range from *Candid Camera* (chapter 1), amateur competitions such as *Ted Mack's Original Amateur Hour* (chapter 3), documentaries such as *An American Family* (PBS, 1973), game shows like *Game for a Laugh* (ITV, 1981–5), *Truth or Consequences* (CBS, 1950–4; NBC,

1954–65) or *All Star Secrets* (NBC, 1979), up to CCTV and home video shows and Bunim/Murray's *The Real World* for MTV, which premiered in 1992 (Clissold, 2004; Kavka, 2012: 13–52; McCarthy, 2004; Ouellette and Murray, 2004). Michael Hill, the creator of *Game for a Laugh* and *All Star Secrets*, explains his intent:

> *Game for a Laugh* [is] a show where the people are the stars . . . let's have fun with people. Let's put people in situations and laugh at the circumstances that befall them . . . In the case of *All Star Secrets* what I really set out to do was create a talk show inside of a game. My trip, my whole trip in everything that I've invented, was not into questions and answers and hard games; my whole trip was into how to do other things disguised as games. So *All Star Secrets*, which in England was with Michael Parkinson [ITV, 1985–6], the game was secondary to the notion that you could get whoever it is to tell secrets about themselves, it was a gossip show. (Hill, interview 2010)

The claim to make a connection with the real world comes from fly-on-the-wall documentaries and docusoaps which are filmed and edited with the intention of giving the audience the sensation of observing a slice of life and providing a 'relatively unmediated view of reality' (Kilborn, 1994: 422). A classic example is those observational shows on police, criminals and emergency services, a sub-genre in its own right that emerged in the late 1980s with titles like *America's Most Wanted*, which debuted on Fox in 1988, *Cops* (Fox, 1989 to time of writing) and *Rescue 911* (CBS, 1989–96) (Kavka, 2012: 51–3; Kilborn, 1994: 426). Each one has inspired foreign versions and, according to Misha Kavka, *America's Most Wanted* was derived from *Crimewatch UK* (BBC One, 1984 to time of writing), which itself was modelled on a ZDF programme called *Aktenzeichen XY . . . ungelöst* [*File Number XY . . . Unsolved*], debuted in 1967 and is still running (Kavka, 2012: 53).

For factual entertainment programming, another related source is the 'lifestyle' shows that began to appear on TV schedules as broadcasters responded to the demand arising from increased leisure time and consumer culture. Examples include BBC's long-running *Gardeners' World* and *Food and Drink*, which first aired in 1968 and 1978 respectively.

All these influences are apparent in the genesis of the first big reality formats, which produced something revolutionary by mixing elements from these various sources and adding devices, rules and situations to engineer drama. This is the case, for instance, with factual entertainment, a reality strand that played a crucial role in the worldwide growth of TV formats. Peter Bazalgette, who was in charge of *Food and Drink* at the BBC, explains the transition to *Ready Steady Cook* (which showed viewers simple recipes but also involved two chefs competing over a half-hour):

Now my modest part in this was sort of creating formats that did not fit into the previous categories, because television entertainment was either drama, or it was a game show or you had kids, or you had documentary. You didn't have sort of formatted reality shows, you didn't have formatted leisure shows and so on and so forth. So kind of what we were doing is we were creating, essentially we were creating hybrids. And *Ready Steady Cook* is, on the one hand, a sort of what the Americans call a how-to show, because it shows you how to cook recipes, on the other hand, it's a game show with a competition, and it's got an element of human interest as well because you get two members of the public in, you talk about their lives and what's happened to them and so on. And again I don't know whether we set out to rewrite the rule book but that's what happened. (Bazalgette, interview 2009)

Many other lifestyle shows went through the same transformation in subsequent years. *Top Gear*, for instance, started life as a car magazine show in 1977 and was relaunched in 2002 as 'an entertainment format about cars' (Duncan Gray, commercial director, *Top Gear*, BBC Worldwide, in Brzoznowski, 2011b: 1). Two years later, *MasterChef*, a pedestrian Sunday afternoon cookery show on air since 1990, was given a reality makeover by John Silver, Shine's then creative director. Today, some of the world's most popular formats mix didactic and entertaining elements and the factual entertainment genre covers everything from makeover and coaching shows to life-swap programmes (chapter 7).

The same fusion of old and new is apparent in the making of *Survivor*, an early reality competition (chapter 3). Charlie Parsons, its creator, was exploring new ways of doing documentaries in a controlled situation. He challenged a reporter to come down from Scotland to London on £5 (he cheated), sent another one to live with a bunch of people in a nuclear bunker, and then filmed four people (a well-known tennis player, a stockbroker, a soap star and an ex-convict) living in very basic conditions on a desert island off the coast of Sri Lanka. *Survive!*, as the project was called, added to these elements an elimination procedure that enabled Parsons to produce a 'winner' and an 'end game' to the island experiment; in other words, 'to have something which was closer to a traditional entertainment show' (Parsons, interview 2009). However, the hybrid nature of the show made it impossible to sell and it was rejected by every single British and American network it was pitched to:

It's difficult to imagine back in those days but in reality the different genres of television were incredibly split. So there was an entertainment department in ITV, there was a factual department in ITV, and there wasn't really a crossover. And actually so when we developed [*Survivor*], I thought it was a mixture of entertainment, factual and soap opera, and was the way to take it forward. And that was our difficulty actually in a way, because when we took it to one department they couldn't see what to do with it. They said well hang on a minute, this doesn't feel like an entertainment programme, because an entertainment programme is *The Generation Game* or it's *Blockbusters*, you know, it didn't feel like an entertainment show. When you took it to the factual department they said well this is very lightweight, it's not a serious documentary, it doesn't tell us anything. Literally it was very difficult to get away. (Parsons, interview 2009)

Survivor was eventually picked by Anna Bråkenhielm in Sweden, who was attracted to the format precisely for its hybridity: 'it was something totally new . . . It was a mix of genres; it was like a documentary and it was like a talk show' (chapter 3) (Bråkenhielm, interview 2009).

The rise of a new unscripted genre played a crucial role in the TV format revolution: as any reality programme can become a format, well over 50 per cent of TV formats in circulation in the 2000s were reality-related (chapter 7). Indeed, the rules and settings these shows use in order to generate storylines and a dramatic arc not only give them a clear structure and distinctive features but transform old programming forms into reproducible and recognizable – and hence formattable – programmes.

Formation of a Global Content Market

The 1990s would see a decade of radical transformation for the TV industry, and the scope and nature of these changes created a global market for TV content. In Europe, most countries were served by a handful of stations, until the liberalization of policy regimes rapidly augmented the pool of broadcasters and the number of commercial channels in the 1980s. New technologies such as communications satellites and the digital revolution enabled cable and satellite platforms to carry channels by the hundreds. The fall of the Iron Curtain and the enlargement of the European Union opened up television markets in Central and Eastern Europe, creating a large European audiovisual space that exceeded 200 million TV households (Chalaby, 2009; Collins, 1998; Gross and Jakubowicz, 2013; Humphreys, 1996; Starks, 2013).

East and West, new broadcasters pressed for content filled their TV channels with cheap imports from Hollywood's back catalogue, complemented by Australian soaps and telenovelas. As competition grew, broadcasters realized that imports would not carry them very far in terms of ratings. They discovered that a higher audience share depended on local content and they had no choice but to turn to local programming. By the second half of the

1990s, domestic production was rising and the proportion of imported programming was falling in all of Europe's key markets, including Spain, Italy, Germany and the UK (Rouse, 2001).

Local programming, however, is not bulletproof: it requires resources and capital and, in truth, most new shows fail. This is why a slice of the content market went to formatted shows: broadcasters needed recipes to bridge the gap between local expertise and demand for local programming.

The same process built up on a global scale in the ensuing years. Democratization (in some territories), digitization and market forces combined effectively to expand the TV industry – and hence the demand for content – worldwide. Television, and the creative industries in general, have shown impressive growth since the mid-1990s across the Middle East, Africa, Asia (including India and China) and Latin America (e.g. Flew, 2013; Moran and Keane, 2004; Page and Crawley, 2001; Sakr, 2007; Sinclair, 1999; Sinclair and Turner, 2004; Thussu, 2013; Zhao, 2008). This growth has been significant in terms of both production (number of TV channels, advertising and subscription revenues) and consumption (e.g. TV viewing time, number of TV sets per territory).

In short, the demand for formats grew exponentially, first in the developed world and then in the emerging markets, because an ever-increasing number of broadcasters operating in an ever-growing number of liberalized broadcasting systems lacked the expertise to create what audiences prefer: local shows.

The global content market has since continued to expand and is conservatively valued at US$50 billion by ITV (ITV, 2014: 7). In Europe alone, the number of TV channels is estimated at 11,474 (including local versions of international brands) and the number of on-demand audiovisual services at 3,695.[2] The TV format industry has managed to secure a growing slice of the market (chapter 4).

Global Information Flow

Correspondence in the BBC Written Archives between BBC executives and agents selling US formats is a reminder of just how cumbersome transatlantic communication was in the early days of the trade. Sometimes they exchanged letters and cables to chase the one and only recording of a show. It could take weeks for these 'kinescopes' to change hands, crossing the Atlantic on board ocean liners.[3]

By the 1990s the pace of the trade quickened as developing communications technologies eased the exchange of information worldwide. New communication networks enabled production companies to monitor the world TV market in real time, detecting trends and successful formats in all corners of the world. For instance, when Endemol expanded internationally they set up a stringers network to observe key markets and report back to the company's top executives on a monthly basis. In the early 2000s, they installed an intranet so managers at the Hilversum headquarters near Amsterdam could watch programmes that had been broadcast the night before in Brazil or Japan.

Today, all TV production majors have digital file-sharing systems that feed the internal flow of information, complemented by email newsletters and online services from information suppliers to the industry. Market fairs, the digital screening rooms of the trade press, YouTube and social media traffic are other means of discovering new trends and formats (chapter 4).

In July 1953, the BBC received a letter from an advertising agency based in Buenos Aires enquiring after *Twenty Questions* – more than six years after the programme had first aired on BBC radio – only to receive the answer that the BBC did not hold the rights to the show.[4] With today's technology, the TV format industry relies on information exchanges that are instantaneous and responsive on a world scale.

Conclusion: The Making of an Entertainment Revolution

The 1950s witnessed the first TV formats and the first contracts to recognize a format as a remake right. The next two decades were rather quiet on the format front as European governments increased their hold on television. Public broadcasters were assigned the task of promoting national culture and elevating public taste. American game shows returned in the 1980s, travelling even further than before.

However, the wheels that were set in motion in the 1990s would later bring the TV format revolution. Large-scale format producers emerged, and an independent TV production sector formed in the UK whose creativity would play a major role in the sector. A new unscripted genre developed – reality – whose structured shows provided a formidable boost to the format trade. US networks began to open up to foreign IP, and elsewhere demand for formats grew as broadcasters sought recipes for local programming. All these factors would eventually combine to create a sharp expansion and globalization of the international format flow in the new millennium. Yet, in the late 1990s, relatively few TV executives were aware of these changes. For the TV format revolution to unfold, all that was needed was for a show to demonstrate its format power.

3 The Advent of the Super-Formats

Although formats were crossing borders in growing numbers just prior to 2000, many TV executives had yet to take notice. The changes bubbling below the surface had yet to break into world television. The role of heralding TV formats to the world fell to four super-formats: *Who Wants to Be a Millionaire?*, *Survivor*, *Big Brother* and *Idols*.

According to Peter Bazalgette, for a format to qualify as super it needs to break new ground in terms of originality, geographical coverage, and revenue generation (Bazalgette, interview 2009). Bazalgette also argues that super-formats changed the TV industry by demonstrating to broadcasters the benefit of adapting concepts with a proven track record (Bazalgette, 2005). True as this is, these concepts also highlight the changes that occurred in the previous decade (chapter 2):

- Three of them originated from the UK, and one from Holland, underscoring the European rise in format production.
- Three were developed by UK-based independent TV production companies, heralding the sector's creativity.
- Two were owned by global production companies formed in the 1990s (Endemol and Pearson Television, which became FremantleMedia).
- Three were in the reality genre.

It is right to argue that these super-formats helped place the TV format trade where it is today – at the heart of the world television industry – but it is equally important to understand how they are the manifestation of changes that took place earlier. The creators of the super-formats were talented enough to create concepts that resonated around the world, even though these concepts reflected wider industry developments.

Millionaire: The Game that Rewrote the Rule Book

Celador was a small British independent production company owned by Paul Smith and specializing in light entertainment. Its mid-1990s production slate included *The Wowfabgroovy Show* and *Talking Telephone Numbers* (two quiz shows), *After the Break* with Patrick Kielty and *The Hypnotic World of Paul McKenna.* Celador's development team, comprising David Briggs, Steve Knight, Mike Whitehill and Paul Smith, set out to create a big-prize game show. The big-money game show was a well-established tradition in the UK – not least because of US formats – and at the time it was *Raise the Roof* (produced by Action Time for ITV) that was giving out the largest-ever prize on UK television: a £100,000 house. The team noticed how much this show lacked in drama and excitement and devised a formula designed to deliver both (Smith, interview 2009).

The first outcome of their endeavour was a show called *Cash Mountain* that Smith pitched to ITV, Channel 4 and Channel 5 (the three British free-to-air commercial networks), which they all turned down (Bazalgette, 2005: 71). After more than two years of rejections, Smith returned to ITV one last time in 1998 to pitch the show to David Liddiment, the new director of programmes, and Claudia Rosencrantz, head of entertainment. He made Liddiment play *Cash Mountain,* so that he experienced first hand how the 'dilemmas and uncertainties grew dramatically' as the game progressed (Bazalgette, 2005: 95). Liddiment also needed to be convinced that, in giving the answers away, the game was not too simple, the odds were not too short, and he would not be bankrupting ITV by giving away too many £1 million prizes. When he opted to cash in at £200 he knew that he should not be unduly worried about this (Liddiment, interview 2011).

The first pilot looked like an old-fashioned Saturday-night variety show, with the heavily lit set and the bouncy music. It also had the appearance of a data-filled Bloomberg screen: around the tiny video box showing the host and contestant were the money tree, the lifelines, the question and the four possible answers (Smith, interview 2009). The structure was in place but the drama was still lacking. The team stripped away all these elements, changed the music and darkened the set, in order to focus on the drama that was being played out on screen:

> What's most appealing about it . . . it's seeing people under genuine pressure . . . making a life changing decision . . . And on the basis of that, of course it is a drama, it's a human drama. And what is most exciting about it is seeing these people wrestle against the questions, the tactics they're going to use. Are they going to use a lifeline or are they not, and when they do use a lifeline are they going to take any notice of the information that is provided to them, or are they going to ignore it, certainly in the case of phone a friend and ask the audience. And are they going to have the guts to go all the way, or the foolishness to go all the way depending on how one looks at it. (Smith, interview 2009)

Contestants would have *two* cameras trained on them, filming close-ups of their agony as the stakes rose:

The most dramatic thing is to look at a close-up of that person when they're under pressure. And so there's two permanent close-up cameras, one with a close-up of the face, and the second one with a slightly looser shot with, down the right-hand side ... the various information about where they are and the ladder as to how far they've climbed up, and also what lifelines they've used. And the director can choose either one at any time, either to provide the drama or to remind people at home exactly what part of the programme a person has managed to get to. (Smith, interview 2009)

The show premiered on ITV on Friday 4 September 1998. By Monday morning, Smith learnt that the show had attracted 44 per cent of audience share, and by the afternoon his PA was getting enquiries from all over the world. Within seven days they had collected forty applications from interested buyers. The first deal was signed with Australia's Channel 9 because a contingent from the network had literally camped in Celador's reception and Smith felt that they 'had demonstrated their commitment to the show' (Smith, interview 2009). Processing approximately one application a week, at least thirty-five deals were signed within a year. One of these agreements was signed with US network ABC, for which *Millionaire* proved such a ratings triumph that the network decided to air it three times a week. This further boosted the format's international profile, and it had sold to ninety countries by March 2001. The format reached 108 territories just before its tenth anniversary, breaking all records (Spencer, interview 2008).

According to Claudia Rosencrantz, *Millionaire* 'single-handedly changed the fortunes of American networks [and] the history of TV' (in Robertson, 2000). As generous as this assessment may be, it is not completely off the mark. *Millionaire* innovated by injecting drama into a genre that was devoid of it and, unlike most other game shows, it was scheduled in primetime. The architecture of the format is also extremely well thought through. At the heart of the game lies the idea that the money prize is financed by calls to a premium-rate number. A media partner was chosen (the *Sun* in the UK) for publicity, without which the line would not have generated sufficient funds. In any case, *Millionaire* was insured against the likelihood of anybody winning a million (Smith, interview 2009). The show also introduced clever format points, not least multiple-choice answers, a device imitated ever since. These answers add an interactive dimension to the game, enabling viewers at home to play along with the contestants.

Millionaire was also the first unscripted entertainment show to be developed as an off-screen franchise (chapter 8). Only minute local variations are allowed on the show as most aspects are defined in the bible, including the music, opening titles, type of host and questions, studio set, lighting, even down to the camera movements. The policy was dictated by a necessity to protect the show's mechanics but also by the need to guard the coherence of the brand across markets. This mattered more than ever before because Smith had had the foresight to retain the show's ancillary rights. In any given territory, the TV broadcast and ancillary rights were sold separately, and the local producer would be given only about 10 per cent of the revenue derived from the exploitation of ancillary rights (Smith, interview 2009). Indeed, *Millionaire*'s merchandising was comprehensive and expanded to 140 product lines – from board games to Christmas crackers – and at one stage represented 40 per cent of the format revenue (Spencer, interview 2008). In terms of both international reach and IP exploitation, *Millionaire* set new benchmarks in international television and was a true game changer for the industry.

Discovering a New Planet: Reality Television

The fate of reality television and the format trade became entwined in the late 1990s when *Survivor* became one of the world's best-travelled shows. The concept was developed by Charlie Parsons and his creative team at Planet 24, then a mid-sized British independent company he controlled alongside Waheed Alli (now Lord) and Bob Geldof (now Sir) (table 2.3, p. 40).

As already seen, Charlie Parsons first experimented with reality TV in 1988 when he filmed a group of celebrities on a desert island off Sri Lanka. The show aired on ITV and attracted little attention, but Parsons understood its significance. His creative team refined the concept, adding a game-show component (competition between two teams, an end game and a winner) but with a revolutionary twist: the competition was to be structured by an elimination procedure whereby contestants voted each other out of the game week after week. The elimination formed an essential part of the show's engine because it dictated contestants' behaviour as to who formed alliances and conspired against each other, delivering drama and tension on a daily basis. Parsons preferred a voting-out mechanism by the contestants themselves – as opposed to a phone vote, which he deemed potentially unfair and unreliable – because 'it wasn't about people being eliminated, it was about who was the hero [and] who would win at the end' (Parsons, interview 2009). The elimination procedure, in different variants, proved highly influential and 'was to dominate most successful reality shows for the next decade' (chapters 6 and 7) (Bazalgette, 2005: 83).

The show was rejected by major networks on both sides of the Atlantic as no one was entirely sure how the elimination procedure would unfold. In 1994, however, Gary Carter, head of the international sales team, managed to sell two multi-territory options to Endemol and Strix, a Swedish production company (Carter, interview 2008). Endemol did nothing with it but Anna Bråkenhielm, Strix's chief executive officer, eventually convinced Sveriges Television (SVT), the Swedish public broadcaster, to commission the show. Bråkenhielm was curious to see how people would cope and although she knew that the elimination system was 'very controversial at the time', she thought that it was also 'thrilling and daring'. SVT called it *Expedition Robinson* and it became a ratings success in Sweden. She subsequently sold the show to Norway, Denmark and Germany (Bråkenhielm, interview 2009).

It would take another three years for the show to air in America, where the rights were picked up by Mark Burnett, creator of *Eco-Challenge*. He began production in March 2000 in Borneo and the show premiered on CBS two months later. The many millions of dollars spent on production and the 400-strong crew involved in the making of each episode helped the show to become a ratings sensation. It was duly recommissioned and the second season, which aired between January and March 2001, beat *Friends* with an average 29.8 million viewers (Burnett, 2005: 119). The glossy US version caused broadcasters to rush to get a local licence and the format finally attained a large geographical footprint. By 2009, there were forty-three local versions of *Survivor*, which covered seventy-three territories because of three pan-regional versions in Africa, the Middle East and the Baltic countries. In Europe and Latin America, the format is often known as *Expedition Robinson* (Parsons, email correspondence 2009). But unlike *Millionaire*, it took the best part of the 1990s before the show turned into an international success.

Big Brother

Big Brother combined the elimination procedure with 24/7 observational reality techniques. It became a global ratings hit and a cultural phenomenon because it was an original concept that pushed the boundaries of acceptability. *Big Brother*, which was devised by John de Mol and his creative team at Endemol, launched on 17 September 1999 on Veronica, a Dutch free-to-air channel. In the Netherlands – as in all the territories it reached – the show faced a barrage of criticism and moral outrage. De Mol, however, expressed different views when he addressed his team on launch day:

Guys – *Big Brother* will be for Endemol what Mickey Mouse is for Disney. We are working on something that is going to be huge: twenty years from now, talking about television, they will talk about TV before *Big Brother* and TV after *Big Brother*. (in Bazalgette, 2005: 143)

There is a hyperbolic side to the pep talk, but it is undeniable that *Big Brother* helped to build one of the world's largest TV production majors and made a significant impact on world television. *Big Brother* was the first show for which a group of US network executives set foot in Europe to look at a TV production. They liked what they saw and CBS launched it in July 2000, recommissioning ever since (Carter, interview 2008). About thirty licences were sold by the mid-2000s, including two pan-regional versions in Africa and the Middle East (where the show was taken off air after a few days) (Bazalgette, 2005: 287–90).

Beyond shock value, there are a few other reasons why *Big Brother* has secured its place in television history. It was the first format to be a multimedia brand that can be delivered on numerous platforms: terrestrial television, cable channel (24-hour coverage and chat shows) and online (24-hour access and forum). And since the show contains many interactive features, each platform has been successfully turned into an income stream (Bazalgette, 2005).

Above all, *Big Brother*, alongside other reality shows such as *Survivor*, made full use of *digital non-linear editing suites* in order to whittle down thousands of hours of footage into a short narrative for the format's flagship evening show. These suites represent a particularly important milestone in the evolution of TV production and have had far-reaching consequences in terms of storytelling techniques for unscripted programming. They began commercialization in the late 1980s by firms such as Editing Machine Corporation, OLE and Avid Technology, the current market leader. Non-linear editing systems removed the artificial linearity of working with tapes by introducing computers and digitizing the editing process. With linear devices the editing was done on VHS tape, with editors fast forwarding or rewinding according to the cuts they wanted to make. If they had twenty tapes they had to change from one and put the next one in. Non-linear systems stored the data from the tapes onto a media drive, and editors were able to manipulate that data within the edit and create the story. By way of analogy, the difference between linear and non-linear systems is akin to writing a novel before and after word processors or making a playlist before and after iTunes. Non-linear editing helped transform the post-production process by making editing incomparably faster, enabling editors to make complex cuts routinely and allowing them to handle a much larger amount of recorded material (Channing, interview 2010; Sargent, interview 2010).

For the first British series in 2000, '200 people were working on *Big Brother,* including a pool of fifty cameramen and thirteen producers' on 24-hour shifts (Ritchie, 2000: 9). The contestants were filmed round the clock by a mix of thirty fixed or operated cameras, and 'the amount of information passing through the five *Big Brother* edit suites was double the whole internet capacity of the UK just three years earlier' (Ritchie, 2000: 19). In the later series, up to twenty non-linear systems were used simultaneously by an army of editors in order to winnow out from this massive amount of footage the best storylines, edit this material as stories unfolded, and keep doing it right up to transmission. This storytelling technique was adopted by all subsequent reality shows: all have a high *shooting ratio* (meaning that they shoot many more hours than they need for the show's edited version) and use digital non-linear editing suites in order to find the storylines and form the series' dramatic arc during the post-production process.

Idols: Opportunity Knocks Again, Again, and Again!

The last super-format that helped to turn the fortunes of the trade was *Pop Idol,* as the original version was named in the UK. *Idols* (its international name) – and just before it, *Popstars* – added a reality element to a genre, the amateur show, that goes back to the sound broadcasting era. The first such show was *Major Bowes' Original Amateur Hour,* which began on WHN New York in 1934 and moved to the major radio networks (NBC, CBS and ABC) in subsequent years (Buxton and Owen, 1972: 192–3). It was adapted by the BBC in 1936 (chapter 1). After Bowes's death in 1946, Ted Mack, who worked on the show, took it to television. It aired as *Ted Mack's Original Amateur Hour* on all the US major networks between 1948 and 1970 (McNeil, 1997: 821). The transition from one medium to another was also made by *Arthur Godfrey's Talent Scouts,* a popular radio show that debuted on television (CBS) in December 1948 and lasted nearly a decade. Young performers were introduced by a celebrity and the evening's winner was determined by a 'clap-o-meter' (Brown, 1992: 226). In Britain, *The Carroll Levis Show,* which aired from 1942 to 1954 and 1956 to 1960 on the BBC Light Programme, put amateurs before a panel of judges.[1]

Godfrey's format formed the basis of Hughie Green's *Opportunity Knocks.* The show first aired on the BBC Light Programme on 18 February 1949, moving on to Radio Luxembourg.[2] It made its TV debut for a short run on ITV in 1956 and came back to the network in 1964 for an almost uninterrupted run that lasted until March 1978. The show was revived by the BBC in 1987 for three years. While the BBC revival introduced telephone voting, it would be a panel of experts that would mark the contestants on ITV's *New Faces* (1973–8). In the show's second version (ITV, 1986–8), the home audience was given the opportunity to vote by postcard, as on the former versions of *Opportunity Knocks*.

Early talent shows (showcasing amateurs) were rooted in the variety genre (professional entertainers): stage-centric and focused entirely on the contestants' on-set performance. Contemporary competitions have kept the twin principles of talent discovery and popularity contest but differ in their reality element. What is offered is a more complex and multi-layered narrative, weaving stories around contestants and their backgrounds, friends and families, judges and mentors. Stories develop in different settings, including the stage, backstage, and locations in recorded segments such as a contestant's primary school or family home. Contemporary talent shows lay the emphasis on drama and emotion and contestants' journey and experiences. They create contrast between success and failure, elation and despair, and new lives and old lives. This storytelling is dependent on these non-linear suites, since the reality element necessitates interweaving hours of footage of contestants at home, at work, on stage and backstage.

There are competing accounts of who created *Pop Idol*, the first being more far-fetched than the second. Simon Cowell claims that he progressively realized the marketing power of television when working as an artists and repertoire (A&R) executive for a variety of record labels. Successes were few and far between until he offered record contracts to established TV stars, including the wrestlers of the World Wrestling Federation, the Power Rangers and the Teletubbies. He also signed up Robson Green and Jerome Flynn, from the popular ITV drama *Soldier, Soldier*, and the cast members of various British soaps, including *Emmerdale Farm*, *Heartbeat* and *Coronation Street* (Bower, 2012: 79–97).

Further success with Westlife, a boyband, finally convinced Cowell that 'the future of the music business is tied to TV', as he said, and in 2000 he allegedly outlined the format of a TV show that would be a platform to sell music (Bower, 2012: 123). He entertained several people about his plans before inviting the interest of Simon Fuller over dinner 'because he's good at these things', Cowell thought (Bower, 2012: 130). Fuller was supposedly enthused by the idea and, mulling over a similar concept, added that 'the audience should decide the winner by telephone voting' (Bower, 2012: 130).

In his own account, Simon Fuller is reluctant to share ownership for the format's origination and presents himself as the man who created *Idols* (Rushfield, 2011: 5). Also starting as an A&R executive, Fuller set up his own company, 19 Entertainment, and went on to manage Annie Lennox and the Spice Girls, and launch S Club 7, a TV and music franchise. Having been involved in auditions for years, he developed the concept of *Fame Search*, an online talent competition that let the audience choose the members of a new band, which ITV turned down in 1999. The following year Fuller was pitching it again as *Your Idol* to Nigel Lythgoe, an entertainment executive at the same network (Rushfield, 2011: 13). In Fuller's own words:

> My show [*Your Idol*] brought together many different elements to one show: Mass auditions, the search for a new star, judges, audience voting. We created this huge live TV event drawing more from a sporting concept of true competition than a conventional talent show. I then added drama of backstories and the real-life soap opera of the unfolding real-time events. It was a reality music competition and soap opera brought together in one massive show that later became known as 'Pop Idol'. (Fuller, 2011)

Lythgoe rejected Fuller's idea for one good reason: he had just signed another talent competition: *Popstars*. The show was conceived by Jonathan Dowling (Essential Productions) in New Zealand in 1999. The show had no studio element and followed a nationwide search to form a band (it became TrueBliss), from the first audition to the recording of their first single. The format rights were acquired by Des Monaghan and Bob Campbell of Screentime, an Australian company, who sold it locally to Seven Network. *Popstars Australia* became a fully fledged singing competition that stretched over a six-month period. It started with nine episodes of auditions, followed by seven quarter-finals and five semi-finals, a process during which 100 contestants were whittled down to twelve. These twelve were put through eleven eviction nights as they were voted off by the public. The format, some fifty episodes long, included a tour of Australia for the final two contestants and five catch-up episodes that revealed backstage moments and the lives of the two finalists after the grand final.

The show came to the attention of Alison Rayson, who had set up a London-based distribution company, Target Entertainment, in 1998. It was sold to her as a 'docusoap' creating pop stars out of ordinary people through a process of audition and selection. Rayson agreed a deal with Screentime to manage the format sales worldwide and placed it first with Lythgoe, who had heard about the format through his son in Australia (Rayson, interview 2010).

Popstars debuted on ITV on 10 January 2001 to yet another stellar ratings performance, and international interest developed for the show. By the end of the year, local versions had been produced in about ten countries, including Argentina, France, Germany, Italy and the USA. A few years later, *Popstars* had been adapted in forty territories, placing it among the fastest-selling formats of its time. Yet, in many countries, *Popstars* was not recommissioned beyond the first or second season. Crucially, the American version fell short because it failed to reach the necessary scale on the WB Television Network. Elsewhere, the franchise suffered because of quality issues (Beale, interview 2008; Jackson, interview 2008; Rayson, interview 2010). The influence and contribution of *Popstars* should not be underestimated, but it lacked the longevity and commercial success in key markets (except Germany) to become a super-format. It was soon to be eclipsed by a format owned by much more powerful promoters.

Preparing for the British version of *Popstars*, Simon Jones, then an ITV business manager, entered into contact with Simon Cowell, sounding him out for a chair on the judges' panel. Cowell accepted and then declined, a decision he briefly regretted after witnessing the growing fame of Nigel Lythgoe, who was riveting audiences with his 'brutal honesty' on hapless performers (Bower, 2012: 129). The two men stayed in touch and when Cowell entertained Jones about his own project of a music-based TV format, the latter, who by then was at Pearson TV (soon FremantleMedia), invited Cowell to meet with Alan Boyd. As Cowell and Fuller had discussed their projects, both turned up to meet Boyd on 13 February 2001 (Jones, interview 2010).

The Simons discussed their plans with Boyd, who was consulted as a TV entertainment executive and tasked to work out the mechanics of the show (Boyd, interview 2009). How many calls could phone companies handle in an hour? How to film 50,000 auditions and where to find storage and a filing system? When and how do the judges and the audience come on board? Once the concept was ready, Rayson heard that the show was being promoted everywhere and was told she had a strong case for a lawsuit. But she did not go to court as she lacked the resources to do so and was convinced not to sue by industry figures, instead obtaining some minor concessions through a FRAPA mediation (Rayson, interview 2010). *Idols* bears strong similarities to *Popstars*, but its improved format has been assembled in a sufficiently original manner to stand just about on its own two feet. It enhanced audience interactivity, searched for a solo star (whereas *Popstars* formed bands at the quarter-final and semi-final stages), laid more emphasis on live shows and went for scale.

Idols illustrates well the contrast between the narrative strategies of pre- and post-reality talent shows. The opening line of the note scribbled during the meeting, which outlines the format of a show called *Your Idol*, reads 'Gone With The Wind'. It was their intent to produce a drama as epic and life-changing as that film (Boyd, interview 2009). They set emotions as the show's bedrock, which was designed to create and document the journey of a champion fighting for success (Boyd, interview 2009). The show was easily sold to ITV (Claudia Rosencrantz commissioning for the network) and debuted in October 2001. By the end of the first series four months later, *Pop Idol* was a phenomenal ratings success and was riveting viewers with the battle between the unassuming and stammering Gareth Gates and the more self-assured Will Young. At the heart of its appeal lay the intertwining of the natural emotive power of music with the emotions engineered by a cleverly constructed dramatic arc.

Next stop was America, where the show struggled to sell. When Cowell, Fuller and Jones crossed the Atlantic to pitch the show, they were turned down by all the networks (Jones, interview 2010). US executives were not as dim as that makes them sound, since quite a few music-based formats had performed poorly, not least WB's *Popstars* and MTV's *Making the Band!*. To them, *Pop Idol* came across as a banal karaoke show that would never work (Boyd, interview 2009). After initially rejecting the proposal, Mike Darnell, Fox's head of alternative programming, reopened the conversation requesting that the show came to the network fully funded. When Cecile Frot-Coutaz, the head of FremantleMedia North America, was putting together a suite of sponsors, Elisabeth Murdoch called her father in New York. Having witnessed first hand the *Pop Idol* phenomenon in London, she urged him to acquire the show at once. Fox's executive team duly obliged, never imagining, recalls one of them, 'that it was going to change the entire fate of the network' (Rushfield, 2011: 46).

American Idol became a cultural institution and the country's top programme for six consecutive years. It was watched by record audiences that reached 37.4 million viewers for the sixth season in January 2007. It made Simon Cowell a household name in America, and he was offered US$300 million to stay with the format and not launch *The X Factor USA* (Bower, 2012: 245). Five years after the debut of *American Idol* in June 2002, forty-one local licences were sold, two of them, in the Middle East and Latin America, covering fifty territories between them. *American Idol* itself, as a finished show, sold in over 180 countries (Clark, interview 2008). By the end of the decade, the format had gone to 156 series in forty-three territories and generated more than 5 billion votes.

Until Fuller sold his majority share to Bob Sillerman in 2005, the format was owned by 19 Entertainment and FremantleMedia. Having been stripped by Fuller of all TV rights, Cowell decided to create his own talent search, *The X Factor* (Bower, 2012: 130–40). It was only in the late 2000s that *Idols* began to falter under the challenge of Cowell's creation, which by then was in twenty-six territories (chapter 8).

Influence and Legacy

The four super-formats have had an extraordinary impact on world television, both culturally and commercially. Before their world conquest, the format as an international distribution mechanism remained relatively unknown in the TV industry, but these shows shifted attitudes by demonstrating the potential of the format and changing the course of TV history.

Each format delivered a distinct message. *Millionaire* established the key principles of a successful TV franchise: internationally consistent branding and the ability to control the IP attached to the brand in order to exploit the ancillary rights (chapter 8). *Big Brother* was a masterclass in multimedia storytelling and multi-platform revenue generation, and *Idols* revealed how a format could also travel as a ready-made show (for the US version). These formats' key points and mechanisms have been borrowed countless times and have inspired numerous shows in their respective genres. Many contemporary game shows duplicate *Millionaire*'s features, such as multichoice answers and the sense of drama, and *Survivor*'s and *Big Brother*'s elimination procedures are fundamental to the reality genre (chapter 7). *Idols* enhanced the interactivity of the amateur talent show and remains a landmark in the history of the genre.

These super-formats launched the TV format revolution and set the stage for the final phase in the history of the format business: it would become, within the wider international trade in audiovisual products, a fully fledged trading system.

Part II

Production and Globalization

4 The Formation of the Format Trading System

The 1990s industry transformations (chapter 2) and the super-formats (chapter 3) laid the foundations for the TV format revolution, which reorganized the TV format business as a global trading *system* that is characterized by two features: rapid international expansion and a systemic element that is underscored by the emergence of a *TV format global value chain*.

A trading system can be defined as a *singular transnational space that brings together interdependent economic agents, institutions, places, networks and commodities*. The value chain that lies at its core, and which is the outcome of the process of *disintegration of production* that took place in the TV industry, determines economic agents' positions and strategies, organizes networks of production and distribution and shapes trade flows within that space. While it is acknowledged that the global trade is only a part of an international trade in audiovisual products, this chapter draws attention to its emerging systemic dimension.

To start with, this chapter examines the international expansion of the trade as the number of formats in circulation has grown exponentially, as has the number of companies and territories involved. The TV format flow has also become more complex and dynamic. The chapter also analyses the key dimensions of the TV format chain: its *input–output structure* (examining economic agents' strategies within it), its *governance* (studying the relationships between buyers and their suppliers), its *geographical configuration* (identifying three tiers of format exporters and specific trade routes along which most formats travel) and finally its *institutional framework* (showing that the TV format trading system has begun to be protected by a fledgling international regulatory regime and that it stands on firmer legal grounds than ever before).

World-Systems Theory and Global Value Chain (GVC) Analysis

Approaching trade as a system was instigated by the scholars studying the long history of the Atlantic as a singular maritime space. The 'Atlantic system' designates the networks of trade and culture, the civilization and values, which have developed across the Atlantic throughout the centuries. Fashioned by a succession of seaborne empires, this system expanded through consecutive phases between the mid-thirteenth and mid-nineteenth centuries. In its last phase, it was marked by the 'Atlantic triangle', which saw manufactured goods leaving Europe for Africa to be exchanged for slaves, who in turn were shipped to work on plantations in the West Indies and the Americas, from where plantation products were exported to Europe (Pietschmann, 2002).

This approach enabled historians to comprehend long-term changes in the structure and patterns of trade flows, identify sets of interdependent relationships and understand the intertwined roles of economic agents, institutions, governments and places within that system. It eventually helped them uncover a singular trans-empire maritime space whose visibility had been partially obscured by national and imperial histories (Pietschmann, 2002: 23). It also allowed them to understand the place – and ultimately the modernizing influence – of the Atlantic system within the world economy (Emmer, 2002).

This approach developed organically but was influenced by Fernand Braudel, who first conceived the Mediterranean as a singular space of commerce and civilization (Braudel, [1979] 1996). Immanuel Wallerstein, a Braudelian scholar, is also cited, as his world-system study is relevant both substantially and methodologically (Canny, 2002; Pietschmann, 2002: 11–18). It is from this perspective that the author of *The Modern World-System* introduced the concept of the *global commodity chain*, defining it as a 'network of labor and production processes whose end result is a finished commodity' (Hopkins and Wallerstein, 1986: 159). This led to the development of a body of literature, initially labelled global commodity chain (GCC) analysis, later evolving into global value chain (GVC) theory (Bair, 2009; Gereffi, 1994).

The GVC theoretical framework brings many benefits, not least the ability to comprehend how the format trading system works: how it informs economic agents' behaviour and how it is continuously reshaped by the interplay between them. It allows us to comprehend corporate strategies in an international context and the way they, in turn, globalize this context. It enables us to assess the role of places and institutions, and identify production patterns and trade routes. It gives us a better understanding of the power distribution within the chain and of the impact of regulation on the format trade.

Globalization

It is in the 2000s that the TV format trade became a global multi-billion-dollar industry: it finally got TV executives' attention with the super-formats, which aired in more territories and generated more revenue for broadcasters than any other TV shows before them. They incited broadcasters to seek out more adaptable programmes and in turn encouraged producers to develop concepts capable of crossing borders. Within a few years, an old licensing right that had lain on the fringes of the TV industry had become a global commodity. From these modest origins, TV format trading grew to an estimated €2.1 billion per year between 2002 and 2004, and €3.1 billion between 2006 and 2008. For 2002–4, 259 formats were counted, leading to 1,310 adaptations and 43,284 hours of formatted programming, while 445 formats led to 1,262 adaptations and a total of 54,383 hours in 2006–8 (Screen Digest, 2005: 19–20; FRAPA, 2009: 8–13). The TV format revolution altered and expanded the world TV format flow in several ways.

A more dynamic and complex flow

First, the format traffic grew exponentially because many more formats crossed borders than ever before and they travelled farther and faster. In the 1980s, only a handful of formats sold in more than ten countries; today the best performers easily pass the thirty-licence mark: *Deal or No Deal* was produced in sixty-seven territories by October 2010 and the following year *Come Dine with Me* and *Money Drop* passed the thirty-mark threshold. Even shows that are expensive to produce travel well: in 2014, *Idols*, *The Voice* and *The X Factor* reached forty-seven, fifty and forty-eight adaptations respectively, *Dancing with the Stars* and *Got Talent* fifty and sixty-three, and *MasterChef* fifty. The record-holder remains *Who Wants to Be a Millionaire?*, with in excess of 100 local versions to date (Marlow, 2014; Stephens, 2013, 2014a).

The dynamic of the format flow is also altered by formats' speed of movement. *The Price is Right*, which had its first screening in 1956 on CBS, waited twenty-six years for its first overseas adaptation. *Jeopardy!*, another classic US game show, had only reached Australia, the UK, France and Italy by the late 1980s. *Family Feud*, which launched on ABC in 1976 and is in nearly fifty countries at the time of writing, was in only a handful of countries before 1990 (Usdan, interview 2010).

Today, a good format can travel at blazing speed. Apart from the super-formats, the first to transit rapidly was Distraction's comedy show *Love Bugs*, which reached almost forty countries by the millennium (Rodrigue, interview 2008). *The Weakest Link* was in nearly seventy territories less than eighteen months after its launch in August 2000 (Jarvis, interview 2008) and *Deal or No Deal* was in forty-six territories within a few years of its premiere (Endemol, 2007: 18). *Dancing with the Stars* was in more than thirty territories not long after it was put on the market in 2004, and it took eighteen months for *The Apprentice*, which started the same year, to equal the number of local versions (twenty-five) that *The Price is Right* gained in almost three decades. FremantleMedia had sold thirty-one local licences of *Hole in the Wall* in under eighteen months by the end of 2008, and *Money Drop* was in thirty-two territories sixteen months after it had premiered on Channel 4 as *The Million Pound Drop* in May 2010 (Clark, interview 2008; Rosser, 2011). Keshet International's *Rising Star* also moved fast and twenty-five local licences were sold in a six-month period between October 2013 and April 2014 (Akyuz, 2014).

However, international roll-outs vary and formats can take different routes to the global market. A classic scenario in the 2000s was for a format to start its international career in the UK, otherwise known as the 'launch pad', and get noticed once picked by a US network – the 'loudspeaker'. Countless formats followed this route, not least *Millionaire*, which Asian and Latin American buyers acquired thinking it was an American game show (Spencer, interview 2008). Another notable instance was Studio Lambert's *Undercover Boss*, which was scheduled by CBS to debut after the Super Bowl in February 2010. *Undercover Boss USA* duly delivered the ratings, and both the format rights and finished tapes have sold widely ever since.

Although most formats travel far only once risk-averse broadcasters are satisfied with the ratings they have obtained in major territories, a few start their roll-out in smaller locations. One such instance of a *reverse roll-out* was Endemol's gameshow *1 vs 100*, which first aired in markets such as Vietnam, Greece, Tunisia and the Czech Republic before being commissioned by BBC One and NBC in 2006. The advantage of this pattern is that the show can be refined before reaching the intense heat of the UK and US markets (C21 Media, 2006).

Finally, there are slow-burners that travel at a more sedate pace. For example, it took a decade for *A Farmer Wants a Wife* to reach fifteen countries because TV executives took a while to realize that this show is popular with the young urban audience that they all want to reach (Clark, interview 2008). Most scripted formats fall into this category as they tend to have a long shelf life and take more time to get adapted than unscripted shows (chapter 9). A case in point is *Yes Minister*, a political comedy that was on BBC Two between 1980 and 1984 and was versioned in several markets twenty years later.

The *structure* of the format flow has also changed since the format revolution to acquire a truly global scope. Virtually all territories import TV formats and the Middle East, Asia and Latin America have all become fast-growing markets in recent years. In Latin America, Brazilian broadcasters have become avid format consumers, and those in smaller markets such as Chile, Panama or Peru have also begun to adapt them in high numbers (Waller, 2013a). The most remarkable development, however, has been Asia. Formerly insular countries are making their first forays into the format trade. In 2014, *The X Factor* sold licences in Cambodia and Myanmar and *Got Talent* in Laos, for instance. Mongolia, Thailand and Vietnam count among the other emerging territories (Daswani, 2014). Until recently, Asia was blighted by a 'blatant disrespect for intellectual property' and local broadcasters simply cloned Western shows on a mass scale (Keane, 2004: 9–10). Chinese firms were particularly adept at borrowing ideas, from *Who Wants to Be a Millionaire?* to *Super Girl* (a copy of *American Idol*). This began to change with the local adaptations of *Dancing with the Stars* (2007) and *Got Talent* (2010), which finally convinced Chinese broadcasters to pay a licence fee and helped the country move away from rampant copy-catting. With the latter show, they witnessed how the transfer of expertise that comes with a legal format contract enabled Shanghai Dragon TV, the broadcaster of *China's Got Talent*, to overhaul its production processes completely and air China's most successful show ever (Yin, email correspondence 2013; see also Fry, 2013b).

Trade data will be examined in detail later, but it can be noted that a growing number of countries are joining the ranks of format exporters, including Australia, Colombia, Poland, South Korea, Turkey and Israel, which has become a sizeable exporter in recent years (chapter 5). More formats are bound to come out of Asia and two Chinese shows, *Sing My Song* and *Not a Star Yet*, are represented by international distributors.

The last structural change of note concerns the North American media market. The US networks began to adapt foreign concepts in greater numbers in the 1990s (chapter 2) but the floodgates opened after *Millionaire*. Since then, *Idols, Survivor, Hell's Kitchen, Dancing with the Stars, Hit Me Baby One More Time, Big Brother, Brat Camp, Wife Swap, Supernanny, Got Talent* and *Undercover Boss*, among others, have all met success with American audiences. In the 2014–15 season, the five US networks (ABC, CBS, Fox, NBC and the CW) transmitted a total of eighteen formats:

nine are unscripted shows from abroad (of which seven can be traced back to the UK, as *Hell's Kitchen* is produced by a British company) (*American Idol, Dancing with the Stars, Hell's Kitchen, MasterChef, Shark Tank, Survivor, Utopia, The Voice* and *Whose Line Is It Anyway?*), three are home-grown contests (*The Amazing Race, The Biggest Loser* and *So You Think You Can Dance*), and six are scripted shows from abroad (chapter 9).[1] The opening of the US market was an important step in the globalization of the TV market. It is a territory that is both influential and financially rewarding for the production companies that export there.

An expanding industry

The number of companies involved in the TV format trade has grown exponentially in recent decades. From a handful before the format revolution, the number has since swollen to hundreds. Media firms progressively saw TV formats as an opportunity for growth and began to specialize in their production and/or distribution. Some companies added formats to their activities while others were purportedly created to trade in the business. In both cases, TV formats often played a crucial role in their growth. As the industry expanded, all had to define a strategy and find a position in the TV format chain (see later section).

Distraction Formats (1997) and Sydney-based Screentime (later Outright Distribution and then part of Shed Media) were among the first in the new breed of format distributors. In the UK, Target Entertainment and 12 Yards Productions (2001) adopted a format-centric business model at the onset, adding to producers (Bazal Productions, RDF Television, Mentorn Barraclough Carey, Hat Trick, Celador, Planet 24) that had already turned their attention to the growing industry segment.

In the USA, while Fremantle sold game show licences overseas, Reveille (2002) was the first company to sell formats both abroad and in its domestic market, where it adapted *The Office* and *Ugly Betty*. Most Scandinavian producers turned their attention to formats, including MTV Mastiff, Jarowskij (*The Empire*), Zodiak Television (*Guillotine, All Stars*), Nordisk Film TV and Metronome Film & TV. Following Endemol's lead, several Dutch firms were created concentrating solely on formats, including Eyeworks (2001) (*Test the Nation, Ticket to the Tribes, Beat the Blondes*), Intellygents (2002) and 2waytraffic (2004). The following year, John de Mol launched Talpa Media.

Elsewhere, early movers have included D&D Entertainment Group (Benelux), Ohm:tv, MME Moviement and Janus TV (Germany),

Adventure Line Productions and Calt International (France), Strand Media (Italy), Lone Eagle Entertainment (Canada) and Cuatro Cabezas (*Caiga Quien Caiga*) and Promofilm (Argentina).

As the decade progressed, format distributors and producers developed in emerging markets, notably Israel's Armoza Formats (*The Bubble, The Frame, Still Standing*) and Turkey's Global Agency (*Perfect Bride*).

Broadcasters had to make a strategic decision whether to stay on the sidelines or invest. While many chose to do nothing, a few decided to grasp the opportunity. The BBC might have created the position of head of format licensing in 1994 (chapter 2), but it took BBC Worldwide more than a decade to strengthen its format team. ITV created a four-strong format development unit called the LWT Greenhouse in 2000 (Morgenstern, interview 2009) and RTL Group acquired Pearson Television (renaming it FremantleMedia) in the same year (chapter 6).

Elsewhere, SVT, the Swedish public service broadcaster, set up its own format development group in 2003 (also called the Greenhouse) and in Japan, Tokyo Broadcasting System (*Funniest Home Videos, Takeshi's Castle, The Chair*) and Fuji TV (*Iron Chef, Dragons' Den*) stepped up their involvement in the trade, as did Globo TV and Televisa (*Dancing for a Dream* and *Singing for a Dream*) in Latin America. It was only later in the decade that the Hollywood majors would expand into the TV format business (chapter 6).

Support systems: market fairs, the trade press and trade associations

The systemic aspect of the TV format trade that we are about to explore is underscored by a set of developing relationships among economic agents. On the one hand the industry is formidably competitive and on the other a 'global village' atmosphere has emerged. Participants' knowledge of – and contact with – one another is on the rise. Several institutions have come into being to create brand awareness, consolidate the profile of the industry and facilitate networking among its members.

MipFormats: a new international event in the diary of TV executives
The calendar year of the world TV industry is punctuated by market fairs where TV executives sell and buy programmes, talk shop and socialize. The most important gatherings listed in table 4.1 are MipTV and MipCom, two events held in Cannes in April and October respectively (see also Havens, 2006: 66–94).

In 2009, MipFormats was created as a stand-alone event preceding MipTV

Table 4.1 Key events in the diary of the international TV industry

Name	Place	Month	Footprint
Natpe	Miami	January	Global
Discop Istanbul	Istanbul	February/March	Regional
MipFormats	Cannes	April	Global
MipTV	Cannes	April	Global
LA Screenings	Los Angeles	May	Global
Banff TV Festival	Banff	June	Regional
Shanghai TV Festival	Shanghai	June	Regional
Natpe Budapest	Budapest	June	Regional
Edinburgh International TV Festival	Edinburgh	August	Regional
MipCom	Cannes	October	Global
Discop Africa	Johannesburg	November	Regional

and caught the attention of the industry right away. The 2014 event attracted 992 participants (570 in 2013) from sixty-seven countries, among them 327 TV buyers. The two-day conference includes seminars, keynotes, networking events, format launches, a pitching competition and an awards ceremony.[2]

The FRAPA Format Awards were launched at the Monte Carlo TV Festival in 2003 and presented at the Rose d'Or Television Festival in Lucerne (Switzerland) between 2005 and 2006, at MipCom until 2011, and moved to MIPFormats in 2012. Renamed the C21 Media/FRAPA Format Awards, the category winners (best comedy format, etc.) are voted for by the 35,000-strong online community of C21 Media.[3]

Trade press and market intelligence firms

The term 'format' barely appeared in the trade press until the late 1990s, but then it all changed, and at present publishing companies devote entire supplements to the business. The first mover was New York-based *World Screen*, which added *TV Formats* to its portfolio of magazines in 2002 (Brzoznowski, 2012c). Two years later, London-based C21 Media opened up a format section on its website www.c21media.net and started an email newsletter, *C21 Formats Lab Weekly*. Television Business International, also in London, has published *TBI Formats* since 2008. Paris-based The Wit provides market intelligence for its subscribers helping them identify trends by tracking format roll-outs and ratings performances in key markets.

Trade associations

The industry's trade association, the Format Recognition and Protection Association (FRAPA), was founded in April 2000 with David Lyle, then at

FremantleMedia, as chairman. FRAPA's foremost objective is to act as an industry pressure group and campaign for the legal recognition of formats and protection of the IP they contain, and to combat plagiarism within the TV industry by means of education and the creation of guidelines for fair competition. The trade association also aims to standardize practices within the format community, and it has created a format price calculator, a standard contract form and a set of guidelines for writing production bibles. In addition, FRAPA offers a format register and a dispute resolution service. Bringing plagiarism disputes to court is a long, expensive and uncertain process, and FRAPA's confidential and voluntary mediation service seems to be appreciated by its members: it claimed to have successfully mediated thirty-five cases of alleged plagiarism by 2011 (FRAPA, 2011: 68–9; Lyle, interview 2009; Rodrigue, interview 2012).

The European Broadcasting Union (EBU) – the Geneva-based organization that has brought together public service broadcasters since the 1950s – runs several format-related activities. Its Eurovision Formats Core Group (previously the Format Unit, launched in 2005) brings its members together to exchange information, explore joint projects and co-develop new formats. In addition, the EBU Creative Forum, held annually, runs a format competition (Waller, 2006).

These associations and publishers offer a range of essential services to the TV format industry. Content creators can promote their IP through paid advertising, digital screen rooms and, at trade fairs, competitions or open pitch sessions. These events provide the opportunity for salespeople to deploy their soft marketing skills and create a 'buzz' around their formats. They turn most interviews and conference workshops into PR exercises that extol the virtues of their latest products. Fairs also allow commissioners to let producers know what their scheduling needs are and what type of shows they are looking for. Finally, these firms and associations help disseminate new practices, industry news and market intelligence, whether it is scheduling trends, technology developments (e.g. second-screen applications) or information about TV genres or territories. All these activities have become essential for an industry that needs to maintain connections and relationships on a global scale in order to thrive.

The TV Format Global Value Chain

As the TV format trade developed as a system, a global chain emerged that structures that system and informs the relationships among agents within it. The formation of this chain is the outcome of a process of *disintegration of production* that has occurred in television and which mirrors developments in other industries (Feenstra, 1998). With the trade in TV formats, broadcasters can outsource some of their production activities, leading to the development of a chain segment that specializes in the supply of content. It also means that a TV format, instead of being produced in-house, travels through a chain of production and consumption that crosses borders.

This section analyses the chain's four dimensions as defined by Gary Gereffi: its *input–output structure* (the shape of its connecting production and distribution processes), *governance structure* (issues of control and power relations among economic agents that determine chain co-ordination), *territoriality* (spatial dispersion) and *institutional framework*, which refers to the impact that policy institutions and regulatory systems have on value chains (Bair, 2009: 9; Gereffi, 1994: 96–7, 1995: 113; Sturgeon, 2009: 130–1).

The input–output structure

The structure of the TV format value chain is composed of four distinct segments (or boxes): a format is, in turn, created, distributed, produced and finally acquired (figure 4.1). This sequence can be played out in many different combinations, depending on economic agents' strategies and resources (table 4.2).

The strategy economic agents choose to pursue within the TV format trading system is dictated by their position in the commodity chain, the relationship with firms located in other segments and their need and/or ability to expand their activities along the chain. These imperatives go a long way towards explaining recent moves by companies located at both ends of the chain. Starting with the production side, licensing was until

Figure 4.1 The TV format global value chain: input–output structure

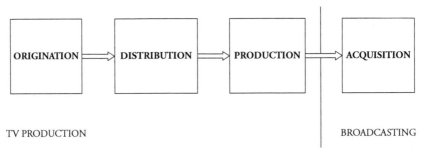

ORIGINATION ⇒ DISTRIBUTION ⇒ PRODUCTION ⇒ ACQUISITION

TV PRODUCTION   BROADCASTING

Table 4.2 Most common combinations within the TV format global value chain

Originator	Distributor	Producer	Buyer
A	A	A	A
A	A	A	B
A	A	B	B
A	A	B	C
A	B	B	C
A	B	C	C
A	B	C	D

recently the most common business model. This implies IP owners selling the international rights of their formats to a distribution company, which in turn sells a licence either to a local production company or directly to a broadcaster that decides to produce the show in-house. The process involves four economic agents in the first case (A/B/C/D) and three in the second (A/B/C/C).

This combination remains common, as most formats are still produced under licence, but leading rights owners have progressively favoured a new model: international production. Wherever feasible, they opt to produce their own shows in order to expand their involvement in the chain and thereby increase their revenue. As will be seen in chapter 6, this strategy has led to the international expansion of TV production companies. Once a concept shows potential these groups keep the format rights and produce it in territories where they have facilities (A/A/A/B). They also have international distribution divisions which acquire third party content, creating an A/B/B/C route through the chain.

Firms at the other end of the chain have reasoned along similar lines and several broadcasters have decided to get involved: BBC Worldwide, RTL (FremantleMedia), ITV (ITV Studios), ProSiebenSat.1 (Red Arrow Entertainment), Modern Times Group (Nice Entertainment Group), Sony Pictures Television and Warner Bros. Television Group are among those that have developed their international TV production capabilities in recent years. These conglomerates have three options: to sell the licence locally (A/A/B/B or A/A/B/C), to produce the format for (or co-produce with) a local broadcaster (A/A/A/B), and in the few countries where they own a TV channel that matches the format's requirements, they can air their own show and achieve full vertical integration in the TV format chain (A/A/A/A). Being involved in TV production lets broadcasters develop their own IP pipeline, sell TV formats and finished programmes to third parties, and diversify their revenues away from advertising. It is a strategy that offers the best of both worlds; they can still access producers' IP and can either use or sell elsewhere the shows they develop.

This evolution has a series of consequences for the format trading system. On the one hand, investment has fed the expansion of the TV format industry and, on the other, as firms from both ends of the chain converge towards its centre, a tension is created between rights owners and licensees. As both parties aim to get involved in the production segment, rights ownership – and rights protection correlatively – remains a live issue in the business. The ensuing power struggle is reflected in the chain's governance structure (see next section). In addition, as economic agents push the system towards an A/A/A/A rather than an A/B/C/D model, independent distributors tend to be squeezed out of the chain: with no rights to own they are left with less IP to offer to broadcasters. Although there is a risk that this situation will lead to a loss of competition, and thereby a creativity deficit, the distribution sector remains very dynamic and evidence shows that the format industry is able to accommodate business models of a different scale (Whittingham, 2014; see also chapter 6).

Governance structure

Governance structure highlights power and co-ordination within chains, and for this purpose a distinction is made between *buyer-* and *producer-driven* value chains. The latter type includes those chains in which large manufacturers remain in control of production and distribution networks and processes, which is 'characteristic of capital- and technology-intensive industries such as automobiles, aircraft, computers' (Gereffi, 1999: 41). By way of contrast, buyer-driven chains prevail in industries that are labour-intensive, and in such cases 'large retailers, branded marketers, and branded manufacturers play the pivotal roles in setting up decentralized production networks in a variety of exporting countries'; the classic example being the fashion industry, which is controlled by a few global marketers in command of large networks of subcontractors across the developing world (Gereffi, 1999: 41–2).

The issue of power has attracted considerable attention in the GCC literature and attempts have been made to expand and soften the terms of the dichotomy. For instance, Philip Raikes and colleagues suggest the existence of 'multi-polar driving' chains with a possible 'diffusion of power between producers and buyers' (Raikes et al., 2000: 397). The more recent GVC framework has highlighted other forms of chain co-ordination and integration (Gereffi et al., 2005; Gibbon and Ponte, 2008; Sturgeon, 2009).

The distribution of power between broadcasters and suppliers in the TV format chain hinges on the answer to these two questions: who is most in control and who benefits most from the chain? It is undeniable that the independent TV production sector has profited from the rise of TV formats. Although this sector is not equally established in every single country, it has witnessed a sharp growth in the UK and USA in recent years, with format sales making a strong contribution. In the UK, the 150 leading TV production companies reached a total turnover of £2.1 billion in 2013 (*Broadcast – Indie Survey*, 2014: 5). Arguably, TV formats represent only a portion of their revenue as the international trade in audiovisual products remains dominated by finished programming. Nonetheless, TV formats have acquired a strategic importance for producers and can make a contribution to several objectives. A recognized entertainment format will raise a company's profile and, as the show develops on the global market, it can help the firm expand internationally, improve income predictability and boost its profit margins. Many TV formats have played a key role in the growth of large production groups, including Endemol's *Big Brother*, RDF's *Wife Swap*, Shed's *Supernanny*, FremantleMedia's and Syco TV's *Got Talent* and *Idols*, and Shine's *MasterChef*.

It is undeniable that TV producers have benefitted from TV formats but on balance the TV format chain is a buyer-driven one. Instances of power diffusion can be found but both control and the lion's share of profit ultimately rest in the hands of broadcasters, the chain's large 'retailers'. The range of benefits TV formats bring in is so vast that broadcasters accept paying licence fees of between 7 and 8 per cent of production costs. By the time a format reaches them, they expect the production model to have been fully refined, all possible short cuts identified and mistakes ironed out in the production process. In addition, broadcasters count on their newly acquired formats to outperform the shows they are replacing, be scalable (adaptable to various budgets) and versatile (able to fit in different slots or be stretched to various lengths).

Above all, broadcasters derive substantial income from TV formats. Well-known franchises never fail to generate a considerable amount of advertising revenue because, notwithstanding their ratings, they are easier to sell to advertisers than generic shows (Lituchy, interview 2014). More often than not, broadcasters get to share extra revenues from voting and licensed products. All the super-formats have made a huge contribution to the balance sheets of TV networks around the world (Bazalgette, 2005). As seen in the introduction to this book, European broadcasters generated US$2.9 billion from the top 100 formats in 2013. Such shows not only become returning brands for channels but become part of their identity and help them to build their profile.

Examining the issue of power, the relationship between broadcasters and their suppliers is determined by three factors: quality of the IP (which is broadly set by a format's ratings record, its originality and complexity); broadcasters' purchasing power; and the supplier–broadcaster ratio.

The importance of IP in contemporary broadcasting means that the suppliers that pass the quality threshold do have a certain amount of leverage on their clients. Broadcasters are desperate to acquire distinctive shows that will help them stand out from the competition, and they compete for the best formats. These companies that control valuable IP, such as a well-known global TV franchise, are arguably in a good negotiating position. It is the uniqueness and originality of a concept that make a TV format difficult to replace and give bargaining power to its rights holders. The complexity of certain formats, in terms of multimedia integration for instance, gives a certain amount of 'competence power' to TV producers (Sturgeon, 2009: 129). Access to good IP being vital, broadcasters are increasingly mindful of their reputation within the TV production community and try to maintain a good relationship with their suppliers.

Even though supplier power is not to be discounted in the TV format chain, ultimately the balance of power lies with the broadcasters. Their significant purchasing power gives them natural leverage on suppliers, a position that is reinforced by the particularly high supplier–broadcaster ratio (there are many more companies selling IP than acquiring it). As such, the position of broadcasters is not dissimilar to that of supermarkets, whose size alone gives them control over large transnational food chains and thousands of farmers.

The UK market, home to some of the world's largest production companies, provides a case in point. Although the number of broadcasters with a commissioning budget has recently expanded to cable and satellite operators such as Sky and Discovery, adding to the country's public service broadcasters and terrestrial channels such as Viacom's Channel 5, they remain far fewer than the hundreds of independent producers that vie for their attention. Broadcasters are also volume buyers of shows for multiple channels, and at times have very large commissioning budgets. Unsurprisingly, each of these broadcasters deals with a large number of producers: in 2013, the BBC worked with 296 independent suppliers (up from 290 in 2012), ITV worked with 89 (up from 81), Channel 5 with 59 (up from 57), Sky with 159 (up from 89), Discovery with 71 (up from 53) and Channel 4 with more than 300 (2012 figure) (*Broadcast – Indie Survey*, 2013: 18–23; *Broadcast – Indie Survey*, 2014: 23–30).

These broadcasters also dwarf the suppliers they are dealing with. ITV's revenues touched £2.7 billion in 2013 and those of the BBC (2012/13) reached £5.1 billion (BBC, 2013: 106; ITV, 2014: 4). By way of contrast, the average revenue of the UK's leading 153 independent production companies stood at £13.1 million in 2013 (*Broadcast – Indie Survey*, 2014: 7–14).

The British government intervened and introduced a Code of Practice that safeguards terms of trade between broadcasters and their suppliers. The Communications Act 2003 established this code to prevent broadcasters from getting hold of all the rights when acquiring a show. It was inspired by the same regulation that prevents supermarkets exploiting their dominant position in the food chain (chapter 5). This Act undoubtedly put the brakes on the most abusive practices that broadcasters indulged in, including price fixing, strong-arming and blackmailing (McVay, interview 2009), but their purchasing power combined with the high supplier–broadcaster ratio means that regulation alone has not fully redressed the balance of power. Indeed, industry surveys regularly paint a picture of a fractious and difficult relationship. A recent survey among Pact's 500 members highlighted once again the difficulties producers face when dealing with their clients. It brought to light a wide range of issues, including broadcasters' not respecting the terms of trade (regarding rights particularly), late payments, lack of concern about producers' cashflow issues, and pressure on financial margins (Khalsa, 2013). Other oft-voiced complaints include unwillingness to pay production costs up front, slow decision process, contradictory feedback, complex commissioning structure, etc. (*Broadcast – Indie Survey*, 2014: 23–9). When another survey asked the top 100 independent producers about commissioning, 69 per cent replied that they had 'overspent on a production due to lack of clear editorial instructions from a commissioner', 23 per cent rated as poor or average the politeness and respect of commissioners, and for 26 per cent of the commissions it was claimed that broadcasters did not set appropriate budget levels for what they were asked to produce (*Broadcast*, 2014). All these complaints are voiced anonymously because the stakes are significant for producers who are willing to jump through hoops to gain a network commission.

The merger that brought together Shine, Endemol and the Core Media Group to form the world's largest TV content creator (chapter 6) was partly motivated by the side effects of buyer power. Alex Mahon, then Shine Group chief executive, stated that production margins in the UK had fallen from 13 per cent in 2010 to 5.3 per cent in 2014 and that 'indies, no matter what their size, are getting less money to make British shows'. Scale was needed, she added, in order to remain sustainable in a 'low-margin business' and expand the firm's capability of deficit-financing projects (in Curtis, 2014b).

A picture emerges: the importance of quality IP and the complexity of production processes in contemporary broadcasting create a certain degree of interdependence among economic agents, and there is evidence of power diffusion in the TV format value chain. However, only suppliers with sought-after IP have a hand to play, and they still need protection through legislation. As already seen, ultimate control resides with a small number of volume buyers that more often than not are in a position to dictate their conditions and that always benefit most from the transaction.

Both broadcasters and producers have developed strategies in order to upgrade their position along the TV format chain. Broadcasters (and Hollywood studios; see chapter 6) have become aware of the benefits of extending their involvement in the chain and have moved upstream by taking control of TV production companies, often across borders. Similarly, many production companies have expanded internationally in order to overcome the inherent limits of their domestic market and exploit their IP across markets. Chapter 6 will further explain these economic agents' strategies, but it is already apparent that the TV format chain is an engine of change that is contributing to the globalization of the TV industry. Before its emergence, media firms invested within national borders and sometimes outside television. Granada, for instance, the former Manchester-based ITV franchise holder, diversified into television rentals, motorway service stations and publishing, and, after being turned down for a bank, purchased an insurance company (Forman, 1997: 243–51). Today, ITV, like all other TV businesses, stays within sector but looks beyond its home shores for investments.

Thus, the chain dynamics not only demand that media firms expand internationally but also, as the number of cross-border transactions between broadcasters and producers continues to grow, increase their transnational – albeit asymmetrical – interdependence. The format business has become a trading *system* since it is being progressively reorganized on the basis of *a transnational network of companies that are increasingly internationally interdependent and whose strategic decisions are informed by their position within the TV format global value chain.*

Geographical scope: trade flows and patterns

The GVC perspective offers us a better account of trade flows in the format trading system than do existing theoretical frameworks. Sociologists such as Ulrich Beck and Arjun Appadurai became influential and contributed to our understanding of contemporary media systems. According to Beck, only a 'boundary-transcending and boundary-effacing' cosmopolitan outlook can investigate a social reality whose inner quality is being transformed by intense cross-border flows and ever-increasing interdependence among states (Beck, 2006: 82). Such theoretical narratives have helped place the stress on the cosmopolitan nature of contemporary media systems, prompting academics to investigate, for instance, the articulation of the local and the global in the media that straddle borders (e.g. Chalaby, 2005: 10–11; McCabe, 2013: 3). Concepts such as hybridization, syncretism and métissage came to the fore as academics grappled with the consequences of interpenetrating cultures (Nederveen Pieterse, 2004: 53).

The cosmopolitan outlook is full of insights but tends to ignore the influence of capitalist power structures on the world TV industry and its growing embedment in international trade. It is a view according to which weightless media float above capitalistic logic, and media products flow seamlessly in all directions. However, from spices to silk and from coffee to IP products, commodities have always travelled along specific routes (Bernstein, 2008). Under the capitalist world economy some routes have disappeared, some have flourished and many new ones have emerged, and on the whole capitalism has intensified trade by encouraging a world-scale division of labour (Hopkins and Wallerstein, 1986; Feenstra, 1998). By letting us bring to light the structure and patterns of trade flows in the world format business, the GVC approach takes the magic out of international communication and replaces it with history.

An examination of the geographical scope of the TV format global value chain reveals tightly structured trade flows. On the basis of data collected in the late 2000s, three tiers of TV format exporters can be distinguished. The UK and the USA precede a group of seven mid-sized exporters (Argentina, Australia, France, Germany, Japan, the Netherlands and Sweden), themselves followed by a third tier of smaller exporters (Canada, Denmark, Italy, Norway and Spain) (table 4.3). Between 2006 and 2008, the UK and the USA exported more formats (431) than all the other exporters put together (386). Their formats generated almost as much revenue (in terms of production costs) as the rest of the exporters (nearly €3.0 billion versus €3.1 billion). Table 4.3 also reveals a clear trade leader, as the UK beats its nearest rival by a margin of 2:1 in terms of the number of exported formats and revenue generated from local production costs. Figure 4.2 highlights the division between countries that are primarily *IP generators* versus those that are *IP consumers*, as four territories only (Argentina, Britain, Japan and the USA) have a positive balance in the TV format trade.

The key to these figures is rooted in history: the trade remains dominated

Table 4.3 Format exports, in terms of number of formats, number of hours, number of episodes and revenue, 2006–8

	No. of exported formats	No. of exported hours	No. of exported episodes	Production costs of format adaptations	Country ranking by number of formats/ revenue
Argentina	55	7,203	6,877	€482 million	4/5
Australia	33	2,510	3,472	€491 million	8/4
Canada	15	274	412	€40 million	13/13
Denmark	20	386	339	€42 million	11/12
France	36	3,252	4,966	€245 million	7/6
Germany	37	2,242	3,340	€136 million	6/9
Italy	19	512	730	€48 million	12/11
Japan	29	1,202	1,470	€147 million	9/8
Netherlands	63	9,677	9,364	€1.1 billion	3/2
Norway	9	151	151	€13 million	14/14
Spain	29	841	750	€78 million	9/10
Sweden	41	1,570	1,706	€233 million	5/7
UK	275	13,781	15,981	€2.0 billion	1/1
USA	156	10,783	13,485	€980 million	2/3

Source: adapted from FRAPA (2009: 11, 13–15).

Figure 4.2 Exported versus imported formats, by country

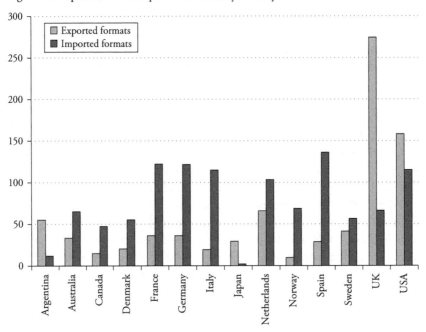

Source: adapted from FRAPA (2009: 11).

Table 4.4 Ranking of TV format exporters versus ranking among exporters in world merchandise trade, 2008

Country	Ranking in TV format trade (in terms of production revenue generated)	Ranking among exporters in world merchandise trade
UK	1	10
Netherlands	2	5
USA	3	3
Australia	4	23
Argentina	5	45
France	6	6
Sweden	7	24
Japan	8	4
Germany	9	1
Spain	10	17
Italy	11	7
Denmark	12	34
Canada	13	11
Norway	14	28

Source: adapted from FRAPA (2009: 11); WTO (2009: 12).

by the two nations that initiated it in the 1950s and several second-tier countries have been latter-day industry pioneers. It is noteworthy that most countries involved in the TV format trade have a long trading history and leading TV format exporters often rank highly in the list of exporters in merchandise trade (2008 data); of the world's top fourteen format exporters, eight also appear among the world's leading eleven exporters, with France and the USA occupying a similar rank in both lists (table 4.4).

Two issues that deserve special attention will be addressed in chapter 5: the sudden rise of the UK as the leading TV format exporter and an assessment of the upgrading strategies of those countries that seek to improve their position in the format trade. For the time being, we note that the geographical configuration of the TV format chain further underscores the systemic aspect of the world format trade: being dominated by a few IP-generating countries, formats do not cross borders haphazardly but follow precise routes that are influenced by history.

Institutional framework: TV formats and the law

A chain's fourth dimension 'identifies how local, national, and international conditions and policies shape the globalization process at each stage in the chain' (Gereffi, 1995: 113). This chapter argues that the TV format trading system has begun to be protected by an emerging international regulatory regime and that it stands on firmer legal grounds than ever before. The viability of this trade rests almost entirely on the recognition of IP rights and these are increasingly acknowledged, in the context of TV formats, by courts of law around the world.

From a legal perspective, a TV format is the right to remake a programme for a given territory (see the introduction to this book). For a show to be formatted, a broadcaster must accept paying for its intangible elements, such as its concept and package (as opposed to a tangible script), and for format rights to be traded, buyers must recognize them as IP rights. This has been a long battle, and it has taken more than a half-century for this right to gain international recognition. As already seen, it was this pressing issue that led to the formation of FRAPA in 2000.

Almost by their nature, TV formats are difficult to protect, and the history of the trade is littered with lawsuits between parties fighting over IP. Some periods have been more acrimonious than others and the first half of the 2000s was particularly so. The height of reality TV brought a flurry of lawsuits involving many of the world's best-known formats. However, despite persistent obstacles, the recognition of TV format rights has progressed by leaps and bounds since the turn of the century and is an increasingly accepted industry norm in regions such as Latin America and Asia. In addition, evidence shows that rights owners have gradually made gains in protecting their formats. Courts are not only more favourable to format owners than in the past, but have a wider choice of options open to them. Five legal routes presently exist (FRAPA, 2011: 6):

- Copyright law protects against copycat formats.
- Laws of unfair competition (or 'passing off' in certain jurisdictions) can provide help against duplicating formats that confuse the public.
- Laws of unfair competition also guard against unfair business practices deemed 'parasitic'.
- The law of confidential information can help safeguard the expertise behind a format.
- The law of registered trademarks helps protect format titles and logos.

Copyright laws

The industry's favourite line of defence has traditionally been copyright laws, but many difficulties reside in their application and the outcome of such cases has been uncertain at best. First, for a TV format to be a 'work' attracting copyright protection, it 'requires that the format (1) has found expression in a certain perceptible form and (2) that originality is expressed' (EBU, 2005: 69). Thus a court must ascertain a format's degree of originality, acknowledging that 'inspiration is allowed' and weighing 'the competing benefits of protecting IP rights against the right of free access to information' (EBU, 2005: 70). Second, a TV show is considered to consist of several 'copyright works' (literary, artistic, musical, etc.), and when 'these elements or other features are combined' they form a 'dramatic work' (FRAPA, 2011: 10–11). It follows that not all formats are equal before the law: scripted formats that come with characters and storylines are easier to protect than quiz shows, themselves easier to protect than variety and reality programmes (FRAPA, 2011: 10–11). To compound the difficulties, concepts, legal practices and interpretations vary considerably from jurisdiction to jurisdiction. The international copyright regime that is underpinned by various treaties such as the Bern Convention and the Budapest Treaty fixes certain general principles, but legislation and its application are still determined by sovereign states (Tingay, interview 2012). For instance, the 'level of inventiveness' or originality that a format must possess to be granted copyright protection varies considerably from one jurisdiction to another (Tingay, interview 2012).

Despite these obstacles, evidence shows that TV formats are increasingly granted legal protection against copyright infringement. After years of fruitless attempts, it was a Spanish court that agreed for the first time that a TV format could be subject to copyright protection. In 1994, Endemol sued the Spanish Antenna 3 over a local version of *Love Letters*. The court found not only that *Love Letters* 'was protected by copyright' but that the '"key elements" of the format had been copied by Antenna 3' (FRAPA, 2011: 16). Since 1994, there have been thirteen instances of a court finding that in principle a TV format can be protected by copyright, whether or not the court upheld the claim of copyright infringement (table 4.5).[4]

In several instances, courts have deemed that TV formats merit protection but have ruled against copyright infringement in a particular case. For example, although the Dutch Supreme Court agreed that 'the combination of 12 elements within *Survive!* when taken together was sufficiently unique and specific to be original', and hence that the whole formed a 'copyright work', it decided that '*Big Brother* was not an infringing copy' (FRAPA, 2011: 17–18).

Other legal options

The laws of unfair competition in civil law jurisdictions (or 'passing off' in the common-law systems that prevail in the Anglo-Saxon world) offer a line of defence that is growing in popularity among format owners. The focal

Table 4.5 Courts that have held that TV formats can be protected by copyright laws

Date and country	Parties	Formats	Outcome
1994, Spain	Endemol vs Antenna 3	*Love Letters/ unknown*	Claimant (Endemol) successful
1999–2004, Netherlands	Castaway Television Productions vs Endemol	*Survive!/Big Brother*	Claimant (Castaway) unsuccessful
2002, Belgium	BVBA Habrasaje en Martin De Jonghe vs VRT	*Golfbreker/ Golfbreker*	Claimant (Martin De Jonghe) successful
2003, USA	Survivor Productions LLC & CBS vs Granada & others	*Survivor/I'm a Celebrity . . . Get Me Out of Here!*	Claimant (Survivor Productions) unsuccessful
2004, Brazil	Globo TV & Endemol vs TV SBT	*Big Brother/Casa dos artistas*	Claimant (Endemol) successful
2005, USA	RDF Media vs Fox Broadcasting	*Wife Swap USA/ Trading Spouses*	RDF's claim of copyright infringement upheld but case did not go to trial
2005, Belgium	Tailor-Made Films vs VRT	*Don't Get Mad . . . Get Even/De Thuisploeg*	Claimant (Tailor-Made Films) unsuccessful
2007, Malta	Endemol vs TVM Malta & others	*Big Brother/L-iSpjun*	Claimant (Endemol) successful
2009, Spain	Maradentro Producciones vs Sogecable	*Epitafios/Epilogo*	Claimant (Maradentro Producciones) unsuccessful
2010, Spain	Atomis Media vs Televisión de Galicia	*No em rattlis, No te enrolles* and *Ya te vale* (all Spanish versions of *What Kids Really Think*)/*O país dos ananos*	Claimant (Atomis Media) unsuccessful
2011, Spain	Sociedad Española de Radiodifusión vs Radio Popular	*Carrusel deportivo/ Tiempo de juego*	Claimant (Sociedad Española de Radiodifusión) unsuccessful
2011, Spain	Corporación Radiotelevisión Española vs Gestevisión Telecinco	*Tengo una pregunta para usted/España pregunta, Belén responde*	Claimant (Corporación Radiotelevisión Española) successful
2011, Canada	Robinson & Les Productions Nilem vs France Animation & others	*Robinson Curiosité/ Robinson Surcroë*	Claimants (Robinson & Les Productions Nilem) successful

Source: EBU (2005: 142–5); FRAPA (2011: 10–29).

Table 4.6 Courts that have held that a TV format can in principle be protected by unfair competition laws

Date and country	Parties	Formats	Outcome
1993, France	Antenne 2 vs TF1	*La Nuit des héros/Les Marches de la gloire*	Plaintiff (Antenne 2) successful
1995, Germany	Developer vs ZDF	*Labyrinth/Goldmillion*	Plaintiff (Developer) unsuccessful
2005, France	Saranga Productions vs Canal Plus	*Crise-en-direct/C'est déjà demain*	Plaintiff (Saranga Productions) successful
2007, Spain	Televisión Autonomia de Madrid vs Televisión Española	*Madrid directo/España directo*	Plaintiff (Televisión Autonomia de Madrid) successful
2011, Spain	Corporación Radiotelevisión Española vs Gestevisión Telecinco	*Tengo una pregunta para usted/España pregunta, Belén responde*	Plaintiff (Corporación Radiotelevisión Española) successful
2013, France	Endemol France vs Banijay	*Dilemma/Loft Story*	Plaintiff (Endemol France) unsuccessful

Source: Brzoznowski (2013a); EBU (2005: 133–6); FRAPA (2011: 30–6).

point here is not the act of copying but the fact that 'the imitation, deliberately or inadvertently, has misappropriated the goodwill such that members of the relevant public would be confused or deceived into thinking that the copy was created by the format owner, causing the format owner loss and damage' (FRAPA, 2011: 30). In this action, the claimant must prove that his or her format has gained a reputation in the country – 'local goodwill' – where the case is brought (Bridge and Lane, 1990: 98).

The first such dispute occurred in France in 1993 (table 4.6). Once Antenne 2 had licensed CBS's *Rescue 911* (*La Nuit des héros*), TF1 poached the production team to make *Les Marches de la gloire* and *Le Défi*. Antenne 2 sued 'for unfair competition on the counts of passing off, disruption of business, acquisition under false pretences and parasitical business practices' and was successful (EBU, 2005: 133). Although the trend is not as marked as for copyright claims, table 4.6 shows that several cases had reached the courts by 2013.

Confidential information about a TV format and the expertise surrounding it can be safeguarded by law. A breach of confidence case can be brought against a party that misuses information received as such. This covers paper formats that are pitched to broadcasters, communications by flying producers and the production bible, which can be seen only by licensees. An important case was won on these grounds by a media consultant against Sony Entertainment Television in India in 2001 (FRAPA, 2011: 42–3).

Finally, the law of registered trademarks can protect format titles and logos. This legal provision is particularly useful when called upon to protect formats with a strong brand element and identity. Several global TV formats, including *Big Brother, Who Wants to Be a Millionaire?* and *Popstars,* have won injunctions to prevent trademark infringement (FRAPA, 2011: 45; see also Pickard, 2011).

The legal protection of IP remains an issue. Perhaps reflecting once more their disadvantageous position in the TV industry, format creators and producers remain adamant that it is difficult to protect ideas and that format theft is a constant threat. For instance, Anna Bråkenhielm exclaimed:

> There's no protection of formats anymore. You can copy anything without risk of getting sued, and there are a couple of examples of this happening in Scandinavia right now. Most broadcasters prefer to buy big formats with a well-proven track record and if they can't get them, they would rather go for a copy than for something completely new. There's a smaller risk associated with copying a big hit than doing something else. (in Waller, 2011a)

Echoing her worries, David Lyle commented when accepting an award in Cannes in 2012: 'Getting [formats] recognised, we've done; getting them protected, we've still a way to go' (in C21 Reporter, 2012). Nonetheless, despite these pending issues, TV rights owners' legal position is stronger than ever. As already seen, all successful copyright cases, bar two, and most successful unfair competition cases have occurred since 2002. Sarah Tingay, FremantleMedia's general counsel worldwide, concurs:

> The case law is improving gradually, yes. If you go back ten years ago there were probably almost no cases that found in favour of a format owner and there are now, and there are an increasing number . . . the courts begin to recognise that there is clearly something here, which people value and pay for and therefore to say it doesn't exist is unconstructive. The courts are beginning to recognise that one way or another it isn't fair if somebody comes along and takes the product of your work and makes money out of it. So I do think there is a positive trending in case law. (Tingay, interview 2012)

FRAPA's chairman, Ute Biernat, also classed the findings of *The FRAPA Report 2011* as 'encouraging' and 'heartening' (FRAPA, 2011: 3). The viability of the format trade rests entirely on the recognition of IP rights, and it can be agreed that they are increasingly recognized by courts of law around the world.

Even within the framework of international treaties, law is always applied by sovereign nation-states, resulting in inconsistencies in the legal protection of TV formats. For instance, Spain saw five copyright cases (two of them successful), compared to none in the UK. Although these discrepancies could be seen as a hindrance for such a global trade, the industry seems to accommodate itself well to the situation. By nature, TV formats are complex works and a workable legal definition would be very difficult to achieve. Legal harmonization also raises the issue of standards and practices that would have to be universally adopted. Media firms would be wary of a harmonization based on civil law because the jurisdictions where it prevails tend to be more protective of authors and artists, and thus a wider range of people would be entitled to copyright. By way of contrast, common-law Anglo-Saxon jurisdictions are more business oriented and assign copyright to those who commercially exploit formats, entitling businesses to take full assignments from authors and actors.

Trade, Television and Globalization

This chapter has argued that the TV format revolution turned the trade into a global system. Although it is located in the broader context of international trade in audiovisual products, this space is *singular* because of the economic interdependence among economic agents, the multiple connections and transactions between them, and the knowledge they have of each other and of the industry as a whole. Common spaces have developed, digital or otherwise, in which industry members can exchange views and develop relationships. These members also increasingly share common values, notably with regard to IP protection.

This trade is *systemic* because it is structured by a global value chain that ascribes roles and relationships, and informs economic agents' commercial and industrial strategies. In addition, commodities do not fly around haphazardly but travel along trade routes that follow patterns.

This space is *global* in scope because it brings together economic agents, organizations, commodities and commercial networks across all borders. More fundamentally, the chain that is at its core plays a dual role of structuring and globalization: it is the engine that stimulates media firms to cross borders and in turn makes them more interdependent internationally.

Finally, this trade is influenced by history and reproduces the patterns and power structures of past trading systems. Formats travel along certain routes because the industry is dominated by a few countries, often the same ones that have dominated trade flows for centuries. However, unlike the case with exporting fuels and minerals, nations have the possibility of joining the ranks of IP exporters. Chapter 5 assesses the industrial upgrading strategies of the countries that have decided to improve their position within the format business.

5 Nations and Competition: Upgrading Strategies in the TV Format Global Value Chain

A startling aspect of the TV format revolution has been the emergence of a new trade leader: Great Britain. In a short time, a nation used to relying heavily on US imports, whose homegrown dramas were once deemed too gritty for export, has turned itself into the world's leading format exporter. This chapter begins with the story of this transformation, as it remains a benchmark for upgrading strategies in the TV industry. Can this process be duplicated elsewhere? Gary Gereffi defines industrial upgrading as a 'process of improving the ability of a firm or an economy to move to more profitable and technologically sophisticated capital- and skill-intensive economic niches' (Gereffi, 1999: 51–2). Indeed, once acquainted with formats, many countries consider their position in the TV format chain and work towards moving from *stage one*: (re)produce foreign IP, towards *stage two*: create local IP for local consumption, and on to *stage three*: export local IP. This chapter assesses the upgrading strategies of a few nations that have embarked on the journey from the *local production of imports* to the *local creation of formats*.

Benchmarking Upgrading Strategies: The British Case

As seen in chapter 4, the UK powered the format revolution and beat its nearest rival by a margin of 2:1 in terms of number of exported formats and revenue generated from local production. Many of the world's most iconic formats originated here including three of the original super-formats (*Millionaire*, *Survivor* and *Idols*), some talent-competition juggernauts (*Dancing with the Stars*, *Got Talent*, *MasterChef*, *The X Factor*), several of the most influential factual entertainment programmes (e.g. *Come Dine with Me*, *Faking It*, *How to Look Good Naked*, *Secret Millionaire*, *Supernanny*, *Undercover Boss*, *Who Do You Think You Are?*, *Wife Swap*), and a few game shows (*Money Drop*, *The Weakest Link*). British TV series, from *The Office* to *Doc Martin*, are also adapted widely (chapter 9). British formats travel far and wide but do particularly well in the USA, with American content aggregators spending nearly half a billion pounds on UK-originated programming (including finished tapes) (Mansfield, 2014). How was this feat achieved? Focusing on factors that impact TV formats specifically, this section shows that policy-making has been a significant ingredient.

Britain's new IP regime

The key to understanding Britain's trade performance is the way it anticipated the disintegration of production in the TV industry that occurred when broadcasters outsourced some of their production activities (chapter 4). It is this process that led to the formation of a distinct production segment, and before anyone else the UK had a small army of independent companies that specialized in IP creation and production. When the format boom came, these firms were in prime position to exploit their IP on the world market.

The story begins with the launch of the UK's fourth channel in 1982. As a commissioning publisher-broadcaster, Channel 4 created a cottage industry of independent companies furnishing it with programmes, essentially documentaries. The nascent sector was provided with further support by a strengthening of this commissioning culture over the years. The Broadcasting Act 1990 introduced 'the statutory independent quota' to other terrestrial broadcasters, stipulating that they must commission at least 25 per cent of their programming from independent producers (Ofcom, 2006: 34). The Broadcasting Act 1996 expanded the principle to digital terrestrial television channels (Ofcom, 2006: 34), helping the sector to reach an annual turnover of over £700 million by the mid-1990s. Most of the early British formats were created by young entrepreneurs such as Peter Bazalgette, Charlie Parsons or Paul Smith, who combined creativity with business flair (chapters 2 and 3). They set up companies that 'were faster, cheaper and more cost-effective than the lumbering in-house production arms of the flabby, heavily unionized broadcasters' (Woodward, 1998; see also Darlow, 2004).

Despite this, many producers remained in a financially precarious position. A financial survey revealed that out of the top 100 producers in the UK, 36 were losing money, 20 were 'heading for trouble' and 27 were facing declining sales in 2002 (Carter, 2002). Pact chief executive John McVay claimed that profit margins of 1 to 3 per cent were 'not uncommon', which was unsustainable in the medium term (Carter, 2002). Hypotheses were proposed to explain the sector's poor financial state, including bad management and poor accounting practices, but fundamentally independents' difficulties stemmed from the unfavourable rights situation. When a producer delivered a programme to a broadcaster, the latter could acquire all the rights attached to it 'in perpetuity' (Pact, 2002: 2). Broadcasters obtained bundled and exclusive rights for the primary window (i.e. the terrestrial showing), cable and satellite distribution, and international sales. For good measure, they also got hold of ancillary and format rights. Pact would later argue that its members' inability to protect their own IP and build up their asset base left the sector 'weak commercially and heavily under-capitalised' (Pact, 2002: 2; see also Carter, 2001).

It was the New Labour government, elected in May 1997, which came to the rescue of an industry that owed a lot to the libertarian ideals of Keith Joseph, a policy advisor to former prime minister Margaret Thatcher (Darlow, 2004: 186–7). The new government immediately paid close interest to the creative industries, first mapping the creative economy, then commissioning a few more studies and finally publishing its Communications Bill, a draft media law, in May 2002 (Freedman, 2003; Garnham, 2005; Hesmondhalgh, 2005; Pratt and Gornostaeva, 2009; Steemers, 2004: 49–73). It was at this point that Pact, often described as a formidable lobbying force, entered the fray. It began by petitioning Parliament, arguing that this legislative exercise would remain useless unless the Bill improved TV programming. Better quality could only be sustained by a healthy supply market, yet, despite the policy initiatives taken by previous governments, this was in a state of terminal decline. Pact claimed that unless a radical change occurred in the basic relationship between buyers (i.e. broadcasters) and suppliers (independent producers), the supply side was effectively going bust. It contended that its members' access to the UK market was restricted by too many exceptions in the quota system and that the very small number of commissioning broadcasters enabled them to negotiate the best possible terms of trade with independent producers (Pact, 2002: 1). At this point Pact compiled a dossier documenting the abuse that independent producers had received from a public broadcaster through price fixing, strong-arming and blackmailing (chapter 4).

Next, the producers' association proceeded to lobby Parliament, targeting the powerful Joint Scrutiny Committee convened by Lord David Puttnam.[1] Their cry was heard and led to a call to the then regulator, the Independent Television Commission (ITC), to launch a review of the programme supply market. The ITC concurred with Pact, and its report made several recommendations that aimed to redress the balance of power between terrestrial broadcasters and producers (Steemers, 2004: 67). In turn, the ITC's views were favourably received by the Department of Culture, Media and Sport (DCMS), and particularly by Kim Howells, a junior minister. Howells recognized that independent producers had a case because he had previously worked at the Department of Trade and Industry

(DTI) where he saw first-hand a handful of dominant buyers – in this case British supermarkets – behaving in a way that was detrimental to suppliers (the farmers). Pact looked at the DTI's approach to this issue and discovered that Howells had overseen a code of practice that aimed to prevent supermarkets from abusing their dominant position. McVay went back to Howells and asked him to do the same for the independent TV production sector. Tessa Jowell, the secretary of state at the DCMS, acquiesced and her department introduced sixty-six amendments to the Communications Act 2003, essentially giving Pact what it wanted (McVay, interview 2009).

The Code of Practice was introduced at the beginning of 2004 and regulates the *terms of trade* between broadcasters and their suppliers. Its core principle is the *disaggregation of rights*, enabling producers to keep all the rights that are not purchased by broadcasters. This includes all the distribution rights (terrestrial, cable and satellite, online and international), the format and ancillary rights. In other words, 'producers should retain rights in the programmes unless they are explicitly sold to a P[ublic] S[ervice] B[roadcaster] and/or other parties' (Pact, 2008: 33).[2] This principle created *a new IP regime* which changed the fundamentals of the production sector.

Specifically, the Code contains three elements which helped British independents propel themselves to the top of the TV format chain. First, the Code does not attempt to constrain market forces and on the contrary reinforces – and even creates – a market for programming rights. In the previous regime, this market was undermined by broadcasters who abused their dominant position in order to amass all the rights 'in perpetuity'. The new regime recalibrates the relationship between commissioners and suppliers, thereby creating a situation where broadcasters are forced to negotiate these rights in a transparent manner.

Furthermore, if the Code sets the framework for negotiating the terms of trade, these terms are still settled by the market: it is down to the broadcasters and suppliers to negotiate sales contracts. Thus, it is incorrect to claim that the Code favours one side over another. If producers do better in the current regime, it is because the Code has ended unfair commercial practices from a handful of dominant players.

Second, this Code improves the programme supply market by encouraging development of the production segment in the chain. Previously, the distribution part of the chain was left to dictate terms to the production sector. The current regime makes it more attractive to supply content and has allowed it to grow through investment in existing producers and new entrants (see next section). Even if there is vertical integration through investment by distributors in the production sector (chapter 6), it now stands up on its own within the chain. The other side of the coin is that the sector has become more competitive, with hundreds of producers vying to have projects green-lighted by broadcasters. So far, the track record of a truly competitive supply side is a positive one, enhancing the quality of programming through creativity and innovation.

Third, the Code has an in-built mechanism that pushes producers to exploit assets in as many ways as possible. John McVay had a clear idea of how he wanted the legislation to work:

> So we wanted to move away from the traditional European model, which is very inward-looking and often dominated by debates around subsidies and cultural issues. We actually wanted to take a more entrepreneurial view of what the sector was for, what it could do. [. . .] So what we wanted to do was arrive at arrangements which incentivised producers to become more international because (a) they get growth, (b) they become more diverse as businesses and (c) ultimately content will become global. (McVay, interview 2009)

Since production companies retain the IP attached to their programmes, it is in their own interests to sweat their assets to the last drop. Indeed, the Code has transformed fee distribution attached to international rights. The commissioning broadcaster once had complete control over these rights (it would even appoint the distributor) and was due 70 per cent of *gross* revenues from any onward sale. It was thus able to deduct expenses, and more often than not the production company would receive next to nothing. With the new Code, the broadcaster's share has been reduced to 15 per cent of net revenues of any show sold overseas. This new rationale played a crucial role in incentivizing British producers to export their IP, notably through their format rights.

The rise of the super-indies

One final aspect of the Communications Act 2003 helped Britain to dominate the TV format trading system: the rise of the super-indies. It was inevitable that among the hundreds of producers a few would grow more rapidly and begin to acquire smaller firms. By 2000, these larger independents included Celador, Chrysalis, Hat Trick, Hit Entertainment, Lion Television, RDF, Tiger Aspect and Wall to Wall (Hogan, 1997; Keighron, 2001). However, in this case also, the Communications Act was a game changer. When producers gained control of their IP it became part of their asset base, which made them attractive to investors interested in content rights. The ensuing influx of capital gave some production companies the opportunity to fund growth through development and acquisitions,

Table 5.1 The leading super-indies, 2008

Company	Overall turnover (£m) 2008	Overall turnover (£m) 2007	Change (%)
All3Media	230.0	202.5	+13.6
Shine Group	216.0	146.0	+47.9
IMG Media	207.5	221.7	−6.4
Endemol UK	170.0	160.0	+6.3
RDF Media	120.6	99.3	+21.5
Tinopolis	68.0	66.0	+3.0
Shed Media	63.0	71.8	−12.3
DCD Media	34.0	42.0	−19.0
Ten Alps	27.0	32.8	−17.7
Target Entertainment	25.0	12.6	+98.4

Source: Broadcast – Supplement (2009: 5).

triggering a process of consolidation. The most acquisitive of these production companies became known as the 'super-indies'. Interest from the City was stimulated by the fact that they gained in scale and centralized costs by bringing in several producers under one roof and adding a distribution arm. Investors also noticed the 'de-risking' strategy these companies pursued by having a foothold in different genres and exploiting formats with international scope (Bonney, interview 2008; Dey, interview 2010).

Henceforth, the independent production sector grew rapidly. The total revenue of the 700 independent producers who are Pact members doubled in a decade to reach £2.0 billion in 2007. The same year, the market share of the top ten companies rose to 65 per cent, and five companies had an annual revenue in excess of £100 million (Mediatique, 2008: 3, 8). Table 5.1 lists the leading super-indies of this period.

Many of these firms played an important role in the history of the format trade because they achieved the necessary scale to make an impact on the world market. Their catalogues spanned different genres and became diverse enough to interest large buyers. They developed enough of a track record to reach the ear of US agents and, through them, the networks. The super-indies also helped foster an export culture in the British TV industry. They adopted a structure consisting of several production companies plus one outfit specializing in international sales and distribution that permitted them to exploit their IP and maximize the value of their rights. They also began to represent third party IP and help smaller independent producers distribute their shows on the international market. These producers also received market intelligence and advice from these distribution divisions, helping them avoid basic mistakes (Millichip, interview 2008; Pedersen, interview 2008). The super-indies that made the biggest impact on the TV format trading system during this formative period are as follows:

1. All3Media was formed in 2003 following a management buy-in of Chrysalis TV. It inherited ten production companies, including Bentley Productions, Cactus TV, IDTV (Netherlands), South Pacific Pictures (New Zealand) and what became North One Television (sports). Within a few years, it added Company Pictures, Lion Television, Lime Pictures, Maverick Television, Objective Productions, MME Moviement and Zoo Productions. Its catalogue of formats (e.g. *Cash Cab*, *Miss Naked Beauty*, *Top Trumps*) expanded when it set up a joint venture with Stephen Lambert (Garvie, interview 2011; Kanter, 2011).

2. Founded by Elisabeth Murdoch in 2001, the Shine Group hit the acquisition trail after five years of organic growth. In 2006, it acquired three prominent British production companies (Firefly, Kudos and Princess Productions) before buying Reveille, a US format producer and distributor. In 2009, Shine pursued its international expansion plans by establishing start-up companies in Germany, France and Australia and acquiring Metronome Film & Television, a pan–Nordic production group based in Sweden (Mahon, interview 2010; Rushton, 2010; see also chapter 6).

3. Endemol UK's library of formats was among the largest in the business, especially with the incorporation in the early 2000s of Brighter Pictures (*Big Brother UK* and derived shows), Cheetah Television (*Deal or No Deal*, *Gok's Fashion Fix*, *Ready Steady Cook*), Initial (*Golden Balls*, *The One and Only*), and Zeppotron (*8 out of 10 Cats*, *Would I Lie to You?*). London's rise as the firm's creative hub was confirmed when Bazalgette became global chief creative officer in 2005. He left the group two years later following a takeover, but Endemol UK briefly became the country's largest independent producer with the acquisitions of Tiger Aspect and Darlow Smithson for £30 million in 2009 (Bazalgette, interview 2009; Endemol, 2007; Rushton, 2009).

4. RDF Media Group was founded in 1993 by David Frank and made its first acquisition twelve years later with Touchpaper Television, a drama specialist. By the end of 2006, RDF had acquired five other independent production companies: Scotland's leading producer IWC Media, Radar, Presentable, The Foundation (children's programming) and The Comedy Unit. RDF developed several classic formats of the 2000s, notably *Wife Swap*, *Location, Location, Location* and Lambert's *Faking It* and *Secret Millionaire* before he joined forces with All3Media (Millichip, interview 2008; RDF Media Group, 2008).

5. Shed Productions was established in 1998 and acquired Ricochet in November 2005, followed by Wall to Wall and Twenty Twenty two years later. Shed Media – as the group was renamed – produced and distributed programming in a variety of genres and was among the first super-indies to be proficient in the US market. Exporting there formats such as *Supernanny, Who Do You Think You Are?* and *The World's Strictest Parents*, Shed was generating 30 per cent of its revenue from the USA by 2008 (Shed Media, 2009: 5).

Britain's broadcasting ecology and commissioning culture

Many of the most-travelled formats of the 2000s were not only developed by British producers but first aired in the UK. What is it about the nation's broadcasting ecology and commissioning culture that is so favourable to the *acquisition* of formats?

First, Britain is the world's second media market and, logically enough, the world's second programming market. In 2013, the total revenue of the British TV industry reached £12.9 billion, an increase of £426 million from the previous year. The main growth driver was pay-TV subscription revenue (£5.9 billion); TV advertising income increased to £3.7 billion, 'other' revenue (e.g. interactive revenues) stood at £736 million, and the BBC allocated about £2.6 billion to its television services (Ofcom, 2014: 159–60). This enabled UK broadcasters to invest a record £5.8 billion in content, the public service broadcasters spending £2.5 billion on first-run originated programming (a 5 per cent decline from 2012) while the commercial multichannel broadcasters invested over £3 billion in content (a 13 per cent increase year on year) (Ofcom, 2014: 159). This money was used to renew sports broadcast rights, acquire film rights, develop in-house projects and also commission new shows. In addition, British broadcasters order short runs, about six episodes in drama (against up to twenty-two or twenty-three in the USA), which leaves room for more commissions.

Furthermore, British broadcasters are less risk-averse than many of their counterparts in Europe, and are among the few willing to try untested ideas. The country's TV ecology is characterized by a healthy balance between competition and diversity. The local TV marketplace is certainly competitive, but with broadcasters relying on distinctive business models (e.g. pay-TV subscription for Sky, licensing money for the BBC and advertising for ITV), revenues flow from a variety of sources. The system's ecology is so designed that competition encourages innovation and does not prohibit risk-taking.

Some public service channels have set out to take risks, such as Channel 4, a testing ground where countless ideas have been tried over the years. The public company claims that it is 'the only broadcaster in the world to source its programming entirely from external production companies' and that its approach to risk-taking is unique (Oliver & Ohlbaum, 2014: 23). It did indeed commission 'on average over 350 new programme titles per year' between 2008 and 2013, more than any other British channel, and first-run commissioned hours represented 29 per cent of the total schedule for the same period, a higher proportion than any other channel (Oliver & Ohlbaum, 2014: 84–5). The broadcaster has gained a lot of kudos from its attitude to innovation: for instance, Simon Andreae, executive vice president at Fox Broadcasting, stated that 'Channel 4 is the single richest source of IP in the world for TV' (Oliver & Ohlbaum, 2014: 19). BBC Three has also been conceived as a nurturing place for talent and programmes, and its dramas are often adapted, especially in the USA (chapter 9).

British television is internationally recognized as a mature and sophisticated market with commissioning practices that may not be perfect but are of a consistently high standard. British commissioners are perhaps not without bias or favouritism, and occasionally come under sharp criticism from producers (chapter 4), but are on average less risk-averse than their foreign counterparts: they know their audience, trust their instincts and remain among the most innovative in the world (Jackson, interview 2008).

Taking into account the overall spend on programming, the ecology of the marketplace and the relatively high tolerance of risk, the volume of innovative shows with international potential is bound to be higher in the UK than in most other countries.

There are a few lesser factors that have helped the UK become a format champion. First, London has risen to become the world's hub for international television. The conglomerates that run their international TV operations – or at least a good chunk of it – from the British capital include Discovery, Lionsgate, NBC Universal, Sony Pictures Television International, Time Warner, Viacom and Walt Disney. Out of these headquarters they run transnational TV networks and local channels overseas (Chalaby, 2009). Many of them, including MTV and Discovery, have installed their international commissioning hub in London. 'London has been, and will continue to be, said Jean–Briac Perrette, Discovery's International President, the creative centre for us' (in White, 2014b).

London also plays a central role in global advertising. Out of the six holding groups that dominate the industry, one is British (WPP), another was established in Japan and is now headquartered in London (Dentsu

Aegis) and the rest are American (Interpublic and Omnicom) and French (Havas and Publicis). Each of these groups encompasses the full spectrum of marketing activities and controls a vast array of companies worldwide, including PR firms, global branding and creative agencies, digital and direct marketers, market research companies and global media networks. These networks, known as media buying and media planning agencies, such as Publicis's Starcom MediaVest, Omnicom's OMD or WPP's Mindshare, plan ad campaigns and then negotiate rates with media owners. These agencies are international networks in their own right but all of them have their European headquarters in London, which is where pan-European advertising accounts are held and pan-European campaigns are planned (Chalaby, 2008; M&M Global, 2015).

The link between TV formats and the advertising industry is not as tenuous as it may seem. These agencies grasped the strategic value of formats many decades ago, so much so that Interpublic owned Fremantle in the first half of the 1990s. Fremantle's game shows provided the perfect setting for advertisers: a controlled environment with a predictable outcome and a returning public whose numbers and demographics can be precisely forecast. This is why media agencies are no longer merely buying airtime but also investing in programming. Leading in this strategy is WPP's GroupM Entertainment, which funded thirty-eight shows for all the major UK networks in 2013 alone. Most programmes fall into the factual entertainment and entertainment genres; they include formats such as *Age Gap Love*, *Celebrity Squares*, *The Jump* and *Let Me Entertain You*.[3] In 2014, GroupM Entertainment hired an executive to accelerate the international distribution of its shows. This type of funding raises issues in terms of leverage, as the parent company of the entertainment division, GroupM, is also the world's largest media investment network, purchasing US$104.5 billion worth of billings in 2013.[4] However, for the time being, it does constitute another local source of investment for the London-based TV content community.

From Local Production of Imports to Local Creation of Formats

The UK has done well for itself, but can this strategy be duplicated elsewhere? This section assesses the strategies of the countries that have initiated an upgrading process in the TV format global value chain and have embarked on the journey from the local production of imports to the local creation of formats.

The rise of local production worldwide

Industrial upgrading in the TV format chain consists of moving upwards from reproducing foreign IP (e.g. adapting *MasterChef* under instruction from flying producers) (stage one) to creating local IP for local consumption (e.g. creating a formatted show for a local broadcaster) (stage two) to developing IP fit for export (stage three). For any territory moving in this direction, the most basic requirement is the development of local TV production expertise and capability. In many developing countries this capacity is being built by the content needs of a growing number of local and regional pay-TV platforms and cable and satellite channels. In the Middle East, for instance, there are more than 600 pan-regional satellite TV channels; in Africa, more than 500 stations are looking for programming (Dickens, 2013). Although these platforms and channels source finished programmes from abroad, their need for local content is inevitably leading to the expansion of a local TV production sector.

In order to produce local content, let alone export it, production standards are required to reach a certain threshold, which can vary from country to country. The good news is that in many places, the TV format trade is contributing to a raising of these standards. Evidence demonstrates that local production communities are learning from imported formats which enable them to up-skill more rapidly than if they were left to their own devices. Bibles and flying producers bring with them skills, knowledge and techniques that can be transferred to other shows. For instance, a Kenyan TV executive from pay-TV company Wananchi Group said she was importing Western formats 'not just to fast-track her way to local content but to train up the emerging local production sector in Africa' (in Waller, 2011b: 1). Twofour Arabia (Emirates) is following a similar path and, according to its general manager, is importing UK formats in order 'to send Emirati producers to the UK to see how we develop and produce programmes there, to bring back skills' (in Waller, 2011b: 1). The same process took place earlier in Israel, a territory that has long adapted Western formats. As Avi Armoza, a leading producer, summarized: 'We started by bringing formats to Israel and producing them locally, and then we began developing our own. The next stage was to give our shows to others to distribute, but we know the formats so we can best do the work ourselves' (in Jenkinson, 2007).

The same learning curve is being followed in territories in Central and Eastern Europe, the Middle East, Asia and Latin America, which have now begun to develop their own formats. Belgium, China, Colombia, Israel, Turkey and South Korea are among those countries that have recently emerged as format exporters. Others, like Australia and Scandinavia, continue to perform strongly in the industry. Among the newcomers, only Israel performs consistently enough to qualify as a tier 2 exporter (chapter 4). Several Israeli producers have managed to sell formats that travel well, notably Armoza Formats, Dori Media Group, Keshet International, Kuperman Productions and The Lab. Two formats helped the country get noticed. The first was *The Vault*, a game show that was picked up by King World, did reasonably well for ITV between 2002 and 2004 and was adapted in six other territories. In the scripted space, it is the 2008 HBO adaptation of *In Treatment* that announced the Israeli wave (Brzoznowski, 2012d; Waller, 2010a). Since then, Israeli formats that have performed well include Armoza's *Connected*, *Upgrade* and *Who's Still Standing?*, Keshet International's *Prisoners of War* (aka *Homeland*) and singing competition *Rising Star*.

Other emerging exporters are not quite in the same league. Turkey's progress has been especially rapid in finished programming, and its TV series have become a TV staple in many markets. By some accounts, the country is now the world's second largest producer of TV drama (Waller, 2014c), but its formats are yet to make such an impact. Turkey's best-travelled formats are Istanbul-based Global Agency's *Perfect Bride* and *Shopping Monsters* (twenty and thirty local versions respectively), and more recently talent competition *Keep Your Light Shining* has been remade in twelve territories (Filiztekin, interview 2014). Adaptations in Western markets remain few and far between. By 2014, Global Agency's *Forbidden Love* had been adapted by the Spanish-speaking US network Telemundo, Ay Yapim's scripted show *The End* was being adapted for Fox, and *Keep Your Light Shining* was being piloted by Nigel Lythgoe for CBS as *In the Spotlight* (Tartaglione, 2014).

South Korea has a similar export profile. It is a strong regional player and the K-drama wave has reached the shores of all Asian countries. Format-wise, Korean exports are mostly in the scripted space. Thirty-one Korean series have been adapted so far, never in more than three territories. The Philippines is the most prolific adapter of K-drama (fourteen titles), followed by Indonesia (seven), China (five) and Japan (two). Examples include *Autumn in My Heart* (Indonesia, Philippines and Thailand) and *My Girl* (Philippines and Taiwan), with the legendary *Winter Sonata* finding only one courageous Indonesian producer to do a remake. Eighteen Korean entertainment shows have been formatted so far, almost exclusively in China (Longnos, 2014).

It was estimated that Asia accounted for as much as 91 per cent of Korean TV exports in 2014, and Korean formats have only begun to venture outside the region. A series called *Yellow Boots* is planned for Italian and Ukrainian remakes, *Good Doctor* from Korean Broadcasting System has been picked up by CBS, and in the unscripted space four formats are showing potential: in 2014, *Three Idiots* was being adapted for the US market, *Crazy Market* in Italy, and *The Genius* and *Grandpas Over Flowers* in the Netherlands (Longnos, 2014; Waller, 2014a; Whittingham, 2015).

Turkey and Korea illustrate the challenges and promises of industrial upgrading in the entertainment industries. Both territories have reached the third stage, but despite rising production standards their exports have not reached the geographical scope and volume of other tier 2 format exporters. Nonetheless, they both perform well in their respective regions, and this is probably a stepping stone to the wider world market.

Upgrading strategies in the TV format global value chain

Industrial upgrading is a demanding process that not all countries manage equally well. As already seen, the journey is arduous for those that aim to become fully fledged exporters. After exporting one or two formats of note, many other territories have not fulfilled their promise. Elsewhere, production standards are often barely good enough for local purposes and the relevance of these producers remains restricted to the domestic market. Thus, the questions are why aren't all countries able to conduct a process of industrial upgrading, and which measures are needed in order to carry it out effectively? This section analyses the lessons that can be learnt from the leading format exporters, paying particular attention to the UK.

Lesson one: vested interests must be challenged

When the British government created the nation's fourth channel as a public company that commissioned its own programming (sanctioning, as we saw, the creation of an independent TV production sector), it did so in the face of formidable pressure from advertisers and ITV companies that had lobbied relentlessly for years for a second service (so certain were they to land their channel that TV sets on sale in the late 1970s already had an 'ITV-2' position on the dial!) (Darlow, 2004: 103). Later, the Communications Act 2003 also challenged the short-term interests of broadcasters by preventing them from warehousing rights for ever and creating a more level playing field between them and producers. These pieces of legislation can only be passed by a government willing to stand up against the vested interests of broadcasters.

Such legislation is currently difficult to envisage even within the European Union as broadcasters would probably be able to block it. European broadcasters do face a certain amount of 'horizontal' competition in distribution, but 'vertically' – along the TV content value chain – their vested interests still prevail and they can secure a total buy-out of rights when acquiring programmes. From a GVC perspective, European broadcasters are rent-seeking organizations whose income is more or less guaranteed while making little investment and taking minimum commercial risk. The greatest risk they face is a change in legislation, and thus logically they expend a substantial amount of energy in manipulating government regulation and maintaining their privileges within the chain. Concretely, this makes format creation and ownership virtually impossible for anyone without a channel on which to air their IP first. It also stifles innovation in Europe's entertainment industry, limits wealth creation and does nothing to address the European Union's substantial trade deficit vis-à-vis the United States in the audiovisual sector.

In the USA, the rights position has equally favoured broadcasters and media conglomerates since the expiration of the Financial Interest and Syndication Rules in 1995 (known as the 'fin-syn rules', they were introduced by the Federal Communications Commission in order to prevent the US networks from owning the programmes they aired in primetime: Kunz, 2007: 77–8; Lotz, 2007: 82–97). It may not affect the country's export capacity as much as is the case in the European Union because of the more competitive nature of the US media market and the dominance of its conglomerates on the world stage, but it remains true that, as seen, US content aggregators have imported more IP since the format revolution.

British broadcasters have not lost out either and have reorganized themselves to get involved in TV production: both BBC Worldwide and ITV now have investments in production, and Channel 4 has started taking stakes in local producers (Campelli, 2014). The country has developed a strong reputation as a place to develop, exploit and protect IP in the TV industry. Many European or American media firms have invested in the UK production sector, or established a British base, in order to take full advantage of the UK rights position (chapter 6).

Short of being able to modify the IP regime, governments can expand local programming obligations to pay-TV channels. This is not always as effective but it doesn't upset the applecart. Such a law was passed in Brazil, for instance, in 2012, leading to a boom in the independent TV production sector (Waller, 2013a).

Lesson two: the whole broadcasting ecology matters
Piecemeal measures to encourage exports tend not to work. In order to perform well in the TV format chain, a country needs to implement media regulation that may not be export-oriented (e.g. South Korea) but that is at least

mindful of the globalization of the IP market in the entertainment industry. Subsidies and export councils that rent booths at MipCom are wasteful unless local media firms have incentives to export and their production values have reached the required standard to do so. The best export incentives are market-driven, which is, again, a strength of the Communications Act 2003: the market for TV rights that the Act helped develop created a 'natural' incentive for rights owners to exploit their IP, internationally or otherwise, leading to a surge of UK export both in formats and in finished programming ever since.

Format creation depends on the ecology of a broadcasting system. As already seen, the British ecosystem strikes a delicate balance between competition and diversity, rewarding innovation and risk-taking from broadcasters. Apart from the UK, both the Dutch and Israeli broadcasting systems present similar characteristics. When such a balance does not exist, these incentives disappear and broadcasters revert to their default position: conservatism. In many European nations, public service broadcasters that are preoccupied with programming costs and commercial broadcasters that are struggling to preserve their audience share are both content with acquiring cast-iron formats with proven track records. In the USA, the cut-throat environment is double-edged as tough competition makes IP investment a necessity but can make broadcasters risk-averse.

As Ed Waller writes: 'The entire edifice of the international format business relies on some networks taking on high levels of risk so that others further down the line, in other countries, don't have to – but pay for the privilege' (Waller, 2013c). Format exporters are in those countries where broadcasters have to take the risks that others are not incentivized to assume.

Lesson three: use trade to hone your skills
Research shows that in several value chains original equipment manufacturers (OEMs) have learnt key skills from the firms they supplied. In East Asia, for instance, several OEMs have used their skills to make the shift to original brand name manufacturing (OBM) (Gereffi, 1999; Gereffi et al., 2005). It seems that a similar process has been taking place in the TV format chain, as four countries that perform well – Britain, Holland, Israel and Japan – share one last feature: all these countries were, and in certain respects remain, heavy importers of American television fare. Since the 1950s, the UK has been among the USA's top TV export markets. From game shows to TV series, there has always been a TV buyer in the UK willing to sign a licence contract for US content. In Holland, companies like Endemol cut their teeth on US game shows, some of which contained the reality element that became the firm's trademark. Israel is also a big importer of US content, and the savvy of the local audience raised on a diet of US programming is

often cited as a factor in 'driving demand for edgy local content' (Waller, 2010a). Even Japan (one of four countries with a positive trade balance in the format business) owes its prowess in the game-show genre to a strong US cultural influence in the aftermath of the Second World War (Ishita, 2000: 29–30). Proximity and familiarity with the birthplace of commercial TV create producers, commissioners and audiences who understand the semiotics of commercial television.

Conclusion

The TV format trade may straddle the planet but its geography remains strikingly unequal and exports are dominated by a few countries. Performance in the TV format chain depends on a multitude of factors and a territory must bring many variables together in order for its companies to perform well in it. If long-range factors were to be considered, it would become apparent that social and cultural values also play a role. IP creators will do better in open cultures where ideas can flow freely than in patriarchal societies that select people on the basis of race or gender for certain roles and positions. The education system also plays a part. For instance, a Hong Kong-based distributor assessed China's efforts towards a more original development in these terms:

> The problem is there is very little creativity in mainland China and this is due to the education system. It's very regimented and opposed to free thinking. People are told what to think and how to live their lives and that kind of atmosphere doesn't encourage innovation. It's a big problem and is one of the reasons Chinese broadcasters turned to Western formats in the first place, as suddenly they had lots of new ideas offered to them on a plate. (in Waller, 2013b)

Nonetheless, the format trade is dynamic and subject to change; inequalities are not written in stone. Already, the trade has enabled new voices to be heard, and more will follow. In addition, although countries like Britain and Holland benefit from historical circumstances that cannot be duplicated, actions can be taken in order to upgrade a territory's standing in the TV format global value chain. An industry motto claims that a good idea can come from anywhere, and while it is not quite true today, it may sound less outlandish in the future.

6   A Globalized Intellectual
Property Market:
The International Production Model

This chapter analyses the modern *production* of TV formats, arguing that a new business model has emerged. In the early decades of the TV format trade, rights holders simply sold a show's licence to a local production company or broadcaster, which would then adapt and produce it for a local audience. Many formats are still produced under licence but firms increasingly favour a new production model: wherever possible, rights holders prefer to adapt and produce their shows themselves in as many markets as possible, a strategy that has in turn led to the international expansion of TV production companies.

First, this chapter offers an overview of the international production model, tracing back its origins and exploring its development in recent years. It shows how it was pioneered by game-show producers before being adopted by British independent production companies and European broadcasters, and eventually by Hollywood studios. The chapter argues that this model is a key factor in the two recent waves of sector consolidation leading to the emergence of *international TV production majors*. The final section contextualizes this, arguing that TV production companies have had to adapt to the *globalization of the IP market* created by the format trading system. Using interviews with TV executives and creative leaders, the chapter analyses the risks and benefits associated with this model in terms of IP generation, exploitation and protection.

Origins: From Grundy to Endemol and Pearson TV

The international TV production model was pioneered by TV format pioneer Reg Grundy. As seen in chapters 1 and 2, Grundy began to adapt US game shows for the Australian market in the late 1950s and branched out into new territories about two decades later, spurred by the representation of the Goodson-Todman catalogue outside Europe and the Middle East. Grundy Worldwide was the first company to set up an international network of subsidiaries, registering its first overseas company in the USA in 1979, followed by New Zealand, the UK and the Netherlands in the second half of the 1980s (Moran, 1998: 47–58). It expanded further in the early

1990s, with the opening of regional offices catering for the Mediterranean area, Latin America and Asia in Monaco, Santiago and Singapore respectively (Moran, 1998: 63–9). Grundy emerged in the mid-1990s with a 'network of owned and operated companies in 17 countries tak[ing] an active hand in the production process' (Fuller, 1994b).

Endemol was the only other firm to adopt this model. Following their 1994 merger (chapter 2), Joop van den Ende and John de Mol combined their international operations and Endemol started life with subsidiaries in Germany, Luxembourg and Portugal (Bell, 1994). By the end of the decade, Endemol owned or partially owned TV production companies in ten territories, notably Spain, Belgium, South Africa, Poland, Scandinavia and the UK (Arris and Bughin, 2009: 104–11; Endemol, 2007: 8). From the outset, Endemol realized that growth required more than just licensing formats, as outlined by Monica Galer, head of international:

> Of course we are interested in taking our formats abroad but that can be in a variety of different ways – producing directly for broadcasters, co-producing with broadcasters, or co-producing with broadcasters and other local producers – whatever the deal demands. (in Fuller, 1994b)

Many of the companies that became part of Endemol, including Joop van den Ende Productions, came from an alliance of producers called Action Group, which was piloted from London. Gestmusic in Spain, Crawford in Australia and Wegelius TV in Sweden were all part of this IP-sharing network, which proved influential in the growth of what would become the format industry (Carter, interview 2008).

Pearson's Greg Dyke subscribed to the model, acquiring Grundy in May 1995 and All American Communications two years later (chapter 2). All American Communications's Fremantle had its own little international network, and combined with that of Grundy, it gave Pearson a footprint that was greater than Endemol's.

A few British TV production companies began to venture overseas in the 1990s. The first to do so was Chrysalis TV, the production company that later formed the backbone of All3Media (chapter 5 and next section). In 1994 it took a 49 per cent stake in IDTV, a leading Dutch production company, and four years later it moved on to South Pacific Pictures, a drama production company based in New Zealand.

Among broadcasters, two ITV franchise holders developed international ambitions. Under the chairmanship of Michael Green (who gave British prime minister David Cameron his only job in the private sector) Carlton Communications purchased two production companies: Hamdon Entertainment in the USA and Tele Films in France. In 1999 Green bought out his German partner from Hamdon and established Carlton America. Granada Media, which was already a large exporter of TV programmes, established its first production outpost in Los Angeles, Granada Entertainment USA, in 1997. It was followed by the purchase of an independent TV production company in Australia and, two years later, the creation of a German subsidiary, Granada Produktion für Film and Fernsehen.

International Consolidation Round 1: The 2000s

The process of internationalization accelerated in the 2000s because of two factors. First, European broadcasters realized that there were benefits in controlling some IP, whether for their own use or for sale to third parties. Second, more production firms pursued a strategy of international production. In the UK, this trend was given added impetus by the Code of Practice that Ofcom published following the Communications Act 2003. As seen in chapter 5, the new IP regime instigated by this Code gave production companies ownership of their content, creating a strong incentive to exploit their IP internationally. These nascent super-indies acquired foreign companies or used their top-selling formats to install outposts in foreign territories (typically the USA). Both factors led to a first round of consolidation in the TV production sector.

Among the super-indies, All3Media provides a case in point. Building on the foundations laid by Chrysalis (chapter 5), All3Media acquired Lion Television in 2004, a UK-based production company with several offices and clients in the USA, and MME Moviement three years later, Germany's largest production company at the time. Once Zoo Productions, a US firm, had joined the company, the super-indie regrouped all its US activities under one banner and launched All3America in June 2008. As Steve Morrison, the chief executive, put it at the time, the objective was to 'scale up from being a largely UK-based company with international reach to becoming more of an international company' (in Campbell, 2007). When All3Media was acquired by Discovery (see next section), it incorporated twenty companies across six territories.

Shine began its international expansion in 2007 with Reveille, an American distribution company noted for adapting *Ugly Betty* and *The Office* for US audiences (chapter 5). Two years later it had start-ups in Germany, France and Australia, before getting hold of Metronome Film & Television, the largest production group of the Nordic region with fifteen companies across Northern Europe. In 2011 Shine established itself in

Spain, bringing the group to twenty-six operating units across ten markets a few years before its merger with Endemol (Mahon, interview 2010).

By the end of the 2000s, even those super-indies without a large international footprint had developed a presence in the USA. Shed Media, RDF Media, Tinopolis and DCD Media opted for a US-focused strategy, opening production facilities in America on the back of successful formats such as RDF's *Wife Swap* and Shed's *Supernanny, The World's Strictest Parents* and *Who Do You Think You Are?* (Wood, 2010a).

Elsewhere in Europe, Endemol continued to expand despite ownership changes, and Zodiak Media Group became one of the fastest-growing firms. The company was brought together by an Italian publishing firm, De Agostini, which had taken over Italy's largest independent producer, Magnolia, followed by Marathon in France and then Stockholm-based Zodiak Television. By the time of its purchase in 2008, Zodiak was present across the Nordic region, and had four companies in the UK and production units in Belgium, Poland, Russia and India. The group spanned thirty companies when it scooped one of the UK-based super-indies, RDF, in spring 2010. This considerably reinforced its presence in the UK and gave it access to the US market. Zodiak was headed by David Frank, RDF's former chief executive, and consisted of forty-five operating units spread across seventeen territories by the end of the decade (Stuart, 2012).

Paris-based Banijay Entertainment was also formed during this period and reached eight territories. Key acquisitions included Nordisk Film TV in Scandinavia – in itself a sizeable international group of companies – and Bunim/Murray Productions, the LA-based company that produced *The Real World* in 1992. In the UK, however, progress stalled following a disagreement with Zig Zag Productions.

On the broadcasters' side, FremantleMedia became the content production division of RTL Group following the merger of Pearson Television and CLT-UFA in 2000. In effect, Pearson had sold its TV division to CLT-UFA but, still being a media company (it also owned the *Financial Times*), the RTL Group could not trade under the Pearson name. Thus, it renamed its content division after one of the businesses Pearson had bought in the 1990s.

ProSiebenSat.1, a German broadcaster, followed suit in 2010, creating Red Arrow Entertainment in order to expand international production capabilities and produce content with international appeal. In addition to its own format producers, Munich-based Redseven Entertainment and Snowman Productions (Stockholm headquarters with offices in Denmark and Norway), the group acquired majority stakes in production houses in Belgium (Sultan Shushi), the USA (Fuse Entertainment, Kinetic), Britain

(Mob Film, CPL Productions and Endor Productions) and Israel (Armoza Formats). On top of this, Red Arrow signed several collaborative partnerships with Dick de Rijk, the creator of *Deal or No Deal*, and Omri Marcus in Israel.

In the UK, the two leading terrestrial broadcasters also developed their own networks. BBC Worldwide, the Corporation's commercial arm, built a network of seven production bases, starting with Los Angeles in 2004, where it produces *Dancing with the Stars* for ABC. This was followed by local production units in Australia, Canada, India, France, Argentina and Germany. Some of these businesses are joint ventures with local companies but the operations in LA, Paris and Mumbai are fully owned by BBC Worldwide (Garvie, interview 2010; Paice, interview 2012).

Despite a history of finished tape exports, it is only at the end of the 2000s that ITV began paying attention to international production. It acquired 12 Yard Productions in London and Stockholm-based Silverback, and, building on its Granada legacy, it added production facilities in Spain and France to its existing ones in Germany, Australia and the USA (east and west coast). A model based on the international co-production of TV formats was in place by the time Adam Crozier, the new chief executive in 2010, made a strong international content business a strategic priority.

Hollywood jets in

International production became a significant trend in the world TV industry in the course of the 2000s. Many independent producers became part of larger businesses, and these groups came to control a growing share of the scripted and unscripted entertainment bought by broadcasters worldwide. Above all, the model was finally adopted by the aristocracy of the cultural industries: the Hollywood studios.

For a good part of the twentieth century, the Hollywood business model was to produce content with universal appeal, and the studios could not foresee that one day they would have to adapt their fare to local taste. As will be seen in chapter 9, they initially perceived the adaptation trade as a threat to their lucrative finished tape business, but had to change tack when they noticed that their TV series were getting less airtime in certain markets. The EU Directive Television Without Frontiers – and the Audiovisual Media Services Directive replacing it in December 2007 – restricted to a maximum of 50 per cent the amount of non-European content a channel could broadcast.[1] In addition, in Europe, as elsewhere, the overwhelming majority of popular TV programmes are locally produced. These factors prompted the studios to move into 'local' TV production – as their executives refer to it – with the aim of producing versions of US scripted series and, where possible, to develop shows that could travel internationally.

Sony Pictures Entertainment was the first Hollywood studio to commit to multi-territory film production, having established local production units in Asia, Germany and the UK by the end of the 1990s (Hazelton, 2001). The studio's TV division, Columbia TriStar International Television (CTIT), took a similar route and was producing local content in the same territories, plus Brazil. By the mid-1990s CTIT was producing about eighty shows locally, including game shows such as *Pyramid* and *The Dating Game* (Hazelton, 2001). After 2000, Sony Pictures Television (under its new name) acquired seventeen production companies (either jointly or solely owned) in fourteen territories, including 2waytraffic, the Dutch company that bought *Who Wants to Be a Millionaire?* from Celador (Abrahams, interview 2011).

Others were to follow. NBC Universal International Television Production was created post-2005. With headquarters in London, the firm subsequently added an Australian and two British production companies, launched a joint venture with a previously acquired film company (Working Title Television) and set up a new production unit (Chocolate Media).

Warner Bros. was to set up its own international production arm in 2009, based in London and headed by a former Endemol executive, Ronald Goes. His first purchase was Shed Media, one of the leading super-indies, for £100 million in 2010. He followed this with the acquisition of a majority stake in BlazHoffski, a Benelux format producer. The UK base is part of Warner Bros. International Television division, whose president, Jeffrey Schlesinger, heralds things to come:

> We set up this division to get into local production. Our goal is to buy or build production companies in the top ten markets of the world just as Endemol and FremantleMedia have done, and be a local producer that will develop local ideas and produce them. We will also plan to take our shows that are formatable, like *The Bachelor*, and produce local versions of them. (in *World Screen*, 2011)

The fourth global media conglomerate to invest in international TV production was 21st Century Fox, which acquired Shine for an estimated £415 million in April 2011.

Thus the international TV production model spread from game-show producers in peripheral territories to Hollywood in the space of a few decades (table 6.1). By the end of the 2000s, in addition to British independents with offices in the USA, and international TV producers of a smaller

Table 6.1 Evolution of the international TV production model, 1980s–2000s

Timeline	Adopters	Key firms
1980s	Pioneers	Grundy
1990s	First global TV production houses	Endemol; Pearson TV
2000s	UK-based super-indies and some integrated producer-broadcasters	Indies: All3Media; RDF Media; Shed Media; Shine Broadcasters: BBC Worldwide; ITV Studios; ProSiebenSat.1; RTL
Late 2000s	Hollywood studios	Sony Pictures Entertainment; NBC Universal; Warner Bros.

size such as John de Mol's Talpa Media, the first TV production majors had emerged. These fourteen groups differed in terms of scope, ethos and type of ownership (five were independent and nine attached to a broadcaster or conglomerate), but all had a sizeable footprint (table 6.2).

International Consolidation Round 2

The global economic recession initially put the brakes on mergers and acquisitions activities, but the interruption was brief and the market became active again. A second round of consolidation is taking place, fuelled by the cheap credit made available by low interest rates. Between the beginning of 2012 and the first half of 2015, the TV production majors made thirty-three acquisitions (majority stake or full ownership, excluding minority participations).

Table 6.3 reveals several trends. First, the most active TV majors were ITV Studios, Modern Times Group, Red Arrow Entertainment and Warner Bros. They are all vertically integrated firms that aim to make inroads into the TV content value chain, internationalize their production capacity and diversify their revenue away from advertising and/or subscription fees. All consolidators, however, seek to diversify their genre base, going for fiction if they were skewed towards unscripted entertainment (e.g. Endemol) and vice versa (e.g. Warner Bros.). Within these broad guidelines, each firm pursues its own distinct objectives. The ITV management, calculating that 29 per cent of the global content market is accounted for by the USA (US$15 billion), has reasoned that it needed a foothold in the country, and their acquisitions have made it the largest US producer of unscripted programming (ITV, 2014: 7). Likewise, Red Arrow Entertainment sought to establish bases in Britain and America. Conversely, Warner Bros. needed to internationalize its revenue base, hence its purchase of a Dutch producer (Eyeworks) with a large international footprint.

Table 6.2 The first fourteen TV production majors, 2010

Company/ division	Owner/type of company	Headquarters	Number of production companies/key brands	International footprint (number of territories)
All3Media	Independent	London	20/IDTV, Lion Television, MME Moviement, Studio Lambert, Zoo Productions	6
Banijay	Independent	Paris	10/Air Productions, Bunim/Murray, Brainpool, Cuarzo, Nordisk Film TV	8
BBC Worldwide	Integrated/BBC	London	–	7
Endemol	Independent	Amsterdam	80/Gestmusic, Remarkable Television, Southern Star, True Entertainment, Zeppotron	31
Eyeworks	Independent	Amsterdam	–	17
FremantleMedia	Integrated/RTL	London	25/Fremantle, Grundy, UFA	22
ITV Studios	Integrated/ITV	London	3/12 Yard, Silverback	7
NBC Universal International TV Production	Integrated/NBC Universal	London	5/Carnival Films, Lucky Giant, Monkey Kingdom	3
Red Arrow Entertainment	Integrated/ ProSiebenSat.1	Munich	3/Fuse Entertainment, Kinetic, Mob Film	8
Shine Group	Integrated/21st Century Fox	London	26/Metronome, Kudos, Princess, Reveille	10
Strix	Integrated/ Modern Times Group	Stockholm	–	4
Sony Pictures Television International Production	Integrated/Sony Pictures Television	London	17/2waytraffic	14
Warner Bros. International TV Production	Integrated/Time Warner	London	2/Shed Media, BlazHoffski	4
Zodiak Media Group	Independent	London	45/Magnolia, Marathon, RDF, Zodiak TV	17

Table 6.3 Acquisitions by TV production majors, 2012–15

TV production major	Acquired companies	Year of acquisition	Origin of acquired company	New territory	Leading proprietary formats or finished programmes acquired
Banijay	Screentime	2012	Australia	Yes	*Underbelly*
	DLO Producciones	2013	Spain	Yes	*El ángel de Budapest, Familia*
	NonPanic	2013	Italy	Yes	*Food Market Battle*
	Stephen David Entertainment	2015	USA	No	*Sons of Liberty*
Endemol	Kuperman Productions	2013	Israel	Yes	*Traffic Light*
	Artists Studios	2014	UK	No	*The Fall*
Eyeworks	Nordisk Film TV	2013	Finland	Yes	Local remakes
	Savage Films	2014	Belgium	No	*Bullhead*
FremantleMedia	Miso Film	2013	Denmark	Yes	*Those Who Kill*
	495 Productions	2014	USA	No	*Jersey Shore*
ITV Studios	So Television	2012	UK	No	*The Graham Norton Show*
	Tarinatalo	2012	Finland	Yes	Local remakes
	Gurney Productions	2013	USA	No	*Duck Dynasty*
	High Noon Entertainment	2013	USA	No	*Cake Boss*
	The Garden	2013	UK	No	*24 Hours in A&E, The Audience*
	Thinkfactory Media	2013	USA	No	*Hatfields and McCoys*
	Big Talk Productions	2013	UK	No	*Rev, Friday Night Dinner*
	DiGa	2014	USA	No	*Celebrity Home Raiders, Ke$sha*
	United	2014	Denmark	Yes	*Pind og Holdt i USA*
	Talpa Media	2015	Netherlands	Yes	*I Love My Country, Utopia, The Voice*
Modern Times Group	Paprika Latino	2012	Romania[a]	Yes	*Fish on the Cake*
	Novemberfilm	2013	Norway	No	*The Insider*
	DRG	2013	UK	No	Distribution
	Nice Entertainment Group (11 companies)	2013	Finland	Yes	*The Grill Masters, Dinner Disasters*

Table 6.3 (continued)

TV production major	Acquired companies	Year of acquisition	Origin of acquired company	New territory	Leading proprietary formats or finished programmes acquired
Red Arrow Entertainment	CPL Productions	2012	UK	No	*A League of Their Own*
	Endor Productions	2012	UK	No	*Cracker, Red Dwarf, State of Play*
	July August Productions	2012	Israel	No	*Still Standing, The Office (Israel)*
	Nerd TV	2012	UK	No	*Inside the Gangsters' Code*
	Left/Right Productions	2012	USA	Yes	*Mob Wives*
	Silver River Productions (incl. Gogglebox Entertainment)	2012	UK	No	*The Big Allotment Challenge*
Sony Television Production International	Left Bank Pictures	2012	UK	No	*Strike Back*
	Playmaker Media	2014	Australia	Yes	*The Code, House Husbands*
Warner Bros. International TV Production	Alloy Entertainment	2012	USA	No	*Gossip Girl, The Vampire Diaries*
	Eyeworks	2014	Netherlands	Yes (13 new territories)	*Test the Nation, Who Wants to Marry My Son?*

[a] Plus nine other countries in Central and Eastern Europe, and Costa Rica.

Overall, the average size of a TV production major increased from seventeen companies in 2010 to twenty-four five years later (table 6.4). Most have expanded their footprint, although they remain conservative in the territories they venture into. They aim at companies in Europe, the USA and Latin America and have yet to show a sustained interest in the Middle East (apart from Israel), Africa or Asia (apart from Australia).

Table 6.4 presents the outcome of this second wave of consolidation. The number of majors goes down to twelve, following Warner Bros.'s purchase of Eyeworks and the 2014 merger between Shine, Endemol and Core Media. Core Media Group is a US-based independent content company that bought several producers, notably 19 Entertainment, and thus co-produces *American Idol* and *So You Think You Can Dance*. The merger was driven by Rupert Murdoch's 21st Century Fox, Shine's owner, and Apollo Global Management, a private equity group, whose affiliates control the other two firms. The new Endemol Shine Group – sometimes referred to as the first 'mega-indie' – brings more than 100 companies under its wing and is certainly the TV production giant of our age.

Only four majors retain independence, as All3Media, Eyeworks and the Nice Entertainment Group all lost theirs. Discovery and Liberty Global, two companies that share a dominant shareholder, John Malone, purchased All3Media for £550 million in 2014. The new Endemol Shine Group, however, must be considered independent by virtue of private–equity co-ownership.

All owners understand the importance of the production segment in the TV industry. Consolidation and even vertical integration do not impact – and indeed are a response to – the disintegration of the production process that has taken place in world television and has led to the emergence of the TV format global value chain (chapters 4 and 5). None of the newly integrated production firms work exclusively for their owners and all can supply content to third parties. There are not always, even, priority deals between the former and the latter, as owners understand that their content people need to be able to operate on the open market. For a start, it is crucial that the programmes of these production divisions find the right home (Wong, interview 2014). Were these divisions perceived not to be behaving with a minimum of integrity, they would irretrievably damage their reputation, lose creative talent (supplying to a sole broadcaster is unattractive) and ultimately see their viability threatened.

Table 6.4 The world's twelve TV production majors, 2015

Company/division	Owner/type of company	HQ	Number of production companies/key brands	International footprint (number of territories)	Leading TV formats
All3Media	Integrated/Discovery-Liberty Global	London	20/IDTV, Lion Television, MME Moviement, Studio Lambert, Zoo Productions	6	Cash Cab, The Fairy Jobmother, Undercover Boss, Skins
Banijay	Independent	Paris	13/Air Productions, Bunim/Murray, Brainpool, Nordisk Film TV	12	71 Degrees North, FC Nerds, Opposite Worlds, Sensing Murder
BBC Worldwide	Integrated/BBC	London	-	7	Dancing with the Stars, Top Gear, The Weakest Link
Endemol Shine Group	Independent/Apollo Global management, 21st Century Fox	London	109/19 Entertainment, Endemol Shine UK's group of companies, Sharp Entertainment, Shine Nordics	30 plus	American Idol, Big Brother, The Biggest Loser, Deal or No Deal, MasterChef, Money Drop, Wipeout
FremantleMedia	Integrated/RTL	London	25/Fremantle, Grundy, UFA	22	Got Talent, Hole in the Wall, Idols, The Price is Right, Take Me Out, The X Factor
ITV Studios	Integrated/ITV	London	12/Gurney Productions, Silverback, Talpa Media, Thinkfactory Media	9	Come Dine with Me, Dancing on Ice, Four Weddings, I'm a Celebrity. . . . Get Me Out of Here!, The Voice

Company	Type/Owner	Location	Production companies	Number	Programs
Nice Entertainment Group	Integrated/Modern Times Group	Stockholm	28/DRG, Novemberfilm, Strix	16	The Bar, Class of..., The Farm, Fish on the Cake
NBC Universal International TV Production	Integrated/NBC Universal	London	5/Carnival Films, Monkey Kingdom	3 (Australia, UK, USA)	Minute to Win It, The Real Housewives of...
Red Arrow Entertainment	Integrated/ProSiebenSat.1	Munich	14/CPL Productions, Endor Productions, Fuse Entertainment, Kinetic, Mob Film	8	My Man Can, Still Standing, We Believe in You, You Deserve It
Sony Pictures Television International Production	Integrated/Sony Pictures Television	London	18/Left Bank Pictures, Silver River Productions	13	The Dr. Oz Show, Dragons' Den, Everybody Loves Raymond, Who Wants to Be a Millionaire?
Warner Bros. International TV Production	Integrated/Time Warner	London	3/Eyeworks, Shed Media, BlazHoffski	17	Brat Camp, Supernanny, Test the Nation, Who Do You Think You Are?, The World's Strictest Parents
Zodiak Media Group	Independent	London	45/Magnolia, Marathon, RDF, Zodiak TV	17	Being Human, Don't Forget the Lyrics, Fort Boyard, Secret Millionaire, Wallander, Wife Swap

TV Production in the Age of Deeper Economic Globalization

The overarching factor behind TV production firms' internationalization is the emergence of the format trading system. Chapter 4 explained how the chain's dynamics encourage media firms to expand internationally, and this section returns to the issue analysing the mechanism from the perspective of economic agents. 'Globalization', Lampel and Shamsie write, 'poses a fundamental challenge to what *constitutes competitive advantage in the cultural industries*' (2006: 278). In the current context, 'competitive advantage' for a TV producer equates to *access to the global content market and ability to develop, exploit and control IP across borders.*

The global content market is born out of the scheduling needs of the thousands of TV and entertainment platforms that exist worldwide today (chapter 2). As for the need to develop IP across borders, it stems from the fact that firms that operate in the format trade operate de facto in a *globalized IP market,* in the sense that, at the same time that the concept of a show can attract interest from around the world, it is in competition with other ideas worldwide. In the context of the format trading system, the 'international' lies at the core of leading producers' business model. They derive the following benefits from internationalization.

Benefits of scale

International expansion pushes up scale, which itself brings several advantages. First, scale is necessary to generate interest from investors. In the past, wooing the City was difficult for British producers. For instance, RDF – listed on the LSE's Alternative Investment Market since 2005 with a £100 million valuation – did not have enough liquidity to draw analysts' attention and become a regularly traded stock (Curtis, 2010). David Frank, Zodiak Media Group's chief executive at the time, used to estimate that a producer needs to reach £1 billion annual turnover and join the FTSE 250 for these analysts to spend time on its strategy (Curtis, 2010). A company with international capability becomes even more attractive to the City by increasing its *cashflow predictability.* Concentration in a single market can leave a firm overexposed to currency fluctuation and the ebb and flow of the local advertising market, whereas a group with a portfolio of businesses can collaterize earnings across multiple territories.

Size is also crucial in distribution, which is inherently a 'scale business' (Graham, interview 2010). A large production company will be able not only to put together a diversified catalogue spanning all key genres but to add third party properties to its books. As with supermarkets, choice is necessary in order to sustain interest from customers. A large distributor can also get involved in deficit financing and can negotiate better terms with large broadcasters (Dey, interview 2010; Graham, interview 2010).

Scale brings two further benefits in terms of development. Large groups have central development funds and development teams to push projects through. The mechanism is not about creating synergies but about supporting local teams in any way they feel will enhance their creativity. As Andrea Wong, president of international production at Sony Pictures Television, explains:

> As a central team, our job is to make our production companies' lives better and easier, so they can do what they do best which is to create content. They should feel like it is a benefit to them to be a part of a big US studio, because we have a strong distribution system, we can help them enter the US, because we can take the operational burden off them, because we have negotiating leverage, because we have a central creative team that can help them both creatively and financially if they need resources, but each of them should feel like they have their own autonomous ability to create and their own cultures. (Wong, interview 2014)

Development funds are used to make pilots better and deficit-finance projects if the broadcaster's money is short of what is required to make a good show. Endemol and Shine have similar facilities. At Shine, when a local producer gets stuck on a project, the central office flies in colleagues from other parts of the group to assist them. It is also the central team's job to distinguish ideas that are merely parochial from those that may gain international resonance (Carter, interview 2014; Hall, interview 2010). International scale also allows for greater flexibility in format development. For instance, once *Pointless* had become an established game show on BBC Two, Endemol funded the pilot for France Télévisions using the BBC's old set. Some paper formats, never taken up in their country of origin, have gone on to do well in other markets. FremantleMedia has turned *Take Me Out* into a global success: created by its French subsidiary and initially rejected by local broadcasters, the format found success in Asia. Some formats can even be brought back to territories where they once failed. ABC originally overlooked Endemol's *Deal or No Deal* after it piloted poorly for the US network. The show became a big hit in the UK and the tape was used to sell the concept to NBC, for which it became an enduring success (Hincks, interview 2010).

IP generation, exploitation and protection

By industry consensus, television is a hit-driven business involving a high level of unpredictability (Picard, 2005: 66). A great international format can change the fortunes of a company and define a career. Endemol grew on the back of *Big Brother*, as did RDF with *Wife Swap*, Shed with *Supernanny* and FremantleMedia with *Idols*. BBC Worldwide developed its international production network on the back of *Dancing with the Stars*. But hits are few and far between and great ideas formidably scarce. Size alone cannot guarantee super-groups the 'next big thing': they need to make themselves bigger than the sum of their parts.

First, all groups ensure that ideas, information and expertise flow across creative teams, what Alex Mahon, ex-Shine's group president, calls 'connecting creativity' (Mahon, interview 2010). Ideas can flow in different ways, but groups try to avoid excessive centralization, and a few have recently dispensed with the role of global creative officer, including Endemol and Zodiak. It is now understood that a global hit cannot be manufactured in a social vacuum (i.e. for an imaginary global market) but always has a local origin and – at first – a local destination. Tim Hincks, former Endemol UK's chief executive (now president of Shine group), explains: 'ideas are incredibly local, even individual' and thus 'you can't really run Endemol's ideas from the centre, you can't really run a creative organization centrally' (Hincks, interview 2010).

Hence the challenge is to *make the local global* – identifying local formats that have the potential to go around the world – and then *make the global local* by assessing the degree of adaptation a format needs in a specific market. TV production majors structure the creative flow of ideas according to these imperatives. Small cross-border teams identify the best ideas and allocate funds once they have decided to champion them. All majors also ensure that conversations take place among local teams so they can learn from each other, share ideas and contrast different approaches. For instance, Endemol runs a scheme called Global Creativity Team whereby the group's ten key territories come together every other month to exchange ideas (Flynn, interview 2014). Shine prizes its international culture, and its central team ensures that an ongoing dialogue takes place among all its creatives (Carter, interview 2014). Majors organize international get-togethers for a similar purpose. Sony, for instance, arranges a once-a-year Creative Leadership Conference whose aim is to highlight some of the projects that the production teams are working on, drive creative collaboration on some ideas that deserve to get off the ground and invite inspiring creative speakers. Actor Seth Morgan, writer Aaron Sorkin, rapper Pitbull and film composer Hans Zimmer all made an appearance in LA in 2014 (Wong, interview 2014).

Making IP travel along the local–global–(multi-)local route is the way super-groups transform local shows into super-formats. It is how Endemol turned *Das Hairdresser* into *The Salon* and *Now or Neverland* into *Fear Factor*, how Shine transformed *MasterChef* and BBC Worldwide *Dancing with the Stars*. The latter was not selling abroad: who else but the Brits would be interested in ballroom dancing? But the US version helped to convince broadcasters that the show could be made locally relevant.

The process of consolidation in the chain's production segment and the formation of TV production majors make the strategy of in-house IP generation doubly important. Since all the majors are equally intent on hanging on to their IP, the market for formats has dried up and it has become virtually impossible to acquire interesting properties at a reasonable price. This makes IP generation – and more fundamentally creativity – essential to the commercial well-being of these TV groups, and places it at the very core of their business model.

It thus raises the issue of whether the control of creative resources – as opposed to mere access – is still necessary for companies to gain a competitive edge. A view has developed, validated by the commercial strategies of the Hollywood studios and game publishers, that 'access to talent' has become more advantageous than 'control of talent' (Lampel and Shamsie, 2006: 279). Likewise, it would not make financial sense for the TV majors to retain well-known presenters and directors on long-term contracts. For the same reason, the majors accept that some of the best ideas will be generated from outside their walls, and all have in place first-look deals with independent producers (White, 2014c).

However, the scarcity of hit ideas and limited availability of IP mean that control over *some* creative talent (including programme makers) and resources remains a competitive advantage. Kees Abrahams, the president of international production at Sony Pictures Television between 2009 and 2011, is emphatic: 'the biggest risk for every company in our business is to lose their key talents, but the biggest opportunity is to attract the right talent' (Abrahams, interview 2011).

The scarcity of hits also dictates that the maximum value must be extracted from any piece of IP. The primary reason that prompted the pioneers to develop their international production capabilities was to boost revenue from their formats. Under the old format licensing model, the IP owner received only a licence fee from the show's local producer, usually falling somewhere between 7 and 8 per cent of total production costs *per episode*. With the exception of a few global brands for which production costs can be exorbitant, daytime quiz shows and factual entertainment pro-grammes that require no studio can be produced very cheaply. Indeed, low production costs sometimes constitute their unique selling point. Thus their licence fee would barely cover distribution costs and a format company would be unable to rely on this income alone. The closure of distribution companies such as Distraction Formats or Target Entertainment provides cases in point.

TV majors have internationalized because there is more value in format production than in licensing. Gary Carter, during his time as FremantleMedia's chief operating officer, explained it clearly: 'there is very little point if you want to be big to just be in the intellectual property busi-ness; you have to be in the production business. And as soon as you get into the production business, intellectual property [and] formats become impor-tant because they allow you to expand into a territory to gain production' (Carter, interview 2008).

In addition to the distribution fee, the revenues that can flow into the group include a share of profits, which can be as high as 40 per cent of the show's total budget in certain territories (Carter, interview 2008). Alternatively, producers can receive a production fee and, depending on the strength of the format and the outcome of negotiations, a ratings bonus and, where applicable, a share of the voting income. Thus, the advantages that international production brings to companies – that is, the ability to capture the value of their IP and expand their stay in the format value chain – justify the risk and overheads involved in the running of an international production network.

Chapter 4 analysed the power relationship between broadcasters and their suppliers and argued that both parties deployed strategies that enabled them to upgrade their position within the TV format chain. The former, as we have just seen, moved upstream (by taking control of TV production companies) while the latter expanded geographically. A key driver that pushed producers across borders is the battle over IP rights. As buyers, broadcasters remain in the driving seat during negotiations (chapter 4), and inevitably try to hold on to the biggest possible share of rights. When a format is produced under licence, they are likely to obtain control over these rights and therefore it is they who will exploit these rights locally. Although the outcome of negotiations always depends on the clout of respective par-ties and local circumstances, a likely result is that the IP owner will be forced to accept a *net* participation in the exploitation of these rights. Since the buyer is entitled to deduct all expenses before passing on its share of the profits to the IP owner, there is often not much left for the latter.

TV majors have various responses to demands for rights and are arguably in a stronger position than smaller producers. Like any other company they can invest in a pilot, giving them more leverage than with a paper format. They can also first produce the show in a country where they can protect their rights – typically the UK – before selling the show in territories where production groups are in full control. International broadcasters can also claim that the rights of a particular show are unavailable because held by a foreign subsidiary that wishes to retain them all, and can then insist on producing or co-producing the show. Not only will their share of profits be considerably higher (even though they may have to share some of the proceeds with the broadcaster) but they can protect their brand by overseeing the commercial exploitation of these rights.

International production capabilities are also valuable for quality control purposes. A format keeps its value only when buyers are reassured that it can be a ratings winner. One single poor adaptation can instil doubts in buyers' minds and irremediably damage an erstwhile valuable franchise. Today, the transfer of expertise between IP owner and licensee is well established and format packages are more complete than ever. Nonetheless, an IP owner takes a risk each time it selects a local producer. The latter may lack experience in the genre, be unfamiliar with certain aspects of the format, or be more concerned about its profit margins than the franchise itself.

TV majors mitigate this risk by designating partners in key territories with whom they collaborate regularly. Ken Starkey and colleagues call this sort of arrangement '*latent organizations* . . . that bind together configurations of key actors in ongoing relationships that become active/manifest as and when new projects demand' and that are based on 'knowledge and trust' among partners (Starkey et al., 2000: 299, 303). But this risk is reduced further by keeping a format within the group. The teams know each other well and can remain in touch throughout the production process, enabling a smoother transfer of expertise, leading to a good-quality execution. Commercially sensitive information is more willingly shared, and if at first the show does not perform as well as expected, issues can be explored without risk of litigation.

A network of production companies can also prevent the over-exploitation of a format. In the USA in the early 2000s, two British shows, *Who Wants to Be a Millionaire?* and *The Weakest Link*, burnt out quickly because the IP owners, Celador and the BBC respectively, had relinquished too much control to the American networks, which overused them. In the case of *The Weakest Link* it taught the BBC a valuable lesson about IP control, and it is partly what spurred BBC Worldwide to turn itself into a global format producer (Jarvis, interview 2010).

Furthermore, global production capabilities are the best line of defence against IP theft. Once a format has proven successful, the chances are that copycat shows will appear. Despite improving legal protection (chapter 4), taking competitors to court remains a costly and unpredictable business. Court cases take a very long time to settle and a case that is won well after the sell-by date of a show is of no value. Thus the best line of defence is commercial, and an international production network enables a company to be 'first to market' by rolling out formats very quickly across borders and thereby pre-empting the appearance of copies (Mahon, interview 2010; see also Singh, 2010). Also, broadcasters think twice before burning bridges with companies like Sony or FremantleMedia by ripping off their formats, knowing that the latter will hand over their next blockbuster to the competition (Abrahams, interview 2011).

Finally, TV production majors have the resources to expand their own *value chain*, in Michael Porter's meaning of the term. Porter's notion of value chain is connected with but distinct from GVC analysis. He defines a value chain as the ensemble of interdependent activities a company performs in order 'to design, produce, market, deliver, and support its product' and ultimately create value for its clients (Porter, 2004: 36, 1998: 40–1). These activities take place *within* the firm, whose activities are embedded in a larger *value system* where its chain connects with that of others (Porter, 2004: 34). Thus developing a new product, or a new way of marketing a product, allows a business to gain a competitive advantage and expand its value chain (Porter, 1998: 41), which is the case with the transformation of TV formats into franchises (chapter 8).

TV majors are investing in new divisions (e.g. FremantleMedia's Digital and Branded Entertainment, Shine 360°) whose role is to realize the full value of their assets by ensuring the exploitation of ancillary rights and the extension of their programmes on to new platforms, from second-screen applications to multi-channel networks. FremantleMedia has also acquired a gaming company (Ludia), a multi-platform producer (RadicalMedia) and Europe's largest multi-channel network (Divimove). In the world television is moving in, the ability to move content across platforms gives a firm a distinct competitive advantage.

Conclusion: Trade, Competition and Innovation

The international production model was pioneered by firms from countries located at the periphery of the global TV trade. It was then adopted by the British super-indies and received its *lettre de noblesse* when embraced by the Hollywood studios. The international model is behind the emergence of TV production majors that grew across borders seeking a competitive advantage in the TV format chain.

The emergence of these majors raises issues about innovation and industry consolidation. Indeed, the second round of consolidation seems to bring closer the prediction of Thomas Dey, a merger and acquisition specialist, that 'the end game is the global consolidation of the production sector into five $1bn businesses – which will ultimately be owned by the studios' (in Wood, 2010b: 25).

In terms of impact on innovation, the commonly held assumption that large media firms are bereft of innovative practices does not square with reality. As we have seen, TV groups innovate in terms of managerial practices, ranging from information flows to productivity gains and multi-platform management. Since they can soak up the cost of failure, they can occasionally take a bet on innovative formats, and when a small producer does come up with a groundbreaking idea, a larger group always has the option of investing into this company.

It can be argued that the cost of expanding and maintaining an international production network has raised the barriers of entry to the industry, confirming the fears of political economists who write about concentrated media ownership (e.g. Bagdikian, 2004; Downing, 2011; Mosco, 2009: 158–69; Schiller, 1992). It is a fact that US capital is investing heavily in TV production, particularly in Britain. However, the TV production industry remains very dynamic and for every producer joining a TV major many more are created. In the UK, Pact claims that 150 new companies join the industry body every year (Kanter, 2014). While some of the acquired firms are well-established businesses, others are start-ups that have literally just switched the lights on. It is not rare either for executives of acquired businesses to leave the group at the end of their lock-in period and start a new venture. There are countless examples of small firms growing rapidly in the context of an expanding global format trade and content market. As large groups expand their activities to respond to market developments, such as ancillary rights exploitation, it creates opportunities for smaller firms to find new niches in which to specialize. Finally, in an IP-driven industry, creativity and intangibles remain as important as commercial clout and industrial prowess. For all their might, the TV production majors have not found the magic formula for the perpetual generation of hits, leaving room for talented individuals and small companies to make an impact. The future of the sector is difficult to predict but it is likely to be able to accommodate all types of businesses.

Part III

TV Formats:
Structuring Narratives

7   Journeys and Transformations: Unscripted Formats in the Twenty-First Century

The remaining part of the book explores key trends in the TV format business from 2000 to the time of writing. This chapter examines unscripted shows, chapter 8 focuses on talent competitions and formats as TV franchises, and chapter 9 looks into TV formats in the scripted space. We open with a brief analysis of the relationship between the format industry and TV genres, examining how the trade has progressed from game shows to reality to fiction. The chapter then provides an overview of key formats in the game-show genre and across three reality strands: observational documentaries, factual entertainment and reality competitions. Close attention is paid to the narrative structure of these shows and, illustrating the argument with material gathered in interviews with format creators, this chapter explains how the TV industry has learnt to tell a story without a script.

Genres and Formats after the Format Revolution

The TV format revolution was powered by reality programming. Early on in the 2000s game shows still constituted nearly half of all traded TV formats, reality 26 per cent (including factual entertainment) and scripted 5.0 per cent (table 7.1).

Later the percentage of game shows dropped to a third, while reality (including factual entertainment and talent shows) continued its inexorable

Table 7.1 Total hours of format programming by genre, 2002–4

Genre	2002	2003	2004	Total	2002–4 (%)
Entertainment	318	226	308	852	2.0
Factual entertainment	96	163	471	730	3.0
Game shows	6,754	7,138	7,655	21,546	48.0
Reality	2,958	3,848	3,608	10,414	23.0
Scripted	625	731	928	2,285	5.0
Variety	642	754	717	2,113	5.0
Other	1,450	1,927	1,968	5,345	14.0
Total	*12,843*	*14,787*	*15,655*	*43,285*	*100*

Source: adapted from Screen Digest (2005: 33).

Table 7.2 Total number of exported episodes by genre, 2006–8

Genre	2006	2007	2008	Total	2006–8 (%)
Factual entertainment	7,452	7,988	8,322	23,762	38.4
Game shows	5,486	6,846	7,302	19,634	31.8
Reality	1,185	1,335	1,265	3,785	6.1
Scripted	2,781	2,972	3,188	8,941	14.5
Talent	1,222	1,330	1,170	3,722	6.0
Other	662	677	671	2,010	3.2
Total	*18,788*	*21,148*	*21,918*	*61,854*	*100*

Source: adapted from FRAPA (2009: 20).

march with more than 50 per cent of formatted episodes (table 7.2). At this stage, the proportion of scripted adaptations doubled to almost 15 per cent.

Game Shows

In 2015, the world's most travelled format remains a game show: *Millionaire* has been adapted in 117 territories, last reaching Kyrgyzstan. It is still on air in at least thirty countries at any one time (Fry, 2014; see also Brzoznowski, 2011a). *Slumdog Millionaire*, which won the 2008 Academy Award winner for Best Picture, has been added to the countless brand extensions. *Millionaire* has been a source of inspiration for many game creators, and several of its features, particularly the multiple-choice answers, are today part and parcel of the genre. *Millionaire* also revived an entire genre; those TV executives who thought that game shows belonged to history changed their mind when they witnessed its success.

No format has reached *Millionaire*'s heights but many game shows have travelled far and wide in the 2000s. In the wake of *Millionaire* came *The Weakest Link*, first aired on BBC Two in August 2000. Its success rested almost entirely on an innovation in the host's demeanour: no longer on the side of contestants and offering the occasional friendly slap on the back, as tradition dictated, she put them under pressure and then scoffed at their failings. Participants were made to feel as intimidated as school children; relieved when the next question moved on. For the public, the pleasure lay in the *Schadenfreude* of watching someone struggle to answer and being scolded in front of millions. The second twist to the genre was the elimination procedure (contestants vote each other off), which was imported from reality programming.

The Weakest Link was an instant hit in the UK, where ratings were helped by tabloid press coverage commenting on the rudeness of local host

Anne Robinson. The show was picked up by NBC and having become a ratings success in the United States it developed into a global phenomenon, even though the host's confrontational attitude did not go down well in a few territories (e.g. Japan and China). The format sold to about seventy territories within three years and was in eighty markets by June 2005 (Beale, interview 2008; Jarvis, interview 2008).

Inventing a game show, Mark Goodson once said, is like inventing a new sport, and the strict rules laid out in the production bible need to be adhered to or the whole enterprise collapses (Usdan, interview 2010). Thus traditionally game-show rights owners have been very cautious with local productions, sending in flying producers to ensure that the format points are understood. As was shown, Paul Smith adopted a similar philosophy with *Millionaire*, with the added incentive for him to create a homogeneous global brand (Smith, interview 2009). Likewise, BBC Worldwide allowed no changes whatsoever to the seventy-odd local versions of *The Weakest Link* (Jarvis, interview 2008).

The first game show to allow more flexibility was *Deal or No Deal*, a Dick de Rijk creation. Originally, the show was a five-minute segment at the end of a ninety-minute quiz show in Holland, funded by one of the national lotteries. Peter Bazalgette, then at Endemol, saw the segment and understood its potential. He told John de Mol that he could transform it into a stripped daily daytime show, giving it a regular time slot throughout the week, but the latter replied that according to the 'Paul Smith principle', it had to remain identical to the original version (Bazalgette, interview 2009).

The Italians were the first to ignore de Mol's advice and went on to expand the five-minute money-box game into a glamorous forty-minute primetime show that they sold to RAI Uno, where it became a hit. The show moved to France and the idea that people could phone in for a cash prize was introduced. Next step was Spain, where Endemol's local subsidiary wanted to save money on production and decided to shoot five shows a day instead of one. They got all the contestants to stay in a hotel and shoot ten shows over a weekend. The unexpected result was that the contestants got to know each other and bonded. Once in the studio with the cameras rolling, they rooted for one another, adding an emotional dynamic to the proceedings that would be duplicated in many other versions.

The show moved to the United States next, where it was given a massive set, with the contestant's family and friends sitting on the front row and celebrity guests coming on to help them make choices. The US network also added the banker as a silhouette behind glass. As *Deal or No Deal* travelled from one territory to another, it evolved into three or four versions that Endemol's subsidiary in the next market could choose between. The UK, for instance, opted for the cheap but intimate Spanish version. This is how the show was produced in seventy territories (and aired in 150) by 2012, at one stage contributing 30 per cent of Endemol's profits worldwide (Bazalgette, interview 2009; Endemol, 2012: 40).

The Dutch company, being one of the world's largest suppliers of game shows, has several other well-travelled titles in its catalogue. First honed in small territories (chapter 4), *1 vs 100* started flying after being picked up by BBC One and NBC in 2006. By 2012 it had been produced in thirty-eight territories, including China and the United Arab Emirates. Endemol was probably disappointed with the pick-up for *The Whole 19 Yards* (five territories by 2012), *101 Ways to Leave a Game Show* (eight countries) and *Bank Job* (one), but fared better with *Wipeout*. *Wipeout* is a *turnkey production*, meaning that teams use the same set (located in this case in Argentina); thus broadcasters need only to find a presenter and add a comedic voiceover. Local teams are flown over to the suburbs of Buenos Aires, where two obstacle courses are set. By 2012, twenty-nine local versions had been produced (Endemol, 2012).

Later, *Money Drop* emerged as Endemol's star format. The game show was created by David Flynn at Remarkable Television, a London-based subsidiary, and launched on Channel 4 as *Million Pound Drop* in May 2010. Flynn's ambition was to reinvent the primetime quiz show, a feat that had not been repeated since *Millionaire*. Looking for an object that could become the show's icon and which could give it its identity, Flynn was struck by the fact that real money had never been used before. He started to plan a show where the money would be visible on set and proceeded to break a rule, one thought to be written in stone, that dictates a game show has to start with a small prize and build up towards a bigger one. His format would open with a £1 million cash prize, the drama being generated by contestants trying to cling desperately to their money (Flynn, interview 2014). As Flynn explained, the tension builds up progressively because 'the nearer [the contestants] get, the more they value the money they do have. £50,000 on question seven is valued much more highly than £1m on question one' (*Broadcast – MipTV Supplement*, 2011a). In truth, viewers enjoy watching people lose money as much as they share their joy when achieving the great prize.

Flynn played the game in Julian Bellamy's office, then head of programming at Channel 4. Flynn gave Bellamy £100 in coins and placed them on four traps cut in a cardboard box. Bellamy lost all his money but was swayed at once, and the deal was clinched when Flynn suggested airing the show live, a real innovation for a pre-recorded genre. Endemol produced showreels before the game aired on Channel 4, and sold in fourteen territories in less than a year. By the end of 2014, the format had seen fifty-two local versions (Flynn, interview 2014).

Many features make game shows – sometimes decried on the grounds of poor taste, either for the excessive prizes they give or just for being mindless junk entertainment – the bedrock of TV schedules. First, a game show can stay on air for decades. In the USA, Sony Pictures Television has produced 5,800 episodes of *Jeopardy!* and 5,200 of *The Wheel of Fortune* since their launches in 1964 and 1975 respectively (Waller, 2010c). In the UK, *University Challenge* (originally an American show called *College Bowl*) has been on air – with a few interruptions – since 1962, and *A Question of Sport* since 1970. In France, *Questions pour un champion* (*Going for Gold*) has been on a public service channel since 1988. Game shows are often scheduled in access primetime, where their 'role is to bridge the gap between the hustle and bustle of daytime and whatever's on in primetime' (Harry Friedman in Waller, 2010c).

Even when taken off air, 'formats never die, they just rest', as they say at FremantleMedia (Clark, interview 2008). The producer has the world's largest catalogue of vintage game shows (*The Price is Right, Family Feud,* etc.), which are regularly taken down from the attic and dusted off for broadcasters. The last economic recession rekindled a taste for 'shining floor shows' – as they are called in the UK – that offer viewers a fuller escape from the daily grind. In Britain alone, broadcasters have commissioned pilots and series of shows such as *Blockbusters, Catchphrase, Mr & Mrs, Play Your Cards Right* and *Surprise, Surprise*. In 2014 ITV revived *Celebrity Squares*, first shown on British screens from 1975 to 1979, which was based on the earlier *Hollywood Squares*, premiered on NBC in October 1966. *The Dating Game,* shown on ABC in December 1965, *The Gong Show* (June 1976, NBC), *Pyramid* (*The $10,000 Pyramid,* March 1973, CBS) and *To Tell the Truth* (December 1956, CBS) are among the shows currently being revived for broadcasters (Fry, 2014; Kanter, 2012).

As evidenced by their importance to the format trade, game shows travel easily and can fit in any culture with the minimum of adaptation. The transfer of expertise is usually straightforward and mechanistic, which is not the case for all genres. Game shows also tend to be highly lucrative as they are produced in series and canned on a production line, and as such they are usually among the first formats acquired by new broadcasters in developing countries.

Finally, only game shows can deliver drama in a *reliable* manner night after night, series after series:

That's what game shows can give you, is that somebody genuinely is doing life-changing decisions, it is a real person, and you then watch whether they make the right call or not, whether that is accepting the offer on *Deal or No Deal*, whether that is choosing to split or to steal on *Golden Balls*, whether that is putting your money on one drop or the other on the final question of *Million Pound Drop*, people make massive decisions either through knowledge or through intuition and then those decisions play out. That kind of natural drama and jeopardy is very difficult to deliver in any other real-life genre. (Flynn, interview 2014)

Reality Programming

Like game shows, reality television is closely bound up with TV formats: the genre is eminently adaptable and most reality shows end up on the format market. This section deals with three of the reality strands identified in chapter 2.

Observational documentaries

Observational documentaries are the most light-touch of reality shows and try to convey a feel for 'authenticity' in the characters and situations they depict. Although the situation is set, it is not artificially created (unlike factual entertainment programmes), and whilst the narrative arc is character-driven it is not pre-structured by fixed format points as in, for instance, *Wife Swap* (see next section). *Duck Dynasty*, *Fat Gypsy Wedding* and *Pawn Stars* are among the strand's most popular programmes and *The Real Housewives of Orange County* the most often adapted. The last of these premiered on Bravo in 2006 and has since been re-versioned several times at home and abroad (Greece and Israel in 2011, Canada the following year, Australia in 2014 and the UK as *The Real Housewives of Cheshire* in 2015). Fixed-rig productions represent an interesting development within the genre. Shows like *24 Hours in A&E*, *One Born Every Minute*, *Educating Essex* or *Gogglebox* use up to seventy remotely controlled fixed cameras in order to capture stories in places where a film crew is too obtrusive.

Observational documentaries are relative newcomers to the format arena because the absence of any formal structure makes them difficult to copyright. Thus they used to be duplicated across markets without licences. It is perhaps a reflection of increasingly shared common values within the international format community with regard to IP protection (chapter 4), as well as the complexity of producing fixed-rig documentaries, that format rights have become sought for such shows. *One Born Every Minute, Educating...* and *The Magaluf Weekender* are all British fixed-rig documentaries that were re-versioned several times in 2014. Among classic observational documentaries, even the format rights of a series with no apparent structure like *Benefits Street* (Channel 4, 2014) have been licensed. It is the strength of the concept behind it, and skill in the ways of delivering it, that are exported. Licensees are told that all the shooting has to be done in a single street, the majority of people must be unemployed, there needs to be a sense of community among its inhabitants, strong characters are essential, and filming must take place over several months (McKerrow, interview 2014).

Factual entertainment

Although factual entertainment programmes do not have a name in America, where they are regrouped under the reality umbrella (also called 'non-scripted' or 'alternative' programming), they can be distinguished from other reality strands. Compared to observational documentaries, factual entertainment shows are lightly structured with clear format points, a possible competitive element but no elimination. Like serial competitions, they have a setting or situation (also called a precinct) that delivers drama, and lead characters who go through a transformation and are hopefully in a better place at the end of the programme than at the beginning. In contrast to competitions that end with the last episode, however, factual entertainment programmes are *closed episodes*. Competitions have the advantage that viewers get attached to the characters over time, but they can be more difficult to sell as finished programmes because they rely on broadcast in a specific order and viewers usually know what the outcome was. As seen in chapter 2, the strand developed in the UK incorporating elements from various genres; it is defined as follows by Stephen Lambert, its most illustrious exponent:

> What is factual entertainment? It's obviously non-scripted programmes but it's where the pressure to be entertaining and popular is as great as the pressure to capture something about the way the world is. So I think to some extent factual entertainment tries to still be informative and revealing about the world and to have some kind of a subtext, but it also has entertainment as an equally core priority. (Lambert, interview 2012)

Within this framework, formatted documentaries are those that have a 'satisfying' beginning, middle and end; hence the need for a situation that can deliver a resolution. Lambert's creations have proven among the most influential. When he joined RDF as an equity partner, his priority was to create returning programmes on which the business could depend. The earliest returning series were half-hour entertaining docusoaps based on popular characters, including *Airport, Children's Hospital* and Lambert's own *Clampers* (traffic wardens) and *Lakesiders* (Lakeside being a shopping centre in Essex).

Lambert, however, grasped the benefits of going one step further. Instead of accessing a situation, he became interested in 'creating' a situation and used his documentary skills to capture the narrative, which, to a large extent, plays itself out once a person has been put in the starting position (Lambert, interview 2012).

The first show created on this premise was *Faking It*, which first aired on Channel 4 in 2000 and was adapted in about ten territories, including the USA. Key to the show's popularity was the idea that fakers have to live for a whole month with their mentors, giving plenty of time for a relationship to develop. At the end of the stay, when the test comes, both the faker and the mentor really care about whether they can pull it off (Lambert, interview 2012).

The inspiration for *Wife Swap* came from the female section of the *Daily Mail*, a British mid-market tabloid. A piece portrayed a nurse, a lawyer and an accountant, comparing their income and the ways they spent it. Lambert and team thought it would be interesting to make them swap homes and live on each other's money for a couple of weeks. The show was pitched on this basis and it is only when making the first episode that they realized that it could be developed into something more than just a personal finance show. It would be about swapping family lives altogether and focus on 'the intensity of people's value systems' (Lambert, interview 2012). The format's key feature became the manual that explains how the household works. It is written by the families but producers ensure that it is done in such a way that it acts as a 'red rag' to the incoming wife (Lambert, interview 2012).

The format had already been sold to five territories before it debuted on Channel 4 in January 2003, and reached twenty territories by the end of that year. By the time *Wife Swap USA* was airing on ABC in 2004, RDF had already launched two spin-off shows, *Boss Swap* and *Husband Swap*. The American version brought many benefits: it helped to establish RDF USA and enabled the outpost to secure further commissions from US networks; the finished tape sold in quite a few territories (the UK included); and the continuing success of *Wife Swap USA* helped sustain the lasting popularity of the format. Local versions have been made in twenty-two territories so far, and the format premiered in Australia in 2013.

A few more Lambert shows made their mark on the international TV marketplace. *Secret Millionaire* was created when the idea of philanthropy was in the air. The programme's first rule is that benefactors give their own money, making them far more invested in the process than if it came from the broadcaster. Second, this money is given to people for whom a few thousand pounds is transformational and can change the whole way in which they are able to conduct the rest of their lives. The show premiered on Channel 4 in November 2006 and the US version aired on Fox two years later.

The inspiration for *Undercover Boss* came from watching the fiasco of British Airways' new terminal in Heathrow in 2008. As the baggage system crashed in the opening days, one of the reporters pursuing Willie Walsh, BA's chief executive, asked him when the last time he travelled on a BA plane as a paying customer was. When Walsh responded that he could not because people would recognize him, Lambert and Holzman, his partner for Studio Lambert USA, 'wondered whether that was true. Would ordinary workers in large corporations recognize their big boss if he or she were dressed like them and they were told that here was a new trainee trying out their kind of job?' (Lambert et al., 2011: 2). *Undercover Boss* is guided by two central ideas. The first is to recognize and *celebrate* the unsung heroes 'who make businesses run' in a storyline that generates emotions (Lambert et al., 2011: 6). The second is to witness the boss awkwardly performing tasks with which he or she is unfamiliar, to comic effect. As one would expect, it can take months to cast a series, as it requires a powerful individual to get down from his or her pedestal and potentially discover unpalatable truths (Lambert, interview 2012).

A UK pilot was shot with the boss of a budget holiday resort company in the summer of 2008, from which a 'sizzle reel' (a five-minute sales tape) for the US networks was produced. The show was pitched to Nina Tassler, president of CBS Entertainment, who immediately grasped its appeal. She liked it so much that she launched it on Super Bowl night, US networks' most desirable slot bar none. The audience on that night in February 2010 reached a cool 38.6 million viewers and the series subsequently settled at 17 million viewers, the highest ratings for a new show during the 2009–10 season (Lambert et al., 2011: 16). More than fifteen local versions have been made since the international launch and finished tapes have sold in over 175 territories, broadcasters often purchasing both the US and UK versions.

Four formats, four situations, yet all underpinned by the same principle: taking a fish out of water. As Lambert explains:

> *Faking It* is going into a world they know nothing about, and it's usually a different value system. And *Wife Swap*'s all about two civilizations, a family is a small civilization and these are two different civilizations with completely

different values. Both *Secret Millionaire* and *Undercover Boss*, it's somebody who's powerful and has limited understanding of those people who are in a less powerful situation, and they are learning what life is like from their point of view, and in the end having much greater empathy or understanding of what life is like for people who are less powerful, and in a small way trying to do something about it. (Lambert, interview 2012)

Studio Lambert's latest hit is *Gogglebox*, a fixed-rig show that captures the public's reactions to TV programmes – as they are watching them – in their living rooms. The concept was imagined by Tim Harcourt, the company's creative director, as he watched the London riots in summer 2011 and wondered how other viewers were reacting to the scenes. The programme launched on Channel 4 in March 2013 and there were more than twenty-five local versions by early 2015 (Brzoznowski, 2015).

Supernanny also counts among the early factual entertainment programmes. It was developed at Ricochet, a British production company that became part of Shed Productions in 2005 (and now Warner Bros. Television Productions UK). The show began a seven-year run on Channel 4 in July 2004 and ten foreign adaptations were made within a couple of years. The American version was particularly successful both domestically and on the international market because it featured the formidable Jo Frost, the original British nanny.

Like many well-travelled formats, *Supernanny* has the distinction of having generated a few copies, notably *Supermamas* in Germany and Granada America's *Nanny 911* for Fox. However, that last show was seemingly different enough to escape legal action and became a successful format in its own right, with more than twenty local adaptations.

Who Do You Think You Are?, an influential format in the genealogy strand, was developed by another Shed company, Wall to Wall. Alex Graham, the company owner, had the idea flying around in his development files for about fifteen years. When the series was finally commissioned by the BBC in 2003, the plan was to make ten episodes retracing the history of Great Britain through the eyes of celebrities. *Who Do You Think You Are?* became an unexpected success aided by its multi-layered narrative. It works like a travel-log, a history programme, a detective story and a journey rich in surprises and emotions for the celebrities discovering their ancestry. In particular, the contrast is always striking between rich, famous and talented people and the hardship and misfortunes of their impoverished forebears (Graham, interview 2010).

The series is relatively expensive to put together, but more than ten adaptations have been made so far. The American one is travelling particularly

Table 7.3 Top titles in Europe, 2012–13

Top five titles by hours broadcast	2012	2013	Change (%)
Come Dine with Me (ITV)	3,742	3,778	+1.0
Fish on the Cake (Red Arrow)	1,765	1,200	–32.0
MasterChef (Shine)	600	1,199	+99.8
Who Wants to Marry My Son? (Eyeworks)	1,037	1,101	+6.2
Big Brother (Endemol)	1,160	1,032	–11.0
Top five titles by value created (US$ million)	2012	2013	Change (%)
Come Dine with Me (ITV)	209.5	205.6	–1.9
Money Drop (Endemol)	224.7	197.5	–12.1
Deal or No Deal (Endemol)	141.7	140.5	–0.8
The Voice (Talpa)	128.1	140.1	+9.4
Dancing with the Stars (BBC Worldwide)	129.1	117.3	–9.1

Source: adapted from *TBI Formats* (2014a: 24).

well because of the global fame of participating Hollywood celebrities. The series has also inspired Wall to Wall to come up with *Long Lost Families*, a series that reunites estranged relatives and was commissioned by ITV in 2010.

Come Dine with Me undoubtedly ranks among the most groundbreaking formats of the 2000s. In a 2013 survey of eighty-four European TV channels, the title came top in terms of both screening hours and value created for broadcasters (table 7.3). Across the world, more than 8,000 episodes have aired so far.

Come Dine with Me debuted on Channel 4 in January 2005 and consists of four or five contestants hosting a dinner party in turn. At the end of each evening the guests mark the host and the winner gets a prize. The series was developed by Nell Butler, then executive producer at Granada Productions (now ITV Studios). Like Lambert, Butler started working on observational documentaries (*Airline* in her case), retaining from the setting the human interest stories and stressful situations. She also produced *Family Exchange*, a daytime show for the BBC involving whole families swapping lifestyles. She liked the domestic setting because it related to her own life and she enjoyed seeing the same people across the week and observing relationships as they develop. On the back of this she developed *Ladies Who Lunch*, a *Come Dine with Me* prototype that was rejected twice by ITV. But Butler struck gold when she combined the domestic setting, the stressful situation (the dinner party) and a competition element. The show blends the joy and stress of entertaining with behind-the-scenes gossip.

Nell Butler honed her idea with Jim Allen, director of factual and entertainment, and Adam McDonald, Channel 4's daytime commissioner.

McDonald duly commissioned a pilot that already included features such as the reading out loud of the menu and the marks out of ten. The series was ordered and did reasonably well but was overshadowed by another newcomer to the daytime schedule: *Deal or No Deal*. The game show was getting huge viewing figures and for a time Channel 4 ceased commissioning *Come Dine with Me*. The show was saved by Granada Germany, which produced it to great ratings, helping it establish itself as an international format (Butler, interview 2009).

As always with successful shows, *Come Dine with Me* works on several levels. First, there is the cooking (the recipes are available online), and contestants must be reasonably good cooks: they are not invited to humiliate themselves if they think opening a tin of baked beans is a great meal. Then, relationships develop among the contestants. Great care is taken with the casting to find the right combination of personalities. The programme makers like outgoing, competitive and slightly eccentric people and do cast for contrast. However, although gender differences and class nuances can generate tension, the atmosphere must remain warm. There is also a strong voyeuristic element and the programme's popularity is partly drawn from its promise of a snoop around people's homes. The *Come Dine with Me* lens zooms in on doorbells, doormats, fridge magnets and coloured loo paper that – viewers like to think – reveal so much about their owners. Audiences also like to see people cook and entertain in their own home because everybody does it differently. The audiences watch what the people eat and how much they drink, and hear what they say, and in a way the programme helps people evaluate their own normality against others' views of what normality is (Butler, interview 2009).

Come Dine with Me also stands out for the number of derivative shows and imitations it has generated. Butler's own team has come up with *House Guest, House Guest in the Sun, Country House Cooking Contest* and *Peace Meal*. ITV Studios also developed *Four Weddings* in 2009, which has since been remade in sixteen territories. The format retains the judging of a ritualized situation as four brides attend each other's weddings and mark the dress, the food, the venue and overall experience. For *Come Date with Me* (2011), the casting is made from contestants trying to find love, and the winner can choose one of the others to take on holiday. Finally, *Fish on the Cake*, a format developed by Paprika Latino (an international production house in Central and Eastern Europe) and ranked second in Europe in terms of broadcast hours (see table 7.3), is based on exactly the same principle, but with celebrities who cook for and entertain their guests in their own homes over the course of one week.

There are hundreds of factual entertainment formats on the market. The themes vary but the basic formula remains the same: a precinct sets a solo character, or a few, on a journey structured by format points. When all goes well, this journey involves a process of discovery and characters use this newly acquired knowledge to change an aspect of their selves or the world that surrounds them. The producers have their story because, as John Yorke explains, 'change is the bedrock of life and consequently the bedrock of narrative' (Yorke, 2013: 46).

Reality competitions

'Reality competitions' are shows that are tightly structured and involve a competition element with an elimination process. This process, however, does not rely on the exhibition of skills or talent in performances such as baking a wedding cake or singing a pop song. In this strand, it is Endemol's *Big Brother* that has proved most influential. The format itself has been produced in forty-four territories at the time of writing and is still going strongly. Indeed, in 2013 it came fifth in the list of European broadcast hours (table 7.3). In the UK, it will continue airing on Channel 5 until at least 2018. In the Americas, it launched in Canada in 2012, where it has been recommissioned since; it is returning for its fifteenth season in Brazil; and it is slated on CBS until 2016. In Asia, it started in Vietnam in 2014 and is scheduled for China in 2015.

Big Brother's engine has inspired countless other titles, such as Strix's *The Farm* (adapted in forty territories since 2001), *The Bar* (over sixty-five territories) and Endemol's own *Loft Story* and *Secret Story*, both created for the French market. Two other shows were deemed too close to the original by Endemol, which began legal action: French judges ruled that Banijay's *Dilemma* did not infringe *Loft Story*'s and *Secret Story*'s copyright (table 4.5), but ABC agreed to pay financial compensation for *The Glass House* in 2012. Banijay also distributes *Opposite Worlds*, a Chilean format that consists of dividing a house by a glass wall, with one side offering an opulent and futuristic life and the other a threadbare existence.

One of the most talked-about reality formats in 2014 was *Utopia*, a year-long show devised by John de Mol, who claimed it took *Big Brother* one step further:

> During 2013, says de Mol, we noticed a fairly constant piece of information: people are really insecure, they're worried about their financial future, and they're unhappy with regulations. So we asked ourselves: what happens if we give people the chance to do it all again? Would they be able to create a mini-society rather than the one we are living in now? (in Curtis, 2014a: 20)

The format rights have been acquired by several important broadcasters since its launch in Holland. After investing a staggering US$50 million in the show (Nededog, 2014), US network Fox premiered it in September 2014, but pulled the plug two months later as the ratings did not hold.

The reality competition engine is simply a platform which can be used to develop shows that differ in many ways. Reality competitions can take place in different surroundings: a Hebridean island (*Castaway*, BBC One, 2000), the jungle (*I'm a Celebrity . . . Get Me Out of Here!*, ITV, 2002–), a beach (*Love Island – 'Big Brother* on a beach') (ITV, 2005–6, ITV2, 2015; Znak, interview 2008) or a kitchen (*Hell's Kitchen*, ITV, 2005–).

Format points and rules can also change. As seen in chapter 4, a New York court had to decide if *I'm a Celebrity . . .* infringed *Survivor*'s copyright, and found substantial differences (table 7.4). Indeed, *I'm a Celebrity . . .* was developed as a celebrity trek through the jungle before *Survivor* went on air in the UK and ITV went back to the show when the ratings of *Survivor*'s second series disappointed. The brief from the commissioners was something 'special' that could be broadcast live, with a public vote and which could be streamed throughout the week (Znak, interview 2008).

In 2015, *I'm a Celebrity . . .* is proving to be a slow-burner as it is getting international success and its highest ratings in its domestic market more than twelve years after its launch. International TV buyers are warming up to the concept even though it is expensive and complex to produce. The British version necessitates 500 staff working round the clock in three shifts, filming 24/7 for three weeks and editing coverage from up to eighty cameras (mostly fixed but a few manned) (Znak, interview 2008). Ten versions have been produced so far. The Germans shoot their show on the same Australian site and immediately after the British version in order to obtain economies of scale, but the Dutch adaptation is shot in Suriname (a Dutch-speaking territory) and the new Australian, Danish and Romanian series are shot in ITV Studios' South African jungle hub.

Hell's Kitchen was developed by the same Znak-led team at ITV Productions, and it is produced and edited 'in a very, very similar way' (Znak, interview 2008). It also rests on the same principle, which consists in taking celebrities away from their pampered lives, putting them in a hostile environment and watching the story unfold:

> It's people under pressure and then, you know, once people are under pressure, whatever pressure that is, whether it's the pressure of being hungry in Australia and wanting some food and not being able to get any or whether it's the pressure of twelve-hour days with a madman screaming at you. It's like how do they cope. We'll find out what those people are really made of in that environment. (Znak, interview 2008)

Table 7.4 A court's comparison of the key elements of *Survivor* and *I'm a Celebrity . . . Get Me Out of Here!*

Expressed element	*Survivor*	*I'm a Celebrity . . . Get Me Out of Here!*
Mood/overall tone	Drama	Comedy
Participant selection	Very dramatic decision-making among the contestants (e.g. the Tribal Council)	Contestants are selected by the viewers. Decisions are passed on in a relaxed manner
Production value	Artistic takes, high level of professionalism	Home video look
Interaction	None: viewers watch an adventure which takes place in the past, with no ability to influence events	Viewers can follow events live (sometimes with 24-hour delay) and decide live what happens next; selection of participants by the viewers
Setting	Dry Australian Outback	Australian rainforest (jungle)
Contestants	Normal people	Celebrities
Presenters	One presenter (Jeff Probst), serious manner, task: judge and presenter appearing twice per episode	Two presenters (Ant and Dec), humorous entertainers: appear throughout the show
Outcome	US$1 million in prize money	King/Queen of the Jungle; prize money goes to a charitable organization
Teams	Two teams: leads to strategic alliances	No teams
Tasks	Necessary: prize money is the motivation	Participation is voluntary
Music	Deep, chanting, tribal music	Upbeat and quick
Animal takes	Dangerous situations and animals (crocodiles, snakes, etc.)	Harmless animals, entertaining
Task difficulty	Contests are physically and mentally strenuous	Contests are not physically strenuous; contestants have to overcome revulsion
Contestants' meals	Contestants have to find their own food, which is limited in quantity	Contestants' meals are provided; contestants can complete tasks in return for better meals

Source: EBU (2005: 113).

Hell's Kitchen remains a popular format and has become a household brand in the USA (for Fox), and with it, Gordon Ramsay.

Finally, the reality engine can be applied to different overarching themes. Several titles focus on couples, the idea being to test the strength of their relationship. One such show was Mentorn's *Paradise Hotel*, which aired several times in the USA in the 2000s and saw about ten adaptations. It was followed by the less successful *Forever Eden*, also from Mentorn and adapted in a few territories. In mid-decade, a Japanese production company went straight to the point with *Fidelity Test*. However, TV history will retain *Temptation Island*, which started the relationship theme and debuted in 2001 on Fox, a channel which, under Mike Darnell, was a pioneering exponent of the reality genre in the USA. The format is still being sold by Banijay and has reached twenty local versions, finding lasting success as *L'Île de la tentation* in France, where TF1 recommissioned it for many years.[1]

Dating is another popular theme. *Average Joe*, which casts male contestants competing for the attention of a 'beauty queen', started on NBC in 2003 and lasted four seasons, ending in 2005. The format generated only a few international versions but in 2011 RTL's M6 revived it as *La Belle et ses princes presque charmants*, with enough success to recommission the series several times. On a similar premise, *Beauty and the Geek* (The WB, 2005) saw local versions in Australia and the UK.

Some format creators decided to introduce a twist to the genre. Following *Who Wants to Marry a Multi-Millionaire?* (Fox, 2000), Darnell developed *Joe Millionaire*, which debuted on the US network in January 2003. Twenty female contestants were tricked into wooing a 'millionaire' who, as revealed to the last remaining contestant, was as poor as a church mouse. The couple were surprised with a cash prize if they decided to stay together. The show was a hit with the American audience but the surprise made it difficult to reproduce since contestants must remain unaware of the ruse. *El, der Millionär*, by UFA for RTL II in Germany, was the most notable adaptation.

As often, the original format proved the strongest, and the global franchise that emerged from the lot is *The Bachelor*. It premiered on ABC in March 2002 and was the first to combine dating with an elimination procedure. The following year, local versions were already in Italy, Poland, Belgium and Germany, and it reached its twenty-fifth adaptation in 2012 (Brzoznowski, 2012b). *The Bachelor* is still performing strongly for ABC, in its eighteenth season at the time of writing, and has delivered several spin-off shows: *The Bachelorette* (tenth season for ABC), *Bachelor Pad* and *Bachelor in Paradise*.

Weight loss is another theme that is often exploited. LWT's *Celebrity Fit Club* (ITV, 2002) and a Dutch show called *The Big Diet* were early in this strand. More recently, the only known Swiss format, *Village on a Diet*, had a few adaptations. In this category, the winning show is *The Biggest Loser*, a weight-loss competition created by David Broome. It first aired on NBC in 2004 and has since clocked up fifteen seasons on the US network alone. Initially distributed by LA-based Reveille (which became independent from NBC Universal in 2005), *The Biggest Loser* was sold into twenty territories by spring 2006. Today, the format has seen more than twenty-five local adaptations, including pan-Asian and pan-Arab versions.

A final popular theme is survival/adventure. *Survivor's* best international days may lie behind it, but the US version has entered American TV folklore by being commissioned by CBS for a thirtieth season at the beginning of 2015. *The Amazing Race* started its US network career a year after *Survivor*, also on CBS, and reached its twenty-fifth season in September 2014. The US version is produced by Jerry Bruckheimer, and is only beginning to travel widely.

In Europe, *Peking Express*, a title from the Netherlands, follows teams of hitch-hikers travelling from Moscow to Beijing on €2 a day. The format has seen eight adaptations in Europe, the latest in Italy in 2012. The newest iteration in the genre is *Dropped*, a 2014 Swedish format that sees contestants dropped in remote locations and tasked to find their way back to civilization (which usually takes them three to four days to do) (*TBI Formats*, 2014b).

The reality wave has reputedly passed by, but many of these shows are well-established international franchises and some still perform strongly for US networks. Although research shows that audiences decrypt reality TV well and understand its codes (Bignell, 2005; Hill, 2002, 2005),[2] fan blogs and the popular press regularly complain about the degree of 'authenticity' of shows in this strand.

As a general rule, relationship-based reality shows tend to be more scripted than others and American producers are inclined to script more than the British;[3] following this logic a show like *The Bachelor* will contain scripted sequences while *I'm a Celebrity* . . . will have none. In principle, however, scripts are not needed, as the entertainment lies in the coming together of certain elements. The first, already touched on, is the setting. As in factual entertainment programming, reality competitions set up contestants in a situation with rules, tasks and missions, making them behave in a certain way and generating drama and storylines that entertain viewers:

> All we can do in these shows is create the environment where you hope it encourages drama. You can't control it. And the whole point about *I'm a Celebrity* . . . is you take people out of their comfort zone, you take away all their luxuries. You put them in a harsh environment and it's real. You don't give them very much food. The whole set-up is designed to push people to their limits, to their edges, and that's where you hope that the drama comes,

you know, but the most important thing is to create the right environment, put interesting people in there, and then hope that it works. That's the key. (Znak, interview 2008)

The second element, mentioned by Natalka Znak, is casting; a process of crucial importance since contestants play themselves. Every reality show sets up its own rules for casting according to its aims and objectives (see also Mayer, 2014). For *I'm a Celebrity . . .*, casting is a year-long process and some celebrities are chased (and some chased away) for several years. Choice is guided by the producers' need to book well-known names but also to include the less famous who are interesting and have a good character. Then, in the interests of diversity, the producers will source from a wide range of people of different backgrounds. Ultimately, what the producers are aiming for is a group of characters whom they cannot imagine together and of whom they cannot predict how they will get on. The objective is perhaps to have not warring celebrities but a cast and characters interesting enough for people to want to watch (Znak, interview 2008).

The third element is editing. As explained in chapter 3, reality shows shoot many more hours than they need for the edited version of the programme (the figure of 90:1 is often floated for some high-end talent competitions). Using a logging system and digital editing suites, producers comb this material in order to construct the storylines, which at times are obvious and sometimes have to be drawn out of the footage. Reality, for Znak, is 'all about storylines', and for Alan Boyd, it is a marriage of two skills, entertainment and 'storytelling [which] was in the drama books' (Boyd, interview 2009; Znak, interview 2008). Boyd mentions a famous episode of *Britain's Got Talent*, a talent competition, to drive home his point about editing and storytelling:

The seven-and-a-half minute Susan Boyle piece was edited by a guy called Ben Thursby. If you had watched Susan Boyle for the performance alone, just alone, you wouldn't have the story. . . .What you saw was the build up of a story before she came on. . . what the public, and sadly what the public expected of her because of the way she looked, not the way she sang, so there was an expectation. And also you have to put it in the context that at that point there was a roll on the show of silly people. . . it was being set up that here's a bad person, here's another bad person and here's another person, and then you see the, aye, you've got to look at the concept of how it was built into the running order. And she came on and you are now, or certainly the British public at this stage were set up to believe here was another. And of course it wasn't, but it was a very effective editing, the use of where the close ups were, and they're all real because it's a ten camera shoot. And you've got them, and you're editing, great editing sees the person you want to see in your imagination at the same time as the producer puts it there. (Boyd, interview 2009)

In reality television, stories are crafted at the pre- and post-production stage: when casting, setting and editing come together, stories flow, viewers are entertained and producers have a hit.

8   Talent Competitions: Myths and Heroes for the Modern Age

This chapter focuses on a fourth reality TV strand: talent competitions. Seeking to understand their global success, it analyses their narrative structure and compares and contrasts them with the hero myths of other civilizations. This chapter also explores the emergence of TV franchises, or formats that no longer merely cross borders but cross platforms.

As a reality strand, talent competitions share many features of the genre but have followed their own evolutionary path and specialize in a type of narrative arc. They involve the following elements:

1. a competition-centric structure
2. skills-based performance
3. a panel of judges and/or mentors
4. a public vote (stage shows only)
5. an elimination process
6. a winner

These six elements are unchanging but can be combined in countless ways. Competitions are structured differently depending on variables such as the setting and the initial number of contestants. Some involve celebrities (*Dancing with the Stars*), some do without (*Got Talent*) and others can do both (*The Apprentice, MasterChef*). Mass competitions pass through a series of stages from auditions to live shows (e.g. *Got Talent*), those with celebrity contestants go through a simple elimination process (*Dancing with the Stars*), while others use a system of heats (*MasterChef*). Contestants are judged on skills-based performances, whether it is cooking, modelling, sewing or singing. For celebrity contestants, their skills are acquired during the series. Judges can be asked to adopt a mentoring role (*The Face, The X Factor*) or can even be replaced by mentors (Banijay's *Mentor*). In all cases, they are central to the show, as viewers side with them and their decisions help shape the narrative. They add an interactive dimension as viewers support their choices, or not. Judges' attitudes can range across the spectrum from the critical and offensive to supportive and nurturing. Panels of four judges offer the most potential for dramatic effect, especially when cast to fill in the roles of alpha male and female, beta male and female. The play of characters is bound to produce a panel prone to arguments and displays of stereotypical behaviour.

Since the format revolution, reality-skewed talent competitions have featured among the world's most popular entertainment programmes and, unsurprisingly, today there is a competition for every talent (table 8.1). *American Idol* was the number one US show for six consecutive years in the 2000s, 'winning audiences of up to 30 million and outperforming Fox's primetime average among 18 to 49 year-olds by more than 200%' (*Broadcast – International Supplement*, 2010). In the UK, the final of *The Great British Bake Off* on 8 October 2014 was the third most-watched show of the year, with 13.5 million viewers and 49 per cent audience (consolidated numbers). (It was beaten only by the World Cup Final and England's first game against Italy.) That same week, *The X Factor Results* was the second most-watched programme, with 8.8 million viewers, followed by *Strictly Come Dancing* and its result show (third and fourth places with 8.7 million and 8.5 million viewers) (Reevel, 2014).

These serial competitions can be seen in all corners of the world: *Dancing with the Stars*, *Got Talent*, *MasterChef*, *The Voice* and *The X Factor* had 308 local versions between them by 2014. Some adaptations also travel extensively as finished programmes: the US versions of *Idols*, *Got Talent* and *MasterChef* have always sold widely and even the British version of *The X Factor* reached 147 territories in the same year. These juggernauts unfold on many platforms and generate many spin-offs (see later section on TV formats as franchises). They are cultural phenomena that hold centre stage in contemporary popular culture and clips of which have been watched billions of times on YouTube.

Stage talent shows involve a public voting system and usually these episodes are broadcast live. Live shows pile on costs but they add scale, a sense of occasion and an interactive element to the series which brings in additional revenue. The public vote and judging decisions can be combined in various ways. Most formats find a way of balancing the public vote against the panel's verdict, as judges bring credibility to the process. The technology that underpins the voting system has moved on from postcards in the 1980s, telephone and texting in the 2000s to second screen and cloud technology today. At least three reality singing contests (*Rising Star*, Univision's *Va por ti* [*Searching for You*] and Telemundo's *Yo soy el artista* [*I Am the Artist*]) and one game show, Endemol UK's *The Singer Takes It All*, have put interactive second-screen applications at the heart of their voting systems.

The elimination process is at the core of these shows and is the dimension that distinguishes them from game show competitions such as *The Singer Takes It All*, Armoza's *I Can Do That!* or Zodiak's *Sing If You Can*. It gives scope and a time-span to the programme and lets the production team wrap the narrative arc along the contestants' journey. It's this part that often

Table 8.1 Leading and upcoming talent competitions, 2000–15

Setting	Title	Country of creation, producer or distributor	Original broadcast
Business	*The Apprentice*	USA – Mark Burnett Productions	2004 – NBC (USA)
Cooking	*Game of Chefs*	Israel – The Lab	2015 – Reshet (Israel)
	The Great Bake Off	UK – Love Productions	2010 – BBC Two (UK)
	MasterChef	UK – Shine	2005 – BBC Two (UK)
	Top Chef	USA – NBC Universal TV Distribution	2006 – Bravo (USA)
	The Taste	UK – Celador	2014 – Channel 4 (UK)
Dancing	*Celebrity Pole Dancing*	Holland – Tévé Media Group	2014 – RTL 5 (Holland)
	Dancing with the Stars	UK – BBC Worldwide	2004 – BBC One (UK)
	So You Think You Can Dance	USA – 19 Entertainment	2005 – Fox (USA)
Drag queens	*RuPaul's Drag Race*	USA – World of Wonder Productions	2009 – Logo (USA)
Fashion/ modelling	*The Face*	USA – Shine	2013 – Oxygen (USA)
	Fashion Star	USA – Electus	2012 – NBC (USA)
	The Great Sewing Bee	UK – Love Productions	2013 – BBC Two (UK)
	Project Runway	USA – Bunim/Murray	2004 – Bravo (USA)
	Next Top Model	USA – CBS TV Distribution	2003 – UPN (USA)
Film-making	*Project Greenlight*	USA – HBO	2001 – HBO (USA)
Gardening	*The Big Allotment Challenge*	UK – Silver River Productions	2014 – BBC Two (UK)
Gymnastics	*Tumble*	UK – BBC Worldwide	2014 – BBC One (UK)
Painting	*The Big Painting Challenge*	UK – BBC Art Productions	2015 – BBC One (UK)
Singing	*Idols*	UK – FremantleMedia	2001 – ITV (UK)
	Rising Star	Israel – Keshet	2013 – Channel 2 (Israel)
	Master Class	Israel – Keshet	2011 – Channel 2 (Israel)
	Mentor	Denmark – Nordisk Film TV	2013 – DR1 (Denmark)
	Keep Your Light Shining	Turkey – Global Agency	2014 – ProSieben (Germany)
	Popstars	Australia – Screentime	2000 – Seven Network (Australia)
	Sing My Song	China – Star China	2014 – CCTV-3 (China)
	The Voice	Netherlands – Talpa	2010 – RTL 4 (Netherlands)
	The X Factor	UK – Syco/ FremantleMedia	2004 – ITV (UK)
Sports	*Celebrity Splash!*	Netherlands – Eyeworks	2012 – SBS 6 (Netherlands)
	Master Athletes	USA – FremantleMedia North America	2014 – SVT (Sweden)
	The Jump	UK – Twofour	2014 – Channel 4 (UK)
Stage craft	*Get Your Act Together*	UK – ITV Studios	2015 – ITV (UK)
	Got Talent	UK – Syco/ FremantleMedia	2006 – NBC (USA)
Tattooing	*First Ink*	USA – Endemol	2005 – TLC (USA)

captivates viewers because they are witness to the transformation of the main characters, a process at the heart of storytelling:

> As the paradigm illustrates . . . learning is central to *every* three-dimensional story: that is *how* the characters change; they learn to overcome their flaw and, what's more, they appear to learn according to a pattern. Their unconscious flaw is brought to the surface, exposed to a new world, acted upon; the consequences of overcoming their flaw are explored, doubt and prevarication set in before, finally, they resolve and conquer it and embrace their new selves. (Yorke, 2013: 51–2)

In Baz Luhrmann's *Strictly Ballroom* (1992), argues Yorke, Scott Hastings, the main protagonist, is a 'great dancer' but also a 'narcissistic, workaholic loner' who is 'crippled emotionally' (Yorke, 2013: 56). Through meeting and dancing with Fran, an amateur dancer, he experiences 'the intimacy of true love' and opens up. After setbacks and trials, Scott overcomes his own 'insecurities and uncertainties', learns about courage and accepts his new self (Yorke, 2013: 56–7).

From the *Iliad* to *Macbeth*, it is a story that has been told countless times. In reality TV, transformations may not always be as complex but characters do embark on a journey of change and sometimes self-discovery. It is the function of the elimination engine to propel this transformation, discriminating between contestants who conquer their own doubts and frailties to overcome challenge and those who stumble at the first hurdle, or the second or third. Thus it also produces the contestant who has embraced change the most: the winner. Alan Boyd on *Idols*:

> It's always a journey. It was designed as a journey . . . music was only one part of the story. It is about creating heroes. It's about creating a hero, and that's what it's about. Basically it says, it's very simple, it's what happens to everyday people who don't give up, yeah, that's what heroes are, that's what you're building. You're building people surviving and winning, defying the odds. (Boyd, interview 2009)

Talking about a reality competition, Znak makes a similar point:

> Well, the show [*I'm a Celebrity* . . .] is all about transformation isn't it, and the winners are always the people that the public feel have gone on a journey. They might start out not liking it, moaning, but then they sort of try hard. The British public likes to see somebody who's trying hard. They like to see somebody who struggles. They like to see somebody suffer and struggle and then they like them. It's very clear what they like. (Znak, interview 2008)

In talent competitions, the story ends when the hero is revealed and viewers are elated by the vision of a character that has fought others, conquered his or her fears and, equipped with a new sense of self, is ready to face a new life. The following sections examine the recent evolution of the genre.

Singing

At the peak of the reality wave, a few talent contests adopted features from across the reality genre. *Operación Triunfo*, a singing competition with a *Big Brother* element, was developed by Endemol's Spanish subsidiary and first aired on TVE in 2001. The show grew a huge following in its domestic market as well as in France, where it became known as *Star Academy*. It made only a brief appearance in the UK as *Fame Academy* in 2003. By the mid-2000s *Operación Triunfo*'s nineteen local versions had good enough ratings to be picked by ABC, where it aired as *The One: Making a Music Star* in 2006. The show has since been eclipsed by other formats and is no longer commissioned.

In 2005, Bea Ballard, creative head and executive producer for BBC Entertainment, applied the talent search recipe to develop a show where the end prize would be a role in a West End musical. Collaborating with composer and music impresario Andrew Lloyd Webber, Ballard and her team came up with *How Do You Solve a Problem Like Maria?*, which aired on BBC One in the summer of 2006. This was followed by *Any Dream Will Do* (a search for the lead role in the musical *Joseph and the Amazing Technicolor Dreamcoat*, BBC One, 2007) and then *I'd Do Anything* (BBC One, 2008), looking for the starring role in *Oliver!*

Avro, the Dutch public service broadcaster, adapted the concept locally in 2007 and set up three shows designed to cast the lead roles in *Evita*, *Joseph* and *Mary Poppins*. The format also travelled to the USA, where NBC adapted it into a talent search for Sandy and Danny in *Grease* (*Grease: You're The One That I Want*, 2007) (Ballard, interview 2009).

Although the US version's fifteenth season in 2016 is set to be its last, *Idols* continues to do well in other territories. Adapted in forty-seven territories so far, it has been watched by 460 million people since its launch, generating more than five billion votes in the process (Stephens, 2014b). It has, however, newer rivals. *The X Factor* was launched in 2004 by Syco Entertainment, a joint venture between Simon Cowell and Sony Music Entertainment. The year before, Cowell had helped launch *Pop Idol* in the UK, a format co-owned between Simon Fuller's 19 Entertainment (two thirds of shares) and FremantleMedia. Cowell did own a stake at first but relinquished it to 19 Entertainment (Jones, interview 2010). Either he did not anticipate the show's success or he thought of the series as primarily a vehicle to sell artists. Without an interest left in the franchise, Cowell proceeded to launch his own talent contest: *The X Factor*. Cowell and Syco's creative team, Nigel Hall and Siobhan Greene, enlarged the search to new categories (groups and over twenty-fives) and linked them to judges who turn mentors for the live stage of the series. Mentoring creates rivalry and often tension among judges, adding a layer of storylines to the narrative arc.

Even though the launch edition of *The X Factor* on ITV in 2004 was a hit, the format's international roll-out was initially slow: as it competed with *Idols*, it was not picked up in a number of markets, even though some stations hedged their bets by alternating between the two (Jones, interview 2010). The format reached its twentieth local version – becoming the number one entertainment show in many territories – before the big jump in the US market in 2011 (*Broadcast – International Supplement*, 2010). The North American adventure lasted three seasons, as Fox did not renew the show for 2014. Despite Cowell's best efforts, *The X Factor* arrived too late to dislodge the leading US singing competition franchise, *American Idol*. It remains a strong franchise, though, with forty-eight local versions to date.

Among the other singing contests launched since, Talpa's *The Voice* is the most widely travelled, with some fifty broadcasters so far adapting the concept, including the BBC. Debuting in Holland in 2010, it benefits from a clear three-act structure (blind auditions, battles and live shows) and an original feature in the shape of swivelling chairs.

While *The Voice* tweaked existing format points, the next step for the genre was real-time public voting. Most competitions that make an extensive use of second-screen applications and social media have turned to real-time voting (see earlier section). The contestants on *Yo soy el artista*, for instance, have 45 seconds to win over 100 social influencers who have all made the trip to Orlando to watch them live (Dickens, 2014). Keshet's *Rising Star* launched in Israel in 2013 and comes with a second-screen application that allows the audience to give instant feedback to performers. If the approval rate exceeds 70 per cent, a screen lifts that reveals the contestant to the judges. After shooting across territories, *Rising Star* stumbled in France and Germany to low ratings and was cancelled by ITV, leaving the show to an uncertain future (Franks, 2014).

Dancing: Blood, Sweat and Glitterballs

Measured against classic format metrics such as number of adaptations and episodes and generated income for broadcasters, the world's top reality format in the late 2000s was a celebrity dance competition: *Dancing with the Stars* (Whittock, 2011a). The show's success has since continued unabated.

In June 2003, BBC One's commissioning team for entertainment convened in order to discuss Saturday nights, always a thorny issue for terrestrial broadcasters. What could be done to give the evening a sense of occasion? In the course of the conversation, Fenia Vardanis, one of the commissioners, remembered watching *Come Dancing* with her mum and suggested that it would be both comedic and glamorous to invite celebrities to do a dance show, which could be called *Celebrity Come Dancing*. The idea went through the wheels and cogs of the channel and it was decided that BBC Production could develop a show along these lines. When the production team pitched the show, it looked like the old *Come Dancing*. It is at this stage that Vardanis and Jane Lush, controller of entertainment commissioning, thought to add an elimination procedure in order to create drama and storylines through emotional attachment: as viewers are drawn to the show, they distinguish between the contestants they like and root for, those they dislike and boot out quickly, and those they feel sorry for. Vardanis and Lush thought that if the eliminations did not solely rest on the public vote (the judges' score weighs in at 50 per cent), it would add gravitas to the show and give those who danced well a chance to stay in. The live band and live singer added to the ballroom feel and the sense of occasion. Bruce Forsyth, a TV veteran whose career stretched back to *Beat the Clock*, added a 'touch of class', as did Len Goodman, lead judge and ballroom expert. The show's name was discussed for a while, as Lorraine Heggessey, the channel's controller, did not want 'celebrity' in the title. After *Come Dance with Me* and *Strictly Ballroom*, they settled for *Strictly Come Dancing* (Vardanis, interview 2009).

The format's brand values are clearly defined and summarized as 'blood, sweat and glitterballs', which covers glamour, fun, humour, dancing, competition and contestants' journeys (BBC sources). Wherever it goes, *Dancing with the Stars* represents one of the broadcaster's biggest entertainment budgets of the year, and local production teams are briefed to deliver a show that looks like a 'flawless, sparkling jewel' that dazzles audiences (Paice, interview 2012). High production values, a visually arresting show, celebrities and a compelling narrative arc go a long way in explaining its enduring popularity.

Strictly Come Dancing first aired on BBC One in May 2004 and immediately attracted foreign buyers. Within a year, fourteen format licences had been sold, including one to US network ABC. The programme that one day would rank among America's premier entertainment shows and reach 350 episodes in nineteen seasons was passed over twice by Andrea Wong, then

ABC's vice president of alternative programming. She initially thought that it was 'uniquely British' and that it would not resonate with her viewers as much as it did in the UK because there is no heritage of ballroom dancing in the USA. She changed her mind when she watched an episode of *Strictly Come Dancing* and could not take her eyes off it; she decided to go for it (Wong, interview 2014).

The format subsequently sold in Latin America (Argentina, Brazil, Colombia and Ecuador) and Asia. It was among the first formats legally obtained by a Chinese broadcaster (Hunan Television), whose stellar ratings taught other local stations that established brands fare better than local copycats. By the time the format reached France in 2011, it had been sold to forty-one countries, totalling 176 series. That year, a version of the show – not necessarily the local one – could be seen in over seventy-five countries, and it was estimated that more than half a billion people watched the programme over a twelve-month period (BBC sources). In spring 2014, Slovenia became the fiftieth country to acquire the format rights.

It was inevitable that BBC lawyers would have to spring into action in order to protect the Corporation's IP. They took offence at *Le Match des étoiles* (Société Radio-Canada), *Das Grosse ProSieben Tanzturnier* [*The Big ProSieben Dance Tournament*], Televisa's *Bailando por un sueño* and Mediaset's *Baila!*

Additional contributions to the dance theme include *So You Think You Can Dance*. The show was created by two British expats, Simon Fuller and Nigel Lythgoe, who had both moved to Los Angeles to set up *American Idol*. The format sets young dancers to compete against each other in a variety of styles and choreographies. Lythgoe, a dancer and choreographer himself, states that the show is 'about the art of dancing' and aims for credibility and integrity within the genre (in Carugati, 2011: 435). *So You Think You Can Dance* debuted on US network Fox in July 2005, where it has been recommissioned ever since, and has twenty-five local versions to date. In the UK, the show was axed by the BBC after its second season in 2011.

A British rival briefly emerged in the guise of *Got to Dance*. Developed by one of Shine's outfits, Princess Productions, the show first aired on Sky 1 in December 2009. Open to all dance acts of any age, *Got to Dance*'s key points and structure are not dissimilar to those of *Got Talent*. CBS's *Live to Dance* was cancelled shortly after its premiere in January 2011 and the format has been adapted only a handful of times.

Got Talent

Got Talent is a British reality talent competition that is co-owned by Syco Entertainment and FremantleMedia. Launched in 2006, its roots are in the amateur discovery show and variety (chapters 1 and 3), two genres that go back to the very early days of broadcasting. In several markets, variety dominated ratings for many years. In the UK, for instance, a long-running series *Sunday Night at the London Palladium* was on ITV from 1955 to 1967 (and revived in 2014).[1]

Some of *Got Talent*'s format points are just as old. A prototype of the judge's buzzer was already in use in the first ever radio talent contest, *Major Bowes' Original Amateur Hour*, which saw the imperious Major Bowes strike a gong to dispatch the untalented (Buxton and Owen, 1972: 193). Developing the idea, *The Gong Show*, first aired on NBC in June 1976, saw 'a panel of three celebrities judge unusual amateur (and professional) talent acts, and any member of the panel could, by banging a large gong, terminate any act before completion' (Buxton and Owen, 1972: 334).

At semi-final stage, *Got Talent* acts are produced and assisted by vocal coaches, stylists and choreographers. Again, the idea of producing amateur acts is as old as *Opportunity Knocks*. In 1949, the BBC and Hughie Green decided that:

> In contrast to previous discovery shows where participants have usually been provided a few stock band parts, in this case [we would] support the discoveries with the best possible orchestrations, and a really polished musical combination, which would enable them to appear against a really strong professional background.[2]

But *Got Talent* also innovates. The elimination rounds give the production team an opportunity to create contrast as the best acts are shown up as raw, bringing along their own costumes and props before being produced. The format is far more than a stage show since it balances four interdependent areas: the stage, the backstage, the judges and the audience. The backstage, which includes the holding area, is a key part of the show that is used to give it a reality feel. It is where the host remains to act as friend and confidant to the contestants and family. Interviews are conducted there, where producers pick up stories. The judges are central characters but are not in as much control of the proceedings as it seems: like the contestants, they are produced. The acts are pre-screened and the judges are briefed on the contestants who are presented to them. Which acts progress, even in the late stages, depends as much on them as on the production team. Finally, the three judges contend with the audience, who are actively encouraged to get involved and voice their opinion.

The formula's key ingredient is the variety and contrasting nature of contestants. The show is open to any act of any age, and producers do their utmost to mix the very young and the very old, the cutest and most hideous, the brilliantly original and the plain weird, the sublime and the shockingly bad. The show thrives on freshness, surprise and contrast. This places casting as the most crucial element of the format, and a great amount of resources and energy is devoted to assembling a wide sweep of talents. There are open calls to auditions, but the production team actively scouts for appropriate acts, who will be invited to participate. Running up and down the country, scouts leave no stone unturned in their frantic search: army and naval bases, booking agencies, cabaret clubs (for burlesque performers and drag queens), church groups, comedy clubs, cruise ships, ethnic societies, local theatres, magicians' societies, music producers, senior citizens' clubs, student unions' entertainment societies, talent agents and wedding planners, among many others, are all given a call.

At the start, Syco shot a pilot but without the right host was unable to get the show commissioned in the UK. The team took it to the USA, where it was picked up by NBC, and commissioners must have recalled *The Gong Show*. It was greenlighted by ITV shortly after, when the format was altered in several respects. But the format had already been picked up by numerous broadcasters and it is the American version that prevailed internationally. The format sales were also helped by the tapes of the US show, as *America's Got Talent* had been shipped to eighty countries by August 2007. Three years later, *Got Talent* was produced in thirty-eight territories and was the highest-rating entertainment series in many of them (Jones, interview 2010). By 2014, it had been commissioned in sixty-three markets and received the accolade of 'most successful reality TV format' from Guinness World Records.

The Apprentice, the Chef and the Model

Mark Burnett claims that he first thought of the concept for *The Apprentice* while in the Amazon shooting a glossy episode of *Survivor*. Camping near the Rio Negro, he lay watching ants in their millions swarming 'over other live insects or the carcass of a dead animal', reminding him 'of the swarms of people living in the urban jungle – everyone crammed into cities and fighting for a place' (Burnett, 2005: 186).

The Hollywood version is rousing but the truth is that most TV programmes are inspired by other TV programmes; *The Apprentice* is no exception. In this case, the incubator was probably *Jamie's Kitchen*, a series that followed British chef Jamie Oliver training fifteen young people from disadvantaged backgrounds. Those who were successful were offered jobs at Oliver's restaurant Fifteen.[3] The five-part documentary, which was co-created by John Silver, then at Talkback – incidentally the same company that produces *The Apprentice* in the UK – aired in 2002 and became a huge ratings hit.

Burnett and team honed their concept, pitched it to Donald Trump and sold it to the highest bidder: NBC. For its first edition, which aired in January 2004, Burnett focused on the '"glass ceiling" concept and pitted women against men' (Burnett, 2005: 203). The idea paid dividends and, following great local ratings, the show was on the road within a few months. It survived a serious casting error in Germany and was in sixteen territories by mid-decade, including Britain, Brazil, Indonesia, the Middle East and South Africa. The series has since been adapted about twenty-five times, including a pan-African version, and is still regularly commissioned by broadcasters.

Fashion and modelling have also proven popular with format creators, as the theme presents strong potential for sponsoring and commercial tie-ins. They are all based on an identical template: contestants face weekly challenges and elimination rounds that produce a winner who is offered a job or contract. The strand's most successful franchise is *Next Top Model*, a format created and developed by Tyra Banks and distributed by CBS Television Distribution. It is a popular format that has seen nearly fifty adaptations since it debuted on United Paramount Network in 2003, reaching countries as diverse as Austria, Mexico and Vietnam. In its home market, it has been on The CW since 2006 and was still attracting half-decent ratings after twenty-one seasons. *America's Next Top Model* does equally well as a completed programme and has been broadcast in well over 100 territories.

Make Me a Supermodel, a British format of the mid-2000s, disappeared without trace but *Next Top Model* may get a run for its money from *The Face*. Developed by Shine America, it launched on Oxygen (USA) in 2013 and has since been produced in five other territories. In the UK, however, Sky Living axed the show's second series due to poor ratings, despite featuring Naomi Campbell.

Fashion design figures in at least four other reality competitions. In 2005, *The Cut* aired for one season only on CBS, with sixteen budding fashion designers vying to create a collection for the Tommy Hilfiger label. Electus' *Fashion Star* has not done much better. Launched first in the USA, its third season was cancelled by NBC in 2013, then in Germany its first season was cut short, and understandably the format is travelling very slowly. Sky-owned, London-based Love Productions is faring better with *The Great British Sewing Bee*, which was renewed for a third series on BBC Two after attracting strong ratings. The show is less expensive to produce than most competitors and has a genteel and 'homely' feel that is in tune with the zeitgeist. Based on an idea by Anna Beattie, the company's co-founder and joint creative head, it borrows the format of *The Great British Bake Off* and has been made in France and Scandinavia (McKerrow, interview 2014).

The strongest concept remains *Project Runway*, an American format created by Eli Holzman that has gone through thirteen seasons in his domestic market to date and has been commissioned in about twenty-five territories. The US version is hosted by Heidi Klum and the finalists prepare a clothing collection for New York Fashion Week.

Cooking shows have been on air since the onset of the broadcasting age. The same year the BBC launched its television service in 1936, it aired a cooking instruction programme fronted by Moira Meighn, the world's first celebrity chef of the TV era. The following year, the Corporation launched the first TV cookery series with French restaurateur Marcel Boulestin (Oren, 2013: 22). In America, NBC got the ball rolling with a show called *Elsie Presents James Beard in "I Love to Eat"*, aired in August 1946 (Collins, 2009: 27). Thereafter, every new show cranked up the genre's entertainment value bit by bit until Bazalgette introduced a competition element to cooking programmes with *Ready Steady Cook* (*Ready. . . Set. . . Cook!* on Food Network).

Today, competitive cooking shows are popular with audiences across the world. In the USA alone, viewers can choose between *The American Baking Competition*, *Chopped*, *Dinner: Impossible*, *Food Network Challenge*, *Hell's Kitchen*, *Iron Chef*, *MasterChef*, *The Next Food Network Star*, *The Taste*, *Throwdown with Bobby Flay*, *Top Chef* and *Ultimate Recipe Showdown* (Collins, 2009: 197). Four of these are formats with a reality element and weekly elimination rounds.

In addition to *Hell's Kitchen* (see chapter 7), *Top Chef* is a US format produced by Magical Elves and has been through eleven seasons since it debuted on Bravo, a cable network, in 2006. It also does well internationally, with more than ten adaptations. *The Taste* is a more recent creation, having debuted on ABC in January 2013. It contains all the classic ingredients of a contemporary reality competition: blind auditions, judges who turn mentors and a combination of individual and team challenges. It is distributed by Red Arrow International and has started to travel well.

The American Baking Competition is the US version of *The Great British Bake Off*, a relative newcomer that premiered on BBC Two in August

2010. Developed by Love Productions, the project was originally called *The Million Pound Bake Off* and was rejected by every single broadcaster in the UK for five years. Finally commissioned by the BBC's documentaries department, the original idea involved a marquee travelling around the country with a group of bakers going through elimination rounds.

As already seen, *The Great Bake Off* is a resounding success in the UK and has passed fifteen local versions. The strength of the format lies in the breadth of the casting, the science of home baking and the fact that it works almost as an antidote to other reality competitions: the pace is rather slow, it is absorbing and many of the contestants would rather bake than be on television. As the show has grown in popularity the production team must sift through many applications, but they also work hard to discover characters. To this end they are actively looking for people who need a lot of persuasion, with help from friends and family, to embark on the journey and who can keep it 'fresh' (McKerrow, interview 2014).

It is *MasterChef* that is still selling most format licences. Its first incarnation was a daytime cookery show fronted by Lloyd Grossman that ran on BBC One between 1994 and 2000. When the Corporation cancelled it, Shine acquired some of the rights with Franc Roddam, the show creator. They gave it a reality makeover and pitched it back to the BBC as a restaurant show mixing elements of *Jamie's Kitchen* and *The Apprentice*. Contestants were tasked with setting up a restaurant, battling it out in challenges involving marketing, interior design, and so on. At this point, John Silver, fresh from Talkback, decided to re-jig the show. He got rid of the 'boring' stuff to focus on the cooking. Commissioners at the BBC were interested but wanted to strip the programme daily over several weeks and demanded that each episode come with a 'beginning, middle and an end' (Silver, interview 2010). Silver worked out a system of heats that produced a winner every day from Monday to Thursday, ensuring that 'every programme [has] a good ending' (Silver, interview 2010). These four winners met for the quarter-final on Friday, and the same pattern was followed in the subsequent weeks, until the closing semi-finals and final were reached.

The new *MasterChef* debuted in spring 2005 on BBC Two and, following good ratings, moved to BBC One four years later. Domestic success helped *MasterChef* become a leading global TV franchise, together with a large-scale Australian version featuring a live final that won a 77 per cent audience share. In 2009, a deal was signed with Fox for a US version featuring Gordon Ramsay. By 2011, the format had been commissioned in more than twenty territories (*Broadcast – MipTV Supplement*, 2011b), and has passed the fifty-mark threshold in 2014. *MasterChef* is adaptable to any culture and any cuisine, from Bangladesh to Norway and from Albania to Peru.

Heroes with a Common Face

Talent competitions are among the most watched TV programmes in the world. These brands are known by hundreds of millions worldwide and they have earned their place in contemporary popular culture. Of the factors that explain their popularity, the process of elimination must rank high because it is the mechanism that allows the construction of hero-centric narratives. Hero myths have always been with humankind and cross so many civilizations that they surely fulfil psychological needs and social functions that are inherent to the human condition. Claude Lévi-Strauss is among many to have painstakingly catalogued, compared and contrasted such myths circulating amid Amazonian tribes (Lévi-Strauss, 1983). The need for myths and heroes transcends time and borders but their roles and duties change with civilizations. The mythologist Joseph Campbell explains these transformations as follows:

> It is not only that there is no hiding place for the gods from the searching telescope and microscope; there is no such society any more as the gods once supported. The social unit is not a carrier of religious content, but an economic-political organization. Its ideals are not those of the hieratic pantomime, making visible on earth the forms of heaven, but of the secular state, in hard and unremitting competition for material supremacy and resources. Isolated societies, dream-bounded within a mythologically charged horizon, no longer exist except as areas to be exploited. And within the progressive societies themselves, every last vestige of the ancient human heritage of ritual, mortality and art is in full decay.
>
> The problem of mankind today, therefore, is precisely the opposite to that of men [sic] in the comparatively stable periods of those great co-ordinating mythologies which now are known as lies. Then all meaning was in the group, in the great anonymous forms, none in the self-expressive individual; today no meaning is in the group – none in the world: all is in the individual. (Campbell, [1949] 2008: 334)

In addition, he explains, 'the center of gravity, that is to say, of the realm of mystery and danger has definitely shifted' (Campbell, [1949] 2008: 336). The issue is no longer to understand the natural order, which used to be a complete enigma, and danger no longer comes from sharing the wilderness with large animals:

> Today all of these mysteries have lost their force; their symbols no longer interest our psyche. The notion of a cosmic law, which all existence serves and to which man himself [sic] must bend, has long since passed through the preliminary mystical stages represented in old astrology, and is now

simply accepted in mechanical terms as a matter of course. The descent of the Occidental sciences from the heavens to the earth (from seventeenth-century astronomy to nineteenth-century biology), and their concentration today, at last on man himself (in twentieth-century anthropology and psychology), mark the path of a prodigious transfer of the focal point of human wonder. Not the animal world, not the plant world, not the miracle of the spheres, but man himself is now the crucial mystery. Man is that alien presence with whom the forces of egoism must come to terms, through whom the ego is to be crucified and resurrected, and in whose image society is to be reformed. (Campbell, [1949] 2008: 336–7)

It is in this context that the phenomenal appeal of reality competitions must be comprehended: they mass-produce heroes for the global age. Viewers follow these contests for multiple reasons: they love the drama and suspense, they get attached to the characters and their stories, they gasp at the dreams that are broken and the contrasts that are created between those who succeed and those who fail. But above all, viewers watch these contests because they manufacture heroes for a culture that is competitive, individualistic and materialistic. Unlike Amazonian tribes' mythical creatures and super-animals, world religions' saints and gods, reality TV heroes are common people with a human face. They elevate themselves through competition, not supernatural forces; they act as saviour and redeemer for themselves, not others; and they overcome challenges and obstacles to change their lives, not to make the world a better place. These personages are individualistic and they fascinate because they are fabricated from the values of contemporary Western culture and for the mysteries of our age.

TV Formats as Franchises

Some of the shows discussed in chapters 7 and 8 are well-established TV franchises, or in the process of becoming so. A TV franchise is a TV format whose IP crosses not only borders but also platforms. As already seen, these competitions travel both as formats and as finished tapes (at least for the American and British versions). They generate online revenue either on broadcasters' catch-up services or on video-sharing platforms such as YouTube. They also spawn innumerable spin-offs, most often involving celebrity and junior versions (table 8.2).

However, for a TV format to become a bona fide franchise, it needs to venture beyond the TV screen and extend onto new platforms. The off-screen activities are based on the ancillary rights that cover merchandising, interactive and online rights (see the introduction to this book). The

Table 8.2 TV formats and their spin-offs, various territories

Franchise	Examples of spin-off show
The Apprentice	*The Celebrity Apprentice*
	Young Apprentice
	The Apprentice: Martha Stewart
Come Dine with Me	*Come Date with Me*
	Couples Come Dine with Me
The Great Bake Off	*Junior Bake Off*
	The Great British Bake Off, Masterclass
	The Great British Wedding Cake
	The Great British Bake Off Christmas Special
MasterChef	*Celebrity MasterChef*
	Junior MasterChef
	MasterChef: The Professionals
Survivor	*Robinson: Love Edition*
Top Chef	*Top Chef Junior*
	Top Chef: Masters
	Top Chef: Just Desserts
Wife Swap	*Celebrity Wife Swap*

exploitation of these rights is emergent and brings two benefits: it extends the value of the IP and permits a firm to expand its activities (chapter 6). A TV franchise can be developed in four directions:

1. *Retail and consumer products.* As seen in chapter 3, Paul Smith was the first with the foresight to retain his show's ancillary rights, enabling him to expand *Millionaire* into more product lines (140) than territories. At one stage, the TV show was simply considered a shop window for all the merchandising behind it (Spencer, interview 2008). This is now more familiar territory for TV formats. For instance, *The Biggest Loser* sells a whole range of diet plans, workout products (DVDs, books, music, plans, etc.) and meal replacement rations. There are also four *Biggest Loser* resorts in the USA. Under the *MasterChef* brand, Shine offers books, magazines, pop-up restaurants, pots, pans and knives (Carter, interview 2014; Liebmann, interview 2013). All the albums and downloads sold by music reality stars can also be considered as part of the show's consumer products.
2. *Brand partnership.* Formats can allow brands to associate themselves with the content through sponsorship and product placement opportunities (where allowed). This gives brands the opportunity not just to advertise on the show but to be part of its narrative.
3. *Digital interactive.* This covers everything from gaming to second-screen applications and is an area of growing strategic importance. A few

companies are now specializing in developing games and second-screen experiences, such as France's Ludia and the UK's Studio Syrup.

Second-screen applications add a play-along element, a new content experience that can drive audience engagement but, as yet, remains difficult to monetize. So far, the poster child of second-screen applications remains Remarkable's *Million Pound Drop*, with 2.7 million apps downloaded and 12.5 per cent of the audience playing along (Strauss, 2014). Today, all talent competitions incorporate second-screen activities in some form, especially those moving into real-time voting territory. These applications have interesting potential and give producers the opportunity to expand their activities with new product lines, but the issue is that, at present, only a minority of viewers feel the need to engage with these applications, and they cannot yet be seen as a significant income stream.

4. *Live experiences.* Live events have become particularly lucrative among these brand extensions, and the growing list includes The American Idol Experience (at Disney World in Orlando), Dancing with the Stars: The Tour and Dancing with the Stars: At Sea (cruise ship), The X Factor Live Tour, MasterChef Live, the Top Gear Live Show, Grand Designs Live and The Price is Right Live (three locations in the USA, including Las Vegas).

In the past, the off-screen exploitation of on-screen brands has been driven most successfully by children's television (to the point where US toy maker Mattel bought HIT Entertainment, the owner of *Thomas the Tank Engine* and other children's brands) and fiction. In the USA, secondary licensing is driven by on-screen personalities such as the Kardashians, who have built a considerable brand licensing business. However, non-scripted shows have proven more difficult to exploit and commercial successes remain few and far between so far. Although TV production majors are keen to turn formats into franchises (chapter 6), they still tend to see licensing activities as part of the marketing of their television brands rather than a business in itself (Carter, interview 2014).

Last Thoughts

There are differences and similarities among the last three strands of reality programming reviewed in chapters 7 and 8. Both reality and talent competitions use an elimination process to deliver a dramatic arc that spreads through the series, but the latter places greater emphasis on the ending and the making of a hero. Factual entertainment formats have a shorter narrative arc (they are produced as closed episodes) and they rely more on social attitudes and differences (class, gender and race) in order to create drama. The journey of a factual-entertainment character is more inward-looking and reflective than for a talent contest. The core ingredients, however, remain similar for all three strands and involve a situation (or a competition), a journey (possibly heroic) and a transformation. Change is both a process and a journey; heroes are those who learn and embrace change the most.

The demise of reality programming is regularly announced (and sometimes called for). Certainly, trends fluctuate, and although the first big wave of reality shows is behind us, reality programming is set to continue. TV producers are continuously developing new ideas: 'I never understand how people think you can reach saturation point,' says Stephen Lambert, 'the only limit is the limit of your imagination and belief of what can be done' (in *TBI Formats*, 2013: 24). Then, as much as fiction, reality programming responds to an insatiable demand for stories and heroes. As seen, the difference between scripted and unscripted programming resides mostly in the method of narrative production, and the TV industry has certainly learnt how to tell a good story without a script.

9   Drama without Drama:
The Late Rise of Scripted Formats

This chapter focuses on the format trade in the scripted space, which covers the full spectrum of serials (soaps, series and telenovelas) and scripted genres from drama and comedy to constructed reality programming. It argues that while the format revolution initially bypassed scripted formats, their number has risen sharply more lately. This chapter identifies and analyses both the causes behind their late rise and their more recent popularity.

Scripted Formats before the TV Format Revolution

As seen, game shows prevailed in the first five decades of the TV format trade, but a few sitcoms and soaps were adapted before the format revolution. The UK emerged as an early source of travelling scripts. In the late 1950s, Associated London Scripts, probably the first British independent TV production company, was headed by Beryl Vertue. Representing her writers' rights when selling series to the BBC, she began crossing out the contract clauses on foreign sales, correctly predicting that the BBC was not interested in selling them abroad (Vertue, interview 2011). Not always being able to sell her shows as finished tapes, it later occurred to her that she could use these international rights in order to get broadcasters to make their own productions. Vertue first travelled to Germany, where she sold the remake rights of a Peter Yeldham play in 1960. The script of *Hancock's Half Hour* (BBC Television, 1956–60) was acquired by a Finnish broadcaster the following year, and her first success came with a local adaptation of *Steptoe and Son* (BBC One, 1962–74) in Holland in 1963 (Vertue, interview 2011).

Other European deals followed, notably in Sweden, but Vertue had set her sights on America. She began with the pilot of *Steptoe and Son*, made for NBC in the mid-1960s (which, with hindsight, she deemed 'quite dreadful') (Vertue, interview 2011). It was not picked up by the US network, but her American breakthrough would come with *Till Death Us Do Part*. The BBC series (1965–75) could not be sold as a finished programme because of the Cockney accents and the peculiarly local nature of its bigotry and prejudice that the protagonists displayed. Vertue settled for an adaptation and sold a format licence to CBS (Vertue, interview 2011). The sitcom was turned into *All in the Family* by Norman Lear and premiered in January 1971. It stayed on air until April 1979 and became one of the most iconic series in the history of US television (McNeil, 1997: 26). Even the spin-off shows, *Maude* (CBS, 1972–8) and *Good Times* (CBS, 1974–9) travelled back to the UK, where they were adapted as *Nobody's Perfect* (ITV, 1980) and *The Fosters* (ITV, 1976–7) respectively (Potter, 2008: 51). On the back of *Till Death*, Vertue managed to sell the rights of *Steptoe and Son*, and the adaptation, *Sanford and Son*, debuted in January 1972 on NBC (Vertue, interview 2011).

Allan McKeown, another British producer who worked for long stretches of his career in the USA, recalled doing 'a US pilot or series of just about every show [he] had done in the UK' (in Baker, 1996a: 25). McKeown's US remakes include *Birds of a Feather* (BBC One, 1989–98) (*Stand By Your Man*, Fox, 1992) and *Porridge* (BBC One, 1974–7), *On the Rocks* (ABC, 1975–6), and pilots of *Auf Wiedersehen, Pet* (ITV, 1983–6), *Fawlty Towers* (BBC Two, 1975–9), *Girls on Top* (ITV, 1985–6) and *Nightingales* (Channel 4, 1990–3) (Baker, 1996b).

In addition to British independents, the second source of scripted formats was Sydney-based Grundy Organization. Grundy was the production company that initially specialized in formatted game shows (chapter 1) but took two Australian soaps to market, *The Restless Years* and *Sons and Daughters*, in the late 1980s. *The Restless Years* led to two long-standing adaptations that still air: *Goede Tidjen, Slechte Tijden* [*Good Times, Bad Times*] started on RTL in the Netherlands in 1990, and a German version (*Gute Zeiten, schlechte Zeiten*), also on a local RTL channel, followed two years later. Attempts to sell adaptations in the USA and France were unsuccessful (Moran, 1998: 56, 62). Six local versions of *Sons and Daughters* were produced (table 9.1).

Table 9.1 *Sons and Daughters*: local versions

Version	Germany	Sweden	Greece	Italy	Croatia	Bulgaria
Local title	*Verbotene Liebe* [*Forbidden Love*]	*Skilda världar* [*Worlds Apart*]	*Apagorevmeni agapi* [*Forbidden Love*]	*Cuori rubati* [*Stolen Hearts*]	*Zabranjena ljubav* [*Forbidden Love*]	*Zabranena lubov* [*Forbidden Love*]
Channel and dates	ARD, 1995–	TV4, 1996–2002	Mega TV, 1998	RAI 2, 2002–3	RTL Televizija, 2004–8	Nova TV, 2008–

Source: Moran (1998: 109, 2013b: 189–93).

Understanding the Late Rise of Scripted Formats

As seen in chapter 7, reality and factual entertainment shows powered the format revolution and it was only later in the same decade that the proportion of scripted adaptations among TV formats doubled to almost 15 per cent (tables 7.1 and 7.2, pp. 131 and 132). This data set is among the latest available at the time of writing, but plenty of anecdotal evidence suggests that scripted formats have pursued an upward trend in more recent years. There are several reasons that explain why the TV format revolution bypassed scripted entertainment at the outset.

First, scripted shows are among the most difficult to adapt, not least because of the complexity of the knowledge transfer. As already seen, format buyers have access to full consulting packages that teach them all they need to know in order to duplicate a show successfully. By the time an unscripted show has crossed a few borders, this transfer of expertise is extensive: the concept has been honed to perfection, every flaw has been ironed out, and every short cut and saving has been squeezed out of the production process.

Although the knowledge transfer for scripted shows has improved in more recent years (see next section), the process cannot be as perfunctory as for other genres. Scripted genres are the most culturally sensitive and a comedy or drama cannot be reproduced as mechanistically as a game show or talent contest. A straight adaptation of the original, such as a mere translation of the script, will not suffice to make a show palatable to local viewers. Any scripted adaptation must go beyond copycat television and re-actualize the script for a new audience. More than for any other genre, a scripted adaptation is a new performance that 'interprets, actualizes, and redefines the format' in order to make it work in a new cultural context (Navarro, 2012: 25). It requires a great deal of talent – and a dose of good fortune – to capture the essence of a comedy or drama and make it work in another culture. The local production team must combine knowledge of the principles of script-writing with an understanding of the show's vision and core values. This complexity explains why TV executives have long been hesitant about commissioning scripted formats, why success can remain elusive, why several attempts may be needed to re-version a script,[1] and why some comedies that are TV classics in their countries of origin never travel (e.g. *Fawlty Towers*).

Second, the entire premise of the TV format trade hinges on two benefits: cost effectiveness and risk management (see the introduction to this book). Formats enable broadcasters to bring down costs by taking out the expense involved in developing a new show. This is realized by (1) the delivery of a ready-made script that in all likelihood has taken a few years to develop, and (2) the transfer of a method of production. TV formats also enable broadcasters to manage risk, as they are acquired on the basis of their ratings track record (see introduction to this book). Today's leading unscripted formats effortlessly pass the twenty mark of local adaptations, and potential buyers can browse ratings data that details the show's performance in a large array of territories, scheduling scenarios, channels and audiences, before committing themselves.

Although drama buyers turn to foreign scripts because it remains easier and cheaper to remake something they can see on tape, the risk is still greater than with any other genre. Whereas it can virtually be guaranteed that a game show with decent ratings in twenty territories will perform well in the next ten, the reception for drama, even if formatted, is more difficult to predict. Not only does drama need to resonate more deeply than unscripted shows, which viewers may only engage with superficially, but its success is dependent to a greater degree on critical reception. In addition, the international ratings history is of less relevance, as scripted shows never travel as extensively and rarely acquire an unblemished ratings record.

Third, trade in scripted entertainment has traditionally been dominated by finished programming. It is a sizeable business worth an estimated US$8 billion per year and is dominated by six Hollywood heavyweights: Warner Bros., Twentieth Century Fox (a 21st Century Fox company), Disney Media Distribution, CBS Studios International, NBC Universal and Sony Pictures Television (Guider, 2013). These companies have long feared that formats could jeopardize their tape sales and, with the exception of Sony, their interest in the trade is recent (see next section).

The last factor is organizational in scope. The TV format trade in the past was ruled by game shows (chapters 1 and 7), a daytime genre long perceived – even within the TV industry – as devoid of artistic merit and character. Game-show producers have never enjoyed much artistic independence and thus easily consented to churning out pre-established formulas coming from abroad. Scripted entertainment entails authorship and drama/comedy producers and writers enjoy more autonomy and creative freedom (Nohr, interview 2013).[2] So, the idea of importing a foreign concept remained incongruous to drama and comedy departments longer than elsewhere. American broadcasters, which, as already seen, have long adapted British scripts, are the exception to the rule. This is probably due to the fact that US scripts are developed by tables of writers already primed to working on ideas that are not their own. However, as the success of a scripted adaptation depends strongly on the local production team, broadcasters everywhere have no choice but to rely on the crew buying into a project and believing in it (Taffner, interview 2013).

Out of the Woods at Last: The Scripted Format Boom

Table 7.2 (p. 132) and evidence given in this section suggest that, since the mid-2000s, scripted adaptations have been on the rise. Furthermore, some of the highest-profile dramas in recent years were adaptations. Both the causes and consequences of this late growth deserve an explanation.

Growth of US demand

The premier factor is the sizeable expansion of the US market for drama. The overall demand for scripts has sharply increased in America because new players have developed an interest in scripted genres, joining the traditional purveyors of drama: the US networks. Following in the footsteps of HBO, fledgling cable channels such as AMC, Bravo, FX, Pivot, Showtime and TLC have been commissioning series in order to secure exclusive content (White, 2013). In addition, subscription-based video-on-demand (SVoD) platforms such as Lovefilm and Netflix are now ordering their own series.

For the new content aggregators, scripted content is an imperative, as only fiction has the pulling power to help them build their brands and make them distinctive, even more so if it is exclusive. In the case of the SVoD platforms, the scripted content alone can justify the monthly subscription fees, and the original series they commission act like marketing tools (Kanter et al., 2014). In the face of all this renewed competition the US networks have been forced to increase investment in scripted genres. Overseas scripted shows come in handy for US buyers who demand not only more scripts but stronger ones. Indeed, while new content aggregators have triggered demand they have also intensified competition for viewers. In such circumstances, all have turned to foreign scripts in order to get hold of solid concepts likely to sustain the interest of fickle audiences.[3]

In 2013 alone, Netflix commissioned its own version of *House of Cards*, originally a BBC One political thriller (1990–5); AMC produced *Low Winter Sun*, also a BBC One drama (2006); HBO opted for yet another BBC One drama, *Criminal Justice* (2008–9); and ABC Family looked further afield for *Chasing Life*, a Mexican series about terminal illness (*Terminales*, Channel 5 – Televisa, 2008) (Waller, 2013c).

The five networks (ABC, CBS, NBC, Fox and The CW) are showing mounting interest in scripted formats (tables 9.2 and 9.3). Every year they pilot scripted shows, out of which about a third are picked for the first season. For the 2011–12 season 88 pilots were ordered, 91 for 2012–13,

Table 9.2 Scripted formats ordered by US networks, statistics, 2012–15

Pilots and formats	2012–13 season	2013–14 season	2014–15 season
No. of pilots ordered	91	104	100
No. of formats included	8	12	15
Percentage of formats	8.8%	11.5%	15.0%
No. of pilots retained (first season)	37	45	51
No. of formats included	3	5	7
Percentage of formats	8.1%	11.1%	13.7%

104 for 2013–14, and 100 for 2014–15 – 12 more than three seasons earlier despite the more recent tendency of bypassing pilot production (Berman, 2013; Waller, 2012, 2014b; White, 2014d). Table 9.2 shows that formats, both in absolute numbers and in proportion to the overall number of pilots and pilots commissioned into first season, are steadily growing, from three among thirty-seven new series in the 2012–13 season to seven for fifty-one new series in the 2014–15 season.

Since Vertue's foray into the American market, US broadcasters have aired 119 scripted format adaptations, most of them originating from the UK (Waller, 2014b). British sitcoms that crossed the Atlantic include Thames TV's *George and Mildred* (ITV, 1976–9) (*The Ropers*, ABC, 1979–80), *Miss Jones and Son* (ITV, 1977–8) (*Miss Winslow and Son*, CBS, 1979), *Keep It in the Family* (ITV, 1980–3) (*Too Close for Comfort*, ABC, 1980–3) and *Tripper's Day* (ITV, 1984) (*Check it Out!*, USA Network, 1988); LWT's *Two's Company* (ITV, 1975–9) (*The Two of Us*, CBS, 1981–2) and *Mind Your Language* (ITV, 1977–86) (*What a Country!*, syndicated, 1986–7); and BBC's *Dear John* (1986–7) (*Dear John*, NBC, 1988–92) (Baker, 1996b; Lituchy, interview 2015; Potter, 2008: 52; Taffner, interview 2013). Some recent adaptations, in addition to those in table 9.3, include *Shameless* (Channel 4, 2004–13) (picked by Showtime in January 2011), *Skins* (E4, 2007–13) and *The Inbetweeners* (E4, 2008–10), the last two aired on MTV in 2011 and 2012 respectively.

In that half-century of British imports, three adaptations became undisputed hits: *All in the Family*; Thames TV's *Man About the House* (ITV, 1973–6), which was turned into *Three's Company* for ABC (1977–88); and *The Office* (2005–13), whose nine seasons on NBC far exceeded the number shown on BBC Two (2001–3). Illustrious casualties, however, include *Ab Fab*, *Fawlty Towers*, *Life on Mars* and *The Vicar of Dibley* (Jackson, interview 2012; Potter, 2008: 52; Taffner, interview 2013; Waller, 2007).

The contrasting fortunes of these adaptations demonstrate that scripted formats do not afford risk-management levels comparable to those offered by unscripted ones. In fact, US networks' worst-performing series of autumn

Table 9.3 Scripted formats ordered by US networks, titles and origin, 2012–15

Network	2012–13 season	2013–14 season	2014–15 season
ABC	US remake: *Family Tools* Original: *White Van Man* UK/BBC Three/2011–12 US remake: *Mistresses* Original: *Mistresses* UK/BBC One/2008–10 US remake: *Red Widow* Original: *Penoza* Holland/KRO/2010–12	US remake: *Killer Women* Original: *Mujeres asesinas* Argentina/Canal 13/2005–8 US remake: *Lucky 7* Original: *The Syndicate* UK/BBC One/2012–	US remake: *Secrets and Lies* Original: *Secrets and Lies* Australia/Network Ten/2014–
CBS	–	US remake: *Hostages* Original: *Hostages* Israel/Channel 10/2013	–
Fox	–	US remake: *Us & Them* Original: *Gavin and Stacey* UK/BBC Three/2007–10	US remake: *Gracepoint* Original: *Broadchurch* UK/ITV/2013– US remake: *Red Band Society* Original: *Polseres vermelles* Spain/TV 3/2011–13
NBC	–	–	US remake: *Allegiance* Original: *The Gordin Cell* Israel/Yes!/2012 US remake: *The Mysteries of Laura* Original: *Los misterios de Laura* Spain/TVE/2009–14 US remake: *The Slap* Original: *The Slap* Australia/ABC1/2011
The CW	–	US remake: *The Tomorrow People* Original: *The Tomorrow People* UK/ITV/1973–9	US remake: *Jane the Virgin* Original: *Juana la virgen* Venezuela/RCTV/2002

2013 was a remake of *The Syndicate* that saw ABC experience a 55 per cent ratings drop between *Lucky 7* and the show it replaced (Andreeva, 2013). Competition, though, forces broadcasters to accept these risks when the rewards for getting scripted content right are higher than in any other genre. ABC, for instance, was undeterred by *Lucky 7* and had six British scripts in development to be piloted in 2015 (White, 2014a).

Inevitably, however, US content aggregators began to diversify their sources and adapt scripts from other territories. Two noted adaptations announced this trend and encouraged US broadcasters to mine new territories for IP. *Yo soy Betty, la fea*, Fernando Gaitán's telenovela (RCN TV, 1991–2001), was adapted into *Ugly Betty* for ABC in 2006. The US version stayed on air for four years (eighty-five episodes), sold in multiple territories and inspired its own local adaptations. In 2008 HBO aired *In Treatment*, a remake of *BeTipul*, an Israeli psychological drama, that won critical acclaim, was recommissioned for three seasons and was re-versioned in other HBO territories. In addition to an increasing number of scripted formats from Israel, Latin America and Scandinavia (see later section on emerging territories), US broadcasters are ordering remakes from countries that have never before sold them a scripted format, including Austria (*Fast Forward* for CBS), Croatia (*Rest in Peace* for Lionsgate), Spain (*The Mysteries of Laura* for NBC and *Red Band Society* for Fox), Norway (*Mammon*, a conspiracy thriller, for Twentieth Century Fox Television and Chernin Entertainment, followed by *Next Summer*, also for Fox), France (*The Returned* for A&E), Turkey (*The End*, at pilot stage at the time of writing, for ABC) and South Korea (*Good Doctor*, for CBS).

Conversely, British series are locally produced in an increasing number of markets. *The Office* (BBC Two, 2001–3) has been made in nine countries so far, and the ITV series *Doc Martin* (2004–) reached its sixth adaptation in 2012 (Jackson, interview 2012). *Yes Minister*, a BBC comedy about political life (BBC Two, 1980–8), has been re-versioned in India, Turkey, the Netherlands and Ukraine (Rosser, 2009).

Hollywood awakes

While the USA is adapting scripts in growing numbers, it has also emerged as the world's second largest supplier of scripted formats (Waller, 2014b). This evolution was sparked by a change of heart from the Hollywood studios, which, as Paul Torre notes, have had to respond to trends that threaten their business model (Torre, 2012: 181). Chief among these threats is the rise in local TV production and the emergence of strong regional production centres (chiefly South Korea, Turkey and the UK for scripted entertainment), which have combined to slow down the global demand for US finished series (Akyuz, 2013; Webdale, 2005). Although the big studios were reluctant at first to exploit their format rights, the inexorable rise in the demand for local programming has led them to revise their assumptions and start mining their vast catalogues.

Sony Pictures Television was the only studio to anticipate the demand for local production and has been selling scripted formats since the early 2000s. Its most widely adapted title is the sitcom *The Nanny* (CBS, 1993–9), which has been re-versioned in ten territories. More recently, *Everybody Loves Raymond* (CBS, 1996–2005) was adapted in Holland, Israel, Russia and the Middle East. Other adaptations include *Married with Children* (Israel), *King of Queens* (Russia) and *Rules of Engagement* (Poland) (Pickard, 2011; Torre, 2012: 189–90).

The other studios have followed suit. Within a few years, NBC Universal cleared the format rights to *Kojak*, *Magnum PI* and *Emergency Room*, and allowed adaptations of *Queer Eye* and *Meet My Folks*. It is, however, the franchise *Law & Order* that has proven most popular with TV buyers. One of the longest-running US crime series (it reached twenty seasons in its final year on NBC in 2010), it has seen adaptations in Russia (NTV, 2007), France (*Paris enquêtes criminelles*, TF1, 2007–8) and the UK (*Law & Order: UK*, ITV, 2009–).

CBS Studios International has put up for sale the format rights of more than twenty titles, including four sitcoms spanning half-a-century: *I Love Lucy* (1950s), *The Honeymooners* (1950s), *The Odd Couple* (1970s) and *Caroline in the City* (1990s). Recent deals include *Cheers*, sold to Spain.

Twentieth Century Fox Television's *Prison Break* (Fox, 2005–9) was adapted by Channel One in Russia, and *24* (Fox, 2001–10) was remade in India on a big budget. Fox sold four titles to Russian broadcasters in 2012 alone: *It's Always Sunny in Philadelphia* (FX, 2005–), *Bones* (Fox, 2005–), *Tru Calling* (Fox, 2003–5) and *Malcolm in the Middle* (Fox, 2000–6).

Walt Disney was equally slow to enter the scripted format market, but then immediately struck gold with *Desperate Housewives* (ABC, 2004–12). Echoing some of the narrative techniques and themes of tele-novelas, *Desperate Housewives* resonated particularly strongly with audiences in Latin America, where three adaptations were made (Argentina, Colombia/Ecuador and Brazil). In 2008 Univision, the Spanish-language US network, produced its own version, and three years later a Turkish series was made (Brzoznowski, 2012a; Rohter, 2006). A sixth local version, *Desperate Housewives Africa*, was launched by a Nigerian broadcaster, EbonyLife TV, in 2015. Other Disney series to have been adapted include

Grey's Anatomy (ABC, 2005–) in Mexico and *Revenge* (ABC, 2011–) in Turkey.

Warner Bros. International Television Production was established only in 2009. The London-based division has tried to make up for lost time since by acquiring large European TV production companies (chapter 6). In the scripted space, *Nip/Tuck* (FX, 2003–10) was turned into a telenovela in Colombia, *Gossip Girl* (The CW, 2007–12) became *Gossip Girl Acapulco* in Latin America, and *The O.C.* (Fox, 2003–7) was adapted in Turkey (Zein, 2014).

Hollywood studios entered the scripted format market belatedly and almost reluctantly, anxious as they were about hurting their finished programming sales. Although they have not thrown caution to the wind, the size of their catalogue, combined with their international footprint and annual output, guarantees them a strong presence in the market for years to come.

Emerging territories

The business in scripted formats is booming because new suppliers are emerging and have begun to make their mark on the trade. As South Korea remakes Japanese dramas and Latin American telenovelas are adapted in China or Russia, the scripted format business has expanded, but has also become more multi-faceted and diverse. From New Zealand came *Outrageous Fortune*, a comedy that was remade in the UK for ITV (*Honest*, 2008) and the USA for ABC (*Scoundrels*, 2010). A version of Radio-Canada's *Les Invincibles* (2005) was made in France for Arte in 2008. From Holland came *Penoza*, which, as already seen, aired as *Red Widow* on ABC in 2013. A few scripted formats have also emerged from Italy, with Mediaset selling format packages for about forty titles. Recent deals include adaptations of the sitcom *Casa Vianello* [*Young Enough*] (Canale 5, 1988–2006) in Serbia, Portugal, Croatia and Turkey, and local remakes of soap opera *Vivere* [*Living*] (Canale 5, 1999–present) in Greece, Portugal and Poland (Fry, 2013a; Mediaset, 2014).

Although the UK remains the leading supplier of scripted formats (Waller, 2014b), two new export territories have attracted attention: Scandinavia and Israel. Following the initial success of finished programmes, many series of the 'Scandi-wave' are being re-versioned. *Wallander* (TV4, 2005–), a Swedish crime series, was remade for the BBC (BBC One, 2008–10), and Danish broadcaster DR's *Forbrydelsen* [*The Killing*] (DR1, 2007) was adapted by Fox Television Studios and Fuse Entertainment for AMC in

Table 9.4 Israeli TV series remakes

Original title	Original broadcast	US remake, broadcaster or production company	Other adaptations
BeTipul [*In Treatment*]	HOT 3, 2005–8	*In Treatment*, HBO, 2008–10	Argentina, Brazil, Canada, Croatia, Czech Republic, Hungary, Italy, Japan, Netherlands, Poland, Romania, Russia, Serbia, Slovenia
Ramzor [*Traffic Light*]	Channel 2, 2008–	*Traffic Light*, Fox, 2011	Russia
Hatufim [*Prisoners of War*]	Channel 2, 2009–12	*Homeland*, Showtime, 2011–13	Brazil, South Korea, Russia, Turkey
The Gordin Cell	Yes!, 2012	*Allegiance*, NBC, 2014	South Korea
Hostages	Channel 10, 2013	*Hostages*, CBS, 2013–14	Russia

2011 (Koranteng, 2012). *Bron* [*The Bridge*] (SVT1, DR1, 2011–), originally from Sweden and Denmark, has been adapted in the USA by Shine America and FX (FX, 2013–) and in the UK and France as *The Tunnel* (Sky Atlantic and Canal Plus, 2013). In spring 2015, both NBC and Twentieth Century Fox Television had yet to produce local versions of, respectively, *Lærkevej* [*Park Road*] (TV2, 2009), a Danish drama series, and *Mammon* (NRK, 2014), a Norwegian thriller, but HBO Europe was producing a Czech and a Polish adaptation of the latter.

Israeli production houses have also developed a strong presence in this market. It began with *BeTipul* [*In Treatment*], which has been re-versioned in fourteen territories since HBO aired the US remake, making it the world's most adapted drama. Following a few other adaptations and US projects that never came to fruition,[4] the next big hit was Keshet's drama *Hatufim* [*Prisoners of War*], which is being adapted in four territories and whose US version, *Homeland*, has sold around the world (table 9.4).

Both Scandinavia and Israel have forged a space in the scripted format trade, yet their approaches differ. As the Israeli market is too small to allow production companies to scale up, the Israelis are investing in an industry whose job is to tell stories that sell worldwide. So far, Scandi-dramas have been primarily aimed at a local audience before they hit the road. For example, the sole ambition of Lars Blomgren, *The Bridge*'s Swedish producer, was to create a co-production that would also work in Denmark (whilst Swedish broadcasters bought Danish series and put them on primetime, the Danish never bought anything from Sweden). The first *Bridge* told the story of two local police forces working across borders; it was only later discovered how ripe this situation was for reinterpretation, being, as it was, of relevance to all those countries that also share interesting borders (Blomgren, interview 2014).

Israeli producers appear adept at stacking up the odds in their favour. By keeping initial budgets low, they create series that can be remade on a small budget, ensuring a record number of adaptations for *BeTipul*. Israeli producers also seem to be flexible in allowing buyers any change they like as long as they understand the essence of the show. Keren Shahar, head of acquisitions and distribution at Keshet International, made it clear that 'a scripted format needs to change and be adapted as much as it needs for that market', allowing a family drama (*Hatufim*) to be transformed into an action series (*Homeland*) (Shahar, 2014).

While Scandinavian producers might prove equally accommodating, it is far from being the case across the industry. Hollywood studios are the least flexible and seek to protect their brand first. Andrew Zein, a senior executive at Warner Bros. International Television Production, stated that 'the overall design concept of a scripted format is something that WBITVP takes very seriously. Our clients have to embrace the original design elements, including costumes, make-up, locations and studio set' (in Stephens, 2014b: 298).

New formatted genres: telenovelas and constructed reality

Adaptations in telenovelas and constructed reality programming are bolstering the volume of scripted formats in circulation. Not taking telenovelas into account would leave unexplained the fact that Argentina has become the world's third largest supplier of scripted formats (Waller, 2014b). Novelas were among the very first programmes to be translated in the sound broadcasting era, and several Cuban scripts for radionovelas travelled across Latin America in the 1940s and 1950s. As seen in chapter 1, the trade was initiated by US advertising agencies and, as Joseph Straubhaar argues, the telenovela genre is in itself a transnational proto-format engineered through a process of hybridization that blended a 'base genre' (the US soap) with local 'traditions of serial fiction' (Straubhaar, 2012: 150–1).

In the television era, the telenovela industry developed in Argentina, Brazil, Colombia, Mexico, Peru and Venezuela, and soon these serials dominated the primetime schedules of broadcasters across Latin America. It was in the late 1980s that telenovelas began to be exported to other world regions (Mato, 2005: 426). Albeit appearing sparsely on broadcasters' schedules in developed markets, telenovelas have found viewers in great numbers in developing countries, particularly in Central and Eastern Europe, the Middle East, and Central and Southeast Asia (Biltereyst and Meers, 2000; Mato, 2005). Until the early 2000s, telenovela exports consisted entirely of finished tapes, but scripts have progressively become popular with local broadcasters eager to develop their local production capabilities and respond to viewers' preference for local content.

The game changer was *Yo soy Betty, la fea* [*Ugly Betty*] (McCabe and Akass, 2013). Written by Fernando Gaitán, *Betty* aired on Canal RCN in Colombia between 1999 and 2001. It was an immediate hit and the series was picked up and adapted by neighbouring broadcasters. In 2006 ABC broadcast a US-made version, confirming the soap's status as a global phenomenon. By 2013, *Ugly Betty* had aired in more than ninety countries and at least twenty versions had been made (Gaitán, 2010; Miller, 2010).

Latin American media firms have since adapted their business model, adding format units to complement their ready-made sales. Early movers include Caracol of Colombia, Telefe of Argentina, Televisa of Mexico and Venevisión of Venezuela, while Globo TV started its format business in 2009. These units' involvement varies from contract to contract, from simple script sales with experienced broadcasters to the full consulting package for those new to the genre. In a few instances, telenovela producers move further along the value chain by co-producing the series with broadcasters (Wasserman, interview 2012).

Caracol Internacional's titles have been adapted thirty times so far, including the popular narco-telenovela *Sin tetas no hay paraíso* [*Without Breasts There Is No Paradise*] (Caracol TV, Colombia, 2006) and *Vecinos* [*Neighbours*] (Caracol TV, 2008–9) (Cabañas, 2012). Telefe International's scripts have passed 100 adaptations, with *Los Roldán* [*The Roldans*] (Telefe, Argentina, 2004–5), *Hermanos y detectives* [*Brothers and Detectives*] (Telefe, 2006) and *Montecristo* (Telefe, 2006) exceeding ten versions each. Outside Latin America, the key markets for telenovela remakes are Central and Eastern Europe (particularly Poland and Russia) and the Spanish-speaking USA. The fastest growth is currently coming from Asian countries, notably China, Indonesia and Malaysia, where a burgeoning taste for the original versions is feeding the adaptation market (Franks, 2013; Middleton, 2015; Waller, 2010b).

Telenovelas have begun to be adapted for the English-speaking US market, the latest example being The CW's *Jane the Virgin* (table 9.3, p. 174). As demand is expected to grow, Televisa has opened a studio in Los Angeles and NBC Universal is developing English-language versions of shows that first aired on its local Spanish networks (Middleton, 2014).

Constructed reality is an emerging strand that blends principles from the reality genre with storytelling techniques from soap opera and consists of 'real' people shot in managed situations and structured scenarios. The strand is divided into two schools. In the Anglo-American variant, producers construct settings but do not use scripts, as dialogues and storylines remain driven by people who play their own character. Genre highlights include MTV's *Jersey Shore* (2009–12), *The Only Way is Essex* (ITV2, 2010–) and *Made in Chelsea* (E4, 2011–) (Woods, 2014).

The second variant was pioneered by German TV production companies and involves the loose reconstruction of real-life events including distressing family incidents, crimes, murders or court cases. These shows are based on scenarios played out by 'ordinary' people (who may not necessarily have been involved in these cases) and sometimes actors, who follow a script in order to deliver the story. For instance, *Das Strafgericht* [*Criminal Court*] (RTL, 2002–) and *Betrugsfälle* [*Wham Bam Scam*] (RTL, 2010–), two constructed reality formats sold by Global Screen, a German distributor, have been picked by broadcasters in a variety of European countries (Smitherman, 2013). The most widely distributed formats are those of Filmpool, an MME Moviement company. So far, 2,600 episodes of constructed reality shows such as *Zwei bei Kallwass* [*Two with Kallwass*] (Sat.1, 2001–13), *Verdachtsfälle* [*Cases of Doubt*] (RTL, 2009–) and *Familien im Brennpunkt* [*Families at the Crossroads*] (RTL, 2009–) have been produced in Europe (All3Media, 2014; Brzoznowski, 2013b).

Telenovelas and constructed reality programmes may not be the most prominent genres, but they matter in terms of volume and their transnational adaptations play a big part in the growth of the scripted format trade.

Improved Knowledge Transfer

As already noted, scripted formats cannot be reproduced as mechanistically as concepts from other genres. Dramas and comedies are culturally sensitive and do not rely on format points and structures that can be duplicated in a routine fashion. There are always cases of game-show rules having to be amended to fit a particular culture and scripts that are translated word for word, but as a general rule scripts need more adaptation than unscripted entertainment. While only the structures of unscripted shows travel, every word and scene of a drama need to sound right to a local audience. Even if, in the best case, these modifications are cosmetic, the full package needs adaptation, including shoot locations, casting, costumes and so on. As local versions of scripted shows tend to differ from one another more than in other genres, lessons learnt in one territory may not apply elsewhere.

Furthermore, in contrast to game shows, for which knowledge transfer mechanisms (production bibles and flying producers) were routinized as early as the 1970s, support practices were until recently not as set for script buyers. Once in possession of the script, the buyers could be left to their own devices. Without guidelines about what made the format work, many scripts ended up being dismembered by local broadcasters. Vertue remembers how US producers tried to do *Fawlty Towers* without malice between Sybil and Basil and *Ab Fab* without the drugs and the drinking. She recollects her first attempt to adapt *Steptoe and Son*:

> They hadn't understood what made *Steptoe and Son* work in the first place, what was the core of it? This love/hate relationship between the father and son, who the son who wanted to break away from but somehow couldn't and the father who stopped him, and they didn't really understand that, and so the pilot had them living in a really lovely place and they didn't have a horse and cart, they had a van, which is fine, but I said to them I don't know why he wants to leave, it's lovely here, you know, where they lived and everything. And so it didn't get picked for series, but it made me think I must not do this again, I must only sell it when I can find that person who I think can see what makes it work, and so I put it in a drawer and I thought one day I'll do it, I'll get it out again. (Vertue, interview 2011)

The knowledge transfer has improved over more recent years and has been catching up with practices common in other genres. Buyers receive more support from consultant producers and production bibles have expanded; buyers get both a storyline *and* a method of production. Today's bibles can detail the series' premise and showrunner's vision of the original series (what the story is about) and include information about key characters, story drivers and dynamics, down to the shooting schedule. It is also increasingly common to see the original creative team included in a consulting package, enabling the adaptation team to hold conversations with the writer and/or producer of the original series (Jackson, interview 2012; Nohr, interview 2013; Stephens, 2014b).

Although knowledge transfer mechanisms have been improved by large distributors with a reputation to protect, scripted formats are even better handled when kept in-house by international production companies with facilities in multiple territories. As seen in chapter 6, most Hollywood studios and newly formed TV production majors have acquired local companies in order to internationalize their production capacity, enabling them, wherever possible, to adapt and produce their scripted shows themselves.

The Bridge, for instance, was co-produced by Filmlance, a Swedish TV production company that became part of Metronome Film & Television, which itself was acquired by the Shine Group in 2009 and has now merged with Endemol and Core Media Group (chapter 6). Both the Franco-British and the American remakes were handled by Shine Companies, and Blomgren acted as executive producer for both adaptations. He read the new scripts and made some comments before becoming 'a fly on the wall' on the production set (Blomgren, interview 2014). He ensured, however, that the changes went in the right direction. For instance, while the Swedes and Danes understand each other in the original series, linguistic and cultural tensions were pushed in the Franco-British show. In the US adaptation, the script highlights cultural differences between police forces from an affluent society versus a developing country (Mexico). The US production team initially planned to reproduce the melancholic Nordic landscapes and planted the story between Canada and the USA. Once they realized where the essence of the drama lay, they transferred the story to the border between Mexico and the USA. The narco-trafficking between the two countries made the story more current and gave it darker undertones (Blomgren, interview 2014).

All in all, the TV industry has a better understanding of the fundamental mechanisms that dictate successful scripted format translation. Any scripted show has a kernel which is the engine of its success. While everything else can be touched, the essence of the story must remain across cultures or else the story crumbles.

Conclusion: A Revolution Comes Full Circle

Scripted formats have come of age but remain different from those in non-scripted genres. They require fuller cultural translation, and the risk of failure stands substantially higher than in other genres. In addition, the underlying economics of their production and distribution differs. Non-scripted genres travel as formats almost exclusively and distributors strive to release them as quickly as possible. Not so with fiction, for which finished tapes remain essential. These programmes are far more expensive to produce than non-scripted fare and many are deficit-funded (requiring distributors to complete the investment from commissioning broadcasters). Since a large part of the funding comes from potential future sales, everything is done to protect the earnings of the completed tape. Consequently, the format rights of scripted shows are often released only once the original version has played out and the initial investment been recouped. If and when adaptations are produced, they are distributed in carefully choreographed sequences of holdbacks and releases (Jackson, interview 2012; Nohr, interview 2013). Hollywood studios remain equally careful and avoid releasing the format rights of series that are too recent, unless these have been cleared by the distribution team.

Finally, the issue of brand purity is particularly acute with scripted shows, as too many adaptations risk diluting a brand and a single poor one can kill a series. The rights holders of series such as *The Bridge*, *CSI* or *Sherlock* receive many more requests for local adaptations than will ever be produced (Blomgren, interview 2014; Gilbert, 2014; Nohr, interview 2013; Vertue, interview 2011).

Nonetheless, the late entry of scripted formats into the TV format trading system is significant. It brings the post-millennial TV format revolution full circle. The trade, now spanning all genres, is no longer confined to the (lower) fringes of the industry. Scripted formats not only add volume and diversity to the TV format business but enhance its credibility as a form of IP exchange. This also establishes how far the TV industry has progressed and learnt to adapt any programme, from the most mundane and formulaic daytime game show to award-winning, primetime, globe-trotting series.

Conclusion:
Trade, Culture and Television

The study of TV formats gives us a better understanding of global media flows in the twenty-first century and enables us to make an intervention in the debate between the proponents of media imperialism and those of cosmopolitan globalization (e.g. Beck, 2006; Chalaby, 2006; Herman and McChesney, 1997; Mattelart, 2002; Nederveen Pieterse, 2004; Schiller, 1992; Sparks, 2007, 2008; Tunstall, 2008). The claims made by both groups need to be disentangled at commercial and cultural level. From an economic perspective, the first issue is to determine the impact of TV formats on international media flows. Have they changed the dynamic of the trade in audiovisual products, and have they made it less Western-centric and more diverse and inclusive – cosmopolitan – than it has been so far? In this context, TV formats represent both change and continuity.

Formats bring change because they deepen media globalization. They add to the ready-made tapes, international TV channels and entertainment platforms that cross frontiers, making trade more important than it has ever been for the TV industry. The international dimension of national TV markets is no longer confined to their fringes but includes the IP that lay within Saturday-night blockbusters. Formats have increased the transnational interdependence of TV firms: they have facilitated the development of the first TV production majors and have connected local broadcasters to a global value chain. Broadcasters that aimed to be self-sufficient outsource a growing amount of their production activities today to a specialist chain segment (the disintegration of the production process; chapter 4), and as they sometimes take programming decisions on the basis of the ratings performances of shows in other territories, they monitor TV schedules beyond their borders.

In terms of the weight of a few Western nations (and the USA in particular) on the trade in audiovisual products, TV formats also bring change but within continuity. The format trade is certainly more inclusive than that in finished programming and has given a voice and commercial opportunities to a new and increasingly large array of countries: Israel, Scandinavia, South Korea and Turkey are among those that are rising through the ranks and joining well-established exporters; Asia too will soon export formats in greater numbers. Since the format revolution, the US market is welcoming foreign IP for the first time and, in a shift towards further de-centring, the industry has a new leader: the UK (chapters 2, 4 and 9). Other nations are following suit, although industrial upgrading in the TV industry is a complex task that necessitates a competitive and diverse media market, and a set of policies that incorporate market-driven incentives and rewards for export (chapter 5). For the time being, the UK's success means that the Anglo-American alliance (Tunstall and Machin, 1999) remains in a strong position in the world media market. As seen in chapter 4, the UK and the USA sell more formats than the next twelve largest exporters. Among the twelve TV majors, nine are based in London and none are outside Europe. In addition, US capital is increasingly present in the Dutch and UK-based international TV production segment, as the recent purchases of Discovery, Fox or Warner Bros. prove (chapter 6). The geography of the TV format trade remains unequal, demonstrating that a more complex and interconnected world can go hand in hand with the economic dominance of a few nations.

At the theoretical level, this evolution underlines the importance of comprehending current globalizing processes within the context of historical capitalism. The commercial and industrial globalization of television has less to do with an alleged cosmopolitization of the world than with the expansion of the capitalist world-system into IP trading. The patterns and structures of the TV format trade clearly show that, in contrast to what Beck claims, borders have not all become 'transparent'; the inequalities among territories, including the division between IP generators and IP consumers (chapter 4), demonstrate that nation-states are more than just 'historical fetishes' (Beck, 2006: 8). The discourse of cosmopolitanism fails to establish the connection between culture and economy, and more fundamentally between culture and history, and thus ultimately fails to understand the nature of globalizing processes.

Immanuel Wallerstein may claim that globalization is nothing new, as the world economy has always been 'marked by a world-scale division of labor' (Hopkins and Wallerstein, 1986: 157), and that 'from the very beginning of historical capitalism' 'almost all commodity chains of any importance have traversed these state frontiers' (Wallerstein, 1983: 31), but the economic interdependence of firms and nations has been accelerating in recent times. World trade has grown rapidly both as a percentage of world GDP and in absolute value, with merchandise exports growing from US$59 billion in 1948 to US$19,930 billion in 2012 (WTO, 2013: 22). Although Wallerstein may overstate his case, history helps explain why a new value chain replicates the features and inequalities of former trading systems and is dominated by the same handful of nations. As seen in chapter 4, TV format exporters also rank high in the list of leading exporters in merchandise trade.

IP trading is a complex business that requires economic capital, knowledge and infrastructure, features that have been accumulated by leading trading nations and enable them to dominate emergent value chains. Calling on history for an explanation does not imply a fixation with the past but allows for a better understanding of the laws and patterns that dictate change.

Finally, the cultural impact of the format trade needs to be assessed. It would be impossible for TV formats developed in the Western world not to convey values. Formats are not created in a social vacuum and always begin life as local shows enjoyed by a local audience. For instance, *Come Dine with Me* strongly reflects British social attitudes towards privacy and social interaction, and talent competitions produce heroes for an individualist and materialist culture. Although the possibility cannot be excluded that some of these values are still carried in the travelling IP that structures these shows, there is little evidence that the TV format trade is having a meaningful impact on local cultures.

Silvio Waisbord, noting the contrast between 'globalized economics' and 'localized cultures', rightly states that 'the contemporary trade of formats puts in evidence that the globalization of media economics and culture are intertwined but are not identical' (Waisbord, 2004: 378–9). The format business may allow TV majors to cross borders with ease but it developed on the back of demand for local programming: local broadcasters, knowing their audience's preferences, always replace imports with local programming as soon as financially possible (e.g. Moran, 1985; Sinclair et al., 1996; Straubhaar, 2007).

The TV format chain may be global, the adaptation process and transfer of expertise may be transnational, but TV formats begin and end their lives as local shows. In fact, they need to become local to stay international, as the only formats that cross borders are those that resonate in each and every territory in which they air. In addition, a format's transnational rules are there to weave narratives and disappear behind the stories they generate. A good format is a platform that vanishes behind the drama it creates. Even though some format rules may convey values that are heterogeneous to some cultures, TV formats are unlikely to be the Trojan horses of global culture that some critics fear.

So far, there is more evidence to show that TV formats benefit local cultures rather than tear them down. Several studies have confirmed Albert Moran's seminal observation that 'television format adaptations are only one small link in the chain that binds viewers in a national community but equally obviously it is an important link all the same' (Moran, 1998: 165). Esser and Jensen concur that 'the popularity of many formats should be seen as proof that they succeed in providing a common reference point for the majority of the population. Many localized adaptations successfully create feelings of belonging and often stimulate debate and reflection at the local/ national level' (Esser and Jensen, 2015: 210). For instance, Joost de Bruin analysed how the New Zealand adaptation of *Idols* was geared to promote local culture, including 'ethnic and cultural diversity; positive representations of young people; and attention for New Zealand popular music' (de Bruin, 2012: 225). His conclusions, that 'the local adaptation of global formats can . . . create opportunities for audiences to recognize themselves as members of national communities', echo those of Moran (de Bruin, 2012: 226).

The immensely popular *Lascia o raddoppia?*, the 1950s Italian adaptation of *The $64,000 Question* (chapter 1), provides another case in point. Chiara Ferrari argues that the show acted as a platform for Italian culture and resonated so strongly that it contributed to the country's linguistic and cultural unification more than half a century ago. The list of questions, she writes, which touched on Italian arts, literature, history, football and opera, 'created among the Italian people the sense of sharing a common heritage and common passions' (Ferrari, 2012: 137). The presenter was Mike Bongiorno, who went on to become one of Italy's most emblematic figures of the second half of the twentieth century; it was claimed that 'Italians have learned their language thanks to Mike's Italian rather than Dante's Italian' (Ferrari, 2012: 142). *Lascia o raddoppia?* even had an impact on the school curriculum, which was reformed once ministers noticed contestants' inability to answer the simplest of questions (Ferrari, 2012: 142).

Lacroix and Tremblay contextualized the emergence of the cultural industries in the long waves of capitalist development and in the history of the production of material and immaterial objects (Lacroix and Tremblay, 1997a). It is the history of trade that is relevant in the rise of TV formats. Trade has become prominent in services and IP commodities, but it has internationalized the production and consumption of many a product in the past. From spices to food staples such as coffee (originally from Ethiopia) and potatoes (modern-day Peru), many crops have made the journey from local to global. Yet these globalized commodities, far from homogenizing cultures, have contributed to differentiate them. There are countless ways of cooking with potatoes and most recipes are specific to a region or a nation, from Tibet's *xogoi momo* to Switzerland's *rösti*. A crop may be global but cuisine is local. In the same way that a basic ingredient can become part of local cuisine, a format can make a contribution to local culture. Trade has been a determining influence in shaping the world we live in, but it is easy to misunderstand its impact on cultures. The fact that the world TV industry is now firmly embedded in international trade does not necessarily mean that local cultures and identities will disappear.

Notes

Introduction

1 Staff, teams and sometimes even companies tend to specialize in one or the other type. In the USA, for instance, where networks were driven by comedy and drama, the first international reality formats were handled by newly established alternative programming departments, as was the case at Fox or ABC (Wong, interview 2014).

Chapter 1 TV Formats as an Anglo-American Invention

1 Pink note from N. Collins to G. L. Marshall, 20 September 1946, File R19/526, Entertainment, *Ignorance Is Bliss*, 1945–53, BBC Written Archives Centre (BBC WAC).

2 File R19/526, Entertainment, *Ignorance Is Bliss*, 1945–53, BBC WAC.

3 'Note from the Programme Contracts Manager', 19 March 1947, in T14/584, TV O.B. *Ignorance Is Bliss*, 1947, BBC WAC.

4 'Note from the Programme Contracts Manager', 19 March 1947, in T14/584, TV O.B. *Ignorance Is Bliss*, 1947, BBC WAC.

5 Unsigned memo, 2 June 1948, R12/230/2, Copyright *Twenty Questions*, March 1948–50, File 1B, BBC WAC.

6 Letter from Ronald Waldman, Acting Head of Television Light Entertainment, BBC, 15 November 1950; Letter from L. P. R. Roche, Assistant Solicitor, BBC, 18 February 1954; both in File 1B, BBC WAC.

7 Unsigned memo, 25 May 1951, T12/457/3, TV Light Entertainment, *What's My Line?*, File 1, 1st Series, 1951, BBC WAC.

8 File R12/2511, Copyright *What's My Line?*, 1955–62, BBC WAC.

9 http://www.ukgameshows.com/ukgs/What's_My_Line%3F.

10 Letter from Ronald Waldman, Head of Light Entertainment Television, to A. H. Cop, 27 May 1955; Memorandum of agreement signed by R. G. Walford, Copyright Department, BBC, and Kenneth Cleveland, MCA England, 27 July 1955, R126/481/1, Copyright *This is Your Life*, 1955–65, BBC WAC.

11 Letter from M. Standing to M. Winnick, 10 December 1948, File R19/526, Entertainment, *Ignorance Is Bliss*, 1945–53, BBC WAC.

12 Letter from M. Standing to M. Winnick, 10 March 1949, File R19/526, Entertainment, *Ignorance Is Bliss*, 1945–53, BBC WAC.

13 G. D. G. Perkins, internal memo, 28 March 1947, File R12/230/1, Copyright *Twenty Questions*, 1947–Feb. 1948, File 1A, BBC WAC.

14 Letter from Perkins to Winnick, 12 November 1947, File R12/230/1, Copyright *Twenty Questions*, 1947–Feb. 1948, File 1A, BBC WAC.

15 Memo from L. Wellington, controller of the Home Service, 23 February 1948, File R12/230/1, Copyright *Twenty Questions*, 1947–Feb. 1948, File 1A, BBC WAC. 'Format' is underlined in the original and it is probably the first time the word is mentioned in such a context in the BBC archives.

16 Letter from Bernard B. Smith to H. F. Burns, BBC New York Office, 28 June 1948, File R12/230/2, Copyright *Twenty Questions*, March 1948–50, File 1B, BBC WAC.

17 Agreement 'Accepting the sum of £1,000 from the BBC for any sound broadcast of Twenty Questions', signed by Maurice Winnick and L. P. R. Roche, the BBC Assistant Solicitor, 18 January 1949, File R12/230/1, Copyright *Twenty Questions*, 1947–Feb. 1948, File 1A, BBC WAC.

18 Letter from Ronald Waldman, 15 November 1950; Letter from B. E. Nicolls, Director of Home Broadcasting, File R12/230/1, Copyright *Twenty Questions*, March 1948–50, File 1B, BBC WAC.

19 Contract between Maurice Winnick and Miss M. T. Candler, Head of Copyright, the BBC, 29 June 1951, in File R12/239/1, Copyright *What's My Line?*, 1951–Oct. 1952, BBC WAC.

20 Contract, File R12/239/1, Copyright *What's My Line?*, 1951–Oct. 1952, BBC WAC.

21 As seen in the introduction to this book, industry lawyers still describe format trading as the selling of remake rights.

22 R. G. Walford, 4 April 1952, File R12/239/1, Copyright *What's My Line?*, 1951–Oct. 1952, BBC WAC.

23 Letter from Ronald Waldman to Maurice Winnick, 6 February 1952, T12/467/1 TV Light Ent, Maurice Winnick 1a: 1950–54, BBC WAC.

24 Internal document from Dennis Main Wilson to the Variety Booking Manager, 21 February 1949, File R19/870, Entertainment, *Opportunity Knocks*, 1948–1960, BBC WAC. *Chance of a Lifetime* already features several attributes of modern talent shows: the contestants, either amateurs or 'pros who haven't hit the big time', the compère who was 'a really well-known name in the entertainment world', the weekly guest star and the show's winner, at the time determined by audience applause. Letter from Winnick to Waldman, 19 December 1951, T12/467/1 TV Light Ent, Maurice Winnick 1a: 1950–54, BBC WAC.

25 Letter from Luker to Ronald Waldman, undated but circa January 1951, File R12/239/1, Copyright *What's My Line?*, 1951–Oct. 1952, BBC WAC.

26 *Superstars* premiered on ABC in January 1974 and aired on Antenne 2 in 1977. The format also reached the UK, Belgium, Sweden and Holland (Leveneur, 2005: 201–8).

Chapter 2 The Making of an Entertainment Revolution

1 The Producers Alliance for Cinema and Television (Pact), the UK trade association that represents the commercial interests of independent producers in film, television and digital media, had 800 members.

2 http://mavise.obs.coe.int.

3 E.g. cable from N. G. Luker, at BBC's New York office, to A. H. Cop, at the BBC in London, 27 February 1951, File R12/239/1, Copyright *What's My Line?*, 1951–Oct. 1952, BBC WAC.

4 In File R12/230/2, Copyright *Twenty Questions*, March 1948–50, File 1B, BBC WAC.

Chapter 3 The Advent of the Super-Formats

1 File R19/639, Entertainment, Levis, Carroll Programmes, 1942–54; Carroll Levis (II) (1947–62), BBC WAC.

2 Internal document from Dennis Main Wilson to the Variety Booking Manager, 21 February 1949, File R19/870, Entertainment, *Opportunity Knocks*, 1948–60, BBC WAC.

Chapter 4 The Formation of the Format Trading System

1 Schedule data from Data.worldscreen/com/season_grid/index.html.

2 See www.mipformats.com.

3 Recipients of the Gold Medal include David Lyle, Merv Griffin, Reg Grundy, Peter Bazalgette, Stephen Leahy and Trish Kinane, and Mark Itkin.

4 This figure includes the RDF Media versus Fox Broadcasting case over *Wife Swap USA/Trading Spouses*, although it was stopped after the first hearing, probably due to an out-of-court settlement (EBU, 2005: 142–5).

Chapter 5 Nations and Competition

1 It is called a 'joint' committee because it brings together Members of the House of Lords and the House of Commons, a rare occurrence.

2 When broadcasters acquire a licence for a programme it will specify a number of uses on a particular channel. Broadcasters can purchase other distribution windows but these have to be negotiated separately.

3 'GroupM Entertainment', *Broadcast Greenlight – The Commissioning Index*, http://greenlight.broadcastnow.co.uk/production-companies/349-groupm-entertainment.

4 http://www.groupm.com.

Chapter 6 A Globalized Intellectual Property Market: The International Production Model

1 See http://ec.europa.eu/archives/information_society/avpolicy/reg/history/historytvwf/index_en.htm.

Chapter 7 Journeys and Transformations: Unscripted Formats in the Twenty-First Century

1 Following a court case in 2010, the show moved to a cable channel, before returning to TF1. Three contestants from the 2003 series argued that the shooting schedule was so constraining that their participation in the show was akin to employment, and that the signed agreement with the production company should be turned into a proper contract of employment. France's Court of Appeal upheld their complaint in June 2003, motivating its decision as follows:

> Analyzing the actual situation and conditions of the filming of *Temptation Island*'s third season, the Social Chamber of the Court of Appeal noted in 2009 that contestants were required to participate in the various activities and meetings, that they had to follow the rules defined unilaterally by the producer, that they were oriented in the analysis of their own behaviour, that some scenes were repeated in order to enhance key moments, that the waking hours and sleep were determined by production, that the regulations imposed on contestants a continuous availability, that they forbade them from leaving the site and communicating with the outside, that they stipulated that any breach of contractual obligations may be sanctioned by discharge . . . [The Social Chamber] deduces that the existence of a link of subordination is thereby highlighted, characterized by the power of the employer to 'give orders and instructions, to monitor their implementation, and to punish breaches of the subordinate'. (Judgment no. 1159, 3 June 2009, Social Chamber, Court of Appeal, my translation; http://www.courdecassation.fr/jurisprudence_2/chambre_sociale_576/1159_3_12905.html)

This decision may rest on the notoriously arcane French labour and employment laws but lifts the veil on the complex production procedures that some reality shows necessitate.

2 'In fact', writes Mark Andrejevic,

> as my own research and Annette Hill's (2005) has revealed, viewers have much the same reaction to reality television as the savvy punditry who reflexively emphasize the mediated artificial character of reality formats. Viewers do search for moments of authenticity, and they recognize a kind of sliding scale of shows from more to less real, but they clearly understand that they are watching an edited, mediated artefact and not an unadulterated, unmediated bit of reality. (Andrejevic, 2014: 42)

3 For instance, when ITV Studios co-produced *Hell's Kitchen* for Fox in 2005, they discovered that their American counterparts had written a script for Gordon Ramsay. They were told that they had 'booked a man who's the definition of spontaneous' and soon discovered that 'you don't tell Gordon what to say' (Znak, interview 2008).

Chapter 8 Talent Competitions

1 From the Victorian era until the 1950s, theatres and music halls across the UK welcomed touring artists and audiences every night. Impresarios put together a variety of acts including music, dance, comedy, magic and speciality acts. The winner of *Britain's Got Talent* gets to perform at the Royal Variety Performance, a fund-raising event organized by the Entertainment Artists' Benevolent Fund since 1912.

2 Letter from Michael Standing to Solicitor, 23 November 1949, R22/193 Legal, Hughie Green, *Opportunity Knocks*, 1949–51, BBC WAC.

3 The training scheme, unlike the show, is still running at the time of writing.

Chapter 9 Drama without Drama

1 For instance, three pilots of *Three's Company* were shot before ABC picked up the show (see next section of the chapter), and more recently CBS piloted *The Ran Quadruplets* twice without commissioning the Israeli series.

2 On the issue of creative autonomy, see Hesmondhalgh (2013: 243–53).

3 The 2007–8 Writers Guild of America strike, however, does not seem to have had an impact on demand for scripted formats (Esser, 2010: 280).

4 Including *The Ran Quadruplets* (Yes!, 2008–9), *Shkufim* [*False Flag*] (Channel 2, 2008–) and *Haverot* [*Little Mom*] (Yes!, 2012).

Personal Communications and Interviews by the Author

(Company names and job titles at time of interview)

Abrahams, Kees (2011) President, international production, Sony Pictures Television, phone interview by author, 11 July. London: tape recording.

Ballard, Bea (2009) Chief executive officer, 10 Star Entertainment, former creative head and executive producer for BBC Entertainment, 2003-7, interview by author, 9 September. London: tape recording.

Bazalgette, Peter (2009) Media consultant and former chief creative officer, Endemol, phone interview by author, 15 July. London: tape recording.

Beale, Mike (2008) Managing director, Alchemy Reality, interview by author, 4 September. London: tape recording.

Blomgren, Lars (2014) Managing director, Filmlance International, phone interview by author, 24 January. London: tape recording.

Bonney, Chris (2008) Managing director, Outright Distribution, interview by author, 3 July. London: tape recording.

Boyd, Alan (2009) Special advisor, FremantleMedia, interview by author, 10 June. London: tape recording.

Bråkenhielm, Anna (2009) Chief executive officer, Silverback, phone interview by author, 17 September. London: tape recording.

Butler, Nell (2009) Executive producer, ITV Studios, interview by author, 4 December. London: tape recording.

Carsey, Steve (2010) Former producer, Mentorn Films, interview by author, 21 May. London: tape recording.

Carter, Gary (2008) Chief operating officer, FremantleMedia, interview by author, 20 November. London: tape recording.

Carter, Gary (2014) Chairman, Northern Europe, and chairman, Shine 360°, Shine Group, interview by author, 10 October. London: tape recording.

Channing, Louise (2010) The Farm Group, interview by author, 23 November. London: tape recording.

Clark, Rob (2008) Senior executive vice president, entertainment and production, worldwide entertainment, FremantleMedia, interview by author, 11 September. London: tape recording.

Dey, Thomas (2010) Chief executive officer, About Corporate Finance, interview by author, 26 October. London: tape recording.

Dyke, Greg (2010) Former chairman and chief executive, Pearson Television, interview by author, 21 July. London: tape recording.

Filiztekin, Senay (2014) Head of drama acquisitions, Global Agency, phone interview by author, 9 October. London: tape recording.

Flynn, David (2014) Chief creative officer, Endemol UK, interview by author, 10 November. London: tape recording.

Fox, Jeremy (2010) Founding managing director, Action Time, interview by author, 2 February. London: tape recording.

Garvie, Wayne (2010) Managing director, content and production, BBC Worldwide, interview by author, 14 June. London: tape recording.

Garvie, Wayne (2011) Managing director, international production, All3Media, interview by author, 7 July. London: tape recording.

Gilbert, Paul (2008) Senior vice president, international formats, CBS Paramount International Television, and founding member, FRAPA, phone interview by author, 23 September. London: tape recording.

Graham, Alex (2010) Chief executive, Wall to Wall, interview by author, 14 September. London: tape recording.

Green, Sue (2010) Former executive producer, Reg Grundy and FremantleMedia, head of Powerlocal, Power Television, interview by author, 4 June. London: tape recording.

Hall, Ben (2010) Managing director, Shine Network, interview by author, 12 October. London: tape recording.

Hallenberger, Gerd (2011) Lecturer at Hamburg Media School, email correspondence with author, 27 October.

Hearsey, Richard (2010) Former executive producer, Talbot Television, Reg Grundy Productions and All American Fremantle, former head of worldwide development and acquisitions at Pearson Television and FremantleMedia, phone interview by author, 31 March. London: tape recording.

Hill, Michael (2010) Game-show producer, phone interview by author, 3 March. London: tape recording.

Hincks, Tim (2010) Chief executive, Endemol UK, interview by author, 13 September. London: tape recording.

Jackson, Andrea (2012) Managing director, acquisitions and formats, DRG, interview by author, 24 May. London: tape recording.

Jackson, Paul (2008) Director of entertainment and comedy, ITV, interview by author, 15 October. London: tape recording.

Jarvis, Colin (2008) Director, programming and international format production, BBC Worldwide, interview by author, 23 July. London: tape recording.

Jarvis, Colin (2010) Director, programming and international format production, BBC Worldwide, interview with author, 9 June. London: tape recording.

Jones, Simon (2010) Senior vice president, operations and international, Syco TV, interview by author, 5 February. London: tape recording.

Kinane, Trish and Stephen Leahy (2010) Former managing directors, Action Time, interview by author, 19 April. London: tape recording.

Lambert, Stephen (2012) Chief executive, Studio Lambert, interview by author, 27 June. London: tape recording.

Liddiment, David (2011) Former director of programmes, ITV, founding member and creative director, All3Media, interview by author, 10 November. London: tape recording.

Liebmann, Ben (2013) Chief executive officer, Shine 360°, interview by author, 2 May. London: tape recording.

Lituchy, Todd (2014) Founder and chief executive officer, New Media Vision, interview by author, 4 February. London: tape recording.

Lyle, David (2009) President, Fox Reality Channel, and founding director, FRAPA, interview by author, 30 September. London: tape recording.

Mahon, Alex (2010) Group president, Shine Group, interview by author, 12 October. London: tape recording.

McKerrow, Richard (2014) Co-founder and creative director, Love Productions, interview by author, 27 October. London: tape recording.

McVay, John (2009) Chief executive, Pact, interview by author, 25 February. London: tape recording.

Millichip, Jane (2008) Chief operating officer, RDF Rights, interview by author, 14 July. London: tape recording.

Morgenstern, David (2009) Producer, 10 Star Entertainment, interview by author, 15 October. London: tape recording.

Nohr, Nadine (2013) Chief executive officer, Shine International, interview by author, 12 December. London: tape recording.

Paice, Matt (2012) Executive vice president, international production, BBC Worldwide, interview by author, 16 May. London: tape recording.

Parsons, Charlie (2009) Chief executive officer, Castaway Television Productions, interview by author, 26 November. London: tape recording.

Parsons, Charlie (2009) Chief executive officer, Castaway Television Productions, email correspondence with author, 2 December.

Pedersen, Louise (2008) Managing director, All3Media International, interview by author, 24 November. London: tape recording.

Rayson, Alison (2010) Founder and chief executive officer, Target Entertainment, interview by author, 9 September. London: tape recording.

Rodrigue, Michel (2008) Chief executive officer, Distraction Formats, and founding member, FRAPA, interview by author, 11 July. London: tape recording.

Rodrigue, Michel (2012) Co-founder, The Format People, and founding member, FRAPA, interview by author, 29 March. London: personal notes.

Sargent, Nicola (2010) Co-founder and chief executive officer, The Farm Group, interview by author, 13 July. London: tape recording.

Silver, John (2010) Former creative director for features, Shine TV, and creative and managing director, Red House, interview by author, 19 March. London: tape recording.

Smith, Paul (2009) Former managing director, Celador, phone interview by author, 8 June. London: tape recording.

Spencer, Graham (2008) Director of sales, 2waytraffic, interview by author, 11 July. London: tape recording.

Taffner Jr, Donald (2013) President, DLT Entertainment, interview by author, 4 November. London: tape recording.

Tingay, Sarah (2012) Director, legal and business affairs, FremantleMedia, interview by author, 31 May. London: tape recording.

Usdan, Pamela (2010) Senior executive producer, FremantleMedia, phone interview by author, 3 June. London: tape recording.

Usdan, Pamela (2010) Senior executive producer, FremantleMedia, email correspondence with author, 9 December.

Vardanis, Fenia (2009) Former senior commissioning executive, entertainment, BBC One, interview by author, 14 December. London: tape recording.

Vertue, Beryl (2011) Producer and chairman, Hartswood Films, interview by author, 6 December. London: tape recording.

Wasserman, Michelle (2012) Head of international business – programming, formats and production services, Telefe, phone interview by author, 24 July.

Wong, Andrea (2014) Vice president of alternative programming, 1998–2007, ABC, currently president of international production, Sony Pictures Television, president of international, Sony Pictures Entertainment, interview by author, 12 November. London: tape recording.

Yin, Vivian (2013) Chief representative and deputy general manager, Star China International Media, email correspondence with author, 2 April.

Znak, Natalka (2008) Controller of factual entertainment, ITV Productions, interview by author, 16 September. London: tape recording.

References

Akyuz, Gün (2013) 'Turkey aims for $1bn TV exports', *c21media.net*, 21 June. http://www.c21media.net/turkey-aims-for-1bn-tv-exports/?ss=Turkey+aims+for+%241bn+TV+exports.

Akyuz, Gün (2014) 'Keshet's star rises in Asia', *c21media.net*, 9 April. http://www.c21media.net/keshets-star-rises-in-asia.

All3Media (2014) 'Cases of Doubt'. http://www.all3media.com/Content/Brand-Zweifelfalle.html.

Andreeva, Nellie (2013) 'Fall 2013 freshman series scorecard: time slot gainers and slackers', *Deadline Hollywood*, 8 November. http://wwwdeadline.com/2013/11/fall-2013-freshman-series-scorecard-time-slot-gainers-and-slackers.

Andrejevic, Marc (2014) 'When everyone has their own reality show', pp. 40–56 in Laurie Ouellette (ed.), *A Companion to Reality Television*. Chichester: Wiley-Blackwell.

Ang, Ien (1985) *Watching Dallas: Soap Opera and the Melodramatic Imagination*. London: Methuen.

Arris, Annet and Jacques Bughin (2009) *Managing Media Companies: Harnessing Creative Value*, 2nd edn. Chichester: Wiley.

Aston, Steve (2001) 'A time for action', *Broadcast*, 7 September: 19.

Bagdikian, Ben (2004) *The New Media Monopoly*, 6th edn. Boston: Beacon Press.

Baget Herms, Josep M. (1993) *Historia de la Televisión en España (1956–1975)*. Barcelona: Feed-Back.

Bair, Jennifer (2009) 'Global commodity chains: genealogy and review', pp. 1–34 in Jennifer Bair (ed.), *Frontiers of Commodity Chain Research*. Stanford: Stanford University Press.

Baker, Matt (1996a) 'Transatlantic transplants', *Broadcast*, 19 January: 24–5.

Baker, Matt (1996b) 'The winter games', *Broadcast*, 19 April: 50.

Bateman, Louise (1995) 'Dyke engineers £175m Grundy Worldwide deal', *Broadcast*, 31 March: 1.

Bazalgette, Peter (2005) *Billion Dollar Game: How Three Men Risked it All and Changed the Face of Television*. London: Time Warner.

BBC (2013) *BBC Annual Report and Accounts. Part 2: The BBC Executive's Review and Assessment*. London: BBC.

Beck, Ulrich (2000) 'The cosmopolitan perspective: sociology of the second age of modernity', *British Journal of Sociology*, 51 (1): 79–105.

Beck, Ulrich (2002) 'The cosmopolitan society and its enemies', *Theory, Culture & Society*, 19 (1–2): 17–44.

Beck, Ulrich (2005) *Power in the Global Age*. Cambridge: Polity.

Beck, Ulrich (2006) *The Cosmopolitan Vision*. Cambridge: Polity.

Bell, Nick (1994) 'Major men', *Television Business International*, April: 18–25.

Berman, Marc (2013) 'Open season', *c21media.net*, 17 April. http://www.c21media.net/open-season/?ss=%22Open+season%22.

Bernstein, William (2008) *A Splendid Exchange: How Trade Shaped the World*. London: Atlantic.

Bettetini, Gianfranco (ed.) (1980) *American Way of Television: Le Origine Della TV in Italia*. Florence: Sansoni.

Bielby, Denise D. and C. Lee Harrington (2008) *Global TV: Exporting Television and Culture in the World Market*. New York: New York University Press.

Bignell, Jonathan (2005) *Big Brother: Reality TV in the Twenty-First Century*. Basingstoke: Palgrave Macmillan.

Biltereyst, Daniël and Philippe Meers (2000) 'The international telenovela debate and the contra-flow argument: a reappraisal', *Media, Culture & Society*, 22 (4): 393–413.

Bjork, Ulf Jonas (2009) '"It's better to steal the idea": Swedish television copies programs from America, 1957–1969', *Historical Journal of Film, Radio and Television*, 29 (2): 219–27.

Black, Peter (1972) *The Mirror in the Corner: People's Television*. London: Hutchinson.

Boddy, William (1993) *Fifties Television: The Industry and Its Critics*. Urbana: University of Illinois Press.

Bourdon, Jérôme (2001) 'Genres télévisuels et emprunts culturels: l'américanisation invisible des télévisions européennes', *Réseaux*, 19 (107): 211–36.

Bourdon, Jérôme (2012) 'From discrete adaptations to hard copies: the rise of formats in European television', pp. 111–27 in Tasha Oren and Sharon Shahaf (eds.), *Global Television Formats: Understanding Television Across Borders*. London: Routledge.

Bower, Tom (2012) *Sweet Revenge: The Intimate Life of Simon Cowell*. London: Faber and Faber.

Brants, Kees and Els De Bens (2000) 'The status of TV broadcasting in Europe', pp. 7–22 in Jan Wieten, Graham Murdoch and Peter Dahlgren (eds.), *Television Across Europe: A Comparative Introduction*. London: Sage.

Braudel, Fernand ([1967] 1992) *Civilization and Capitalism, 15th–18th Century. Vol. I: The Structures of Everyday Life: The Limits of the Possible*. Berkeley: University of California Press.

Braudel, Fernand ([1979] 1996) *The Mediterranean and the Mediterranean World in the Age of Philip II. Vol. 1*. Berkeley: University of California Press.

Bridge, Richard McDee and Shelley Lane (1990) 'The protection of formats under English law: part 1', *Entertainment Law Review*, 1 (3): 96–102.

Broadcast (2014) 'Indie relations: the verdict', 22 August: 14–15.

Broadcast – Indie Survey (2013) 'The definitive report on the UK independent production sector', 22 March.

Broadcast – Indie Survey (2014) 'The definitive report on the UK independent production sector', 21 March.

Broadcast – International Supplement (2010) 'The dealmakers – format kings', 1 October: 44–5.

Broadcast – MipTV Supplement (2011a) '*Money Drop*: Endemol moves fast to build brand', 1 April: 36.

Broadcast – MipTV Supplement (2011b) '*MasterChef*: Shine Group breathes life into 20-year-old format with major rollout', 1 April: 38.

Broadcast – Supplement (2009) 'The annual survey of the UK independent TV producers', 20 March.

Brown, Les (1992) *Les Brown's Encyclopedia of Television*, 3rd edn. Detroit: Visible Ink.

Brzoznowski, Kristin (2011a) 'Case study: *Who Wants to Be a Millionaire?*', *WorldScreen*, October 2011: 446.

Brzoznowski, Kristin (2011b) '*Top Gear* firing on all cylinders', *TV Formats Weekly*, 1 August: 1–3.

Brzoznowski, Kristin (2012a) '2011: year in review', *TV Formats Weekly*, 2 January: 1–3.

Brzoznowski, Kristin (2012b) 'Case study: Warner Bros.' *The Bachelor*', *TV Formats Weekly*, 7 May: 1–4.

Brzoznowski, Kristin (2012c) 'Celebrating a decade of *TV Formats*', *World Screen – TV Formats*, October: 379.

Brzoznowski, Kristin (2012d) '*In Treatment* in session in Central Europe', *TV Formats Weekly*, 27 February: 1–2.

Brzoznowski, Kristin (2013a) 'French court rejects Endemol appeal in dilemma suit', *WorldScreen.com*, 27 November. http://www.worldscreen.com/articles/display/42366.

Brzoznowski, Kristin (2013b) 'Real or fake?', *WorldScreen.com*, 30 September.

Brzoznowski, Kristin (2015) 'Case study: *Gogglebox*', *TV Formats Weekly*, 12 January: 1–3.

Burnett, Mark (2005) *Jump In! Even If You Don't Know How to Swim*. New York: Ballantine.

Buxton, Frank and Bill Owen (1972) *The Big Broadcast: 1920–1950*. New York: Viking.

C21 Reporter (2012) 'Changing the meaning of success', *c21media.net*, 9 April. http://www.c21media.net/changing-the-meaning-of-success/?ss=%22changing+the+meaning+of+success%22.

C21 Media (2006) 'Endemol quiz reverses into BBC1', *c21media.net*, 20 July. http://www.c21media.net/endemol-quiz-reverses-into-bbc1.

Cabañas, Miguel (2012) '*Narcotelenovelas*, gender, and globalization in *Sin tetas no hay paraíso*', *Latin American Perspectives*, 39 (3): 74–87.

Campbell, Joseph ([1949] 2008) *The Hero With a Thousand Faces*, 3rd edn. Novato: New World Library.

Campbell, Lisa (2007) 'All3Media moves into Germany', *Broadcast*, 1 March: 12.

Campelli, Matthew (2014) 'First indies win C4 investment', *Broadcast*, 22 August: 1.

Camporesi, Valeria (2000) *Mass Culture and National Traditions: The BBC and American Broadcasting 1922–1954*. Fucecchio: European Press Academic.

Canny, Nichola (2002) 'Atlantic history, 1492–1700: scope, sources and methods', pp. 55–64 in Horst Pietschmann (ed.), *Atlantic History: History of the Atlantic System, 1580–1830*. Göttingen: Vandenhoeck & Ruprecht.

Carter, Meg (1996) 'Auntie sets the pace abroad', *Broadcast*, 19 April: 42–3.

Carter, Meg (2001) 'Who has the right?', *Broadcast*, 1 June: 16.

Carter, Meg (2002) 'Indies' bad trip', *Broadcast*, 18 October: 15.

Carugati, Anna (2011) 'Interview with Nigel Lythgoe', *WorldScreen*, October: 434–6.

Chalaby, Jean K. (2002) *The De Gaulle Presidency and the Media: Statism and Public Communications*. Basingstoke: Palgrave Macmillan.

Chalaby, Jean K. (2005) 'Towards an understanding of media transnationalism', pp. 1–13 in Jean K. Chalaby (ed.), *Transnational Television Worldwide: Towards a New Media Order*. London: I.B. Tauris.

Chalaby, Jean K. (2006) 'American cultural primacy in a new media order: a European perspective', *International Communication Gazette*, 68 (1): 33–51.

Chalaby, Jean K. (2007) 'Beyond nation-centrism: thinking international communication from a cosmopolitan perspective', *Studies in Communication Science*, 7 (1): 61–83.

Chalaby, Jean K. (2008) 'Advertising in the global age: transnational campaigns and pan-European television channels', *Global Media and Communication*, 4 (2): 139–56.

Chalaby, Jean K. (2009) *Transnational Television in Europe: Reconfiguring Global Communications Networks*. London: I.B. Tauris.

Clissold, Bradley D. (2004) '*Candid Camera* and the origins of reality TV: contextualising a historical precedent', pp. 33–53 in Su Holmes and Deborah Jermyn (eds.), *Understanding Reality Television*. London: Routledge.

Collins, Kathleen (2009) *Watching What We Eat: The Evolution of Television Cooking Shows*. New York: Continuum.

Collins, Richard (1998) *From Satellite to Single Market: New Communication Technology and European Public Service Television*. London: Routledge.

Committee on Broadcasting (1962) *Report of the Committee on Broadcasting, 1960*. London: HMSO.

Cooper-Chen, Anne (1994) *Games in the Global Village: A 50-Nation Study of Entertainment Television*. Bowling Green: Bowling Green State University Popular Press.

Curtis, Chris (2010) 'Plotting a stellar course for Zodiak', *Broadcast*, 24 September: 23.

Curtis, Chris (2014a) 'John de Mol, Talpa Media', *Broadcast*, 31 January: 20–3.

Curtis, Chris (2014b) 'Mahon lifts lid on Endemol deal', *Broadcast*, 12 September: 1.

Darlow, Michael (2004) *Independent Struggle: The Programme Makers Who Took On the TV Establishment*. London: Quartet.

Daswani, Mansha (2014) 'Format fever', *WorldScreen.com*, 24 November.

Davies, Simon (1998) 'A slice of American pie', *Broadcast*, 22 May: 16–17.

De Bruin, Joost (2012) '*NZ Idol*: nation building through format adaptation', pp. 223–41 in Tasha Oren and Sharon Shahaf (eds.), *Global Television Formats: Understanding Television Across Borders*. London: Routledge.

Dickens, Andy (2013) 'Continental drift', *c21media.net*, 18 December. http://www.c21media.net/continental-drift.

Dickens, Andy (2014) 'Social gathering', *c21media.net*, 3 October. http://www.c21media.net/telemundos-social-gathering.

Downing, John D. H. (2011) 'Media ownership, concentration, and control: the evolution of debate', pp. 140–68 in Janet Wasko, Graham Murdock and Helena Sousa (eds.), *The Handbook of Political Economy of Communications*. Chichester: Wiley-Blackwell.

Dyke, Greg (2005) *Inside Story*. London: Harper Perennial.

EBU (2005) *Trading TV Formats: The EBU Guide to the International Television Format Trade*. Geneva: EBU.

Elliott, Katy (2001) 'The deal maker', *Broadcast*, 19 January: 9–10.

Emmer, Peter (2002) 'In search of a system: the Atlantic economy, 1500–1800', pp. 169–78 in Horst Pietschmann (ed.), *Atlantic History: History of the Atlantic System, 1580–1830*. Göttingen: Vandenhoeck & Ruprecht.

Endemol (2007) *Annual Report 2006*. Hilversum: Endemol.

Endemol (2012) *Format Catalogue: MIPCom 2012*. Amsterdam: Endemol.

Esser, Andrea (2010) 'Television formats: primetime staple, global market', *Popular Communication*, 8: 273–92.

Esser, Andrea (2013) 'The format business: franchising television content', *International Journal of Digital Television*, 4 (2): 141–58.

Esser, Andrea and Pia Majbritt Jensen (2015) 'The use of international television formats by public service broadcasters in Australia, Denmark and Germany', *International Communication Gazette*, online pre-publication: 1–25.

Febvre, Lucien (1997) 'Preface', pp. 9–14 in Lucien Febvre and Henri-Jean Martin, *The Coming of the Book: The Impact of Printing 1450–1800*. London: Verso.

Feenstra, Robert C. (1998) 'Integration of trade and disintegration of production in the global economy', *Journal of Economic Perspectives*, 12 (4): 31–50.

Fejes, Fred (1981) 'Media imperialism: an assessment', *Media, Culture & Society*, 3 (3): 281–9.

Ferrari, Chiara (2012) '"National Mike": global host and global formats in early Italian television', pp. 128–47 in Tasha Oren and Sharon Shahaf (eds.), *Global Television Formats: Understanding Television Across Borders*. London: Routledge.

Flew, Terry (2012) 'Media as creative industries: conglomeration and globalization as accumulation strategies in an age of digital media', pp. 84–100 in Dwayne Winseck and Dal Yong Jin (eds.), *The Political Economies of Media: The Transformation of the Global Media Industries*. London: Bloomsbury.

Flew, Terry (2013) *Global Creative Industries*. Cambridge: Polity.

Forman, Denis (1997) *Persona Granada: Some Memories of Sidney Bernstein and the Early Days of Independent Television*. London: André Deutsch.

Franks, Nico (2013) 'Adapting novellas', *c21media.net*, 8 July. http://www.c21media.net/adapting-novelas/?ss=%22Adapting+nov%22.

Franks, Nico (2014) '*Rising Star* falls in Germany', *c21media.net*, 16 September. http://www.c21media.net/rising-star-falls-in-germany.

FRAPA (2009) *The FRAPA Report 2009: TV Formats to the World*. Cologne: FRAPA.

FRAPA (2011) *The FRAPA Report 2011: Protecting Format Rights*. Cologne: FRAPA.

Freedman, Des (2003) 'Who wants to be a millionaire? The politics of television exports', *Information, Communication & Society*, 6 (1): 24–41.

Fry, Andy (2013a) 'Sticking to the scripts', *c21media.net*, 7 May. http://www.c21media.net/sticking-to-the-scripts/?ss=%22Sticking+to+the+scripts%22.

Fry, Andy (2013b) 'Talent management', *c21media.net*, 29 April. http://www.c21media.net/archives/109579.

Fry, Andy (2014) 'The rush to reboot', *c21media.net*, 27 October. http://www.c21media.net/the-rush-to-reboot.

Fuller, Chris (1994a) 'Dutch double', *Broadcast*, 28 October: 13.

Fuller, Chris (1994b) 'Winning games', *Broadcast – MipTV Supplement*, 16 April: 14.

Fuller, Simon (2011) 'Simon Fuller on how "Idol" began: Brit music maven discusses the show's launch', *Variety*, 20 May. http://variety.com/2011/tv/news/simon-fuller-on-how-idol-began-2-1118037190.

Gaitán, Fernando (2010) Interviewed by *WorldScreen*, in *WorldScreen*, October: 136.

García Canclini, Néstor (1995) *Hybrid Cultures: Strategies for Entering and Leaving Modernity*. Minneapolis: University of Minnesota Press.

Garnham, Nicholas (2005) 'An analysis of the implications of the "creative industries" approach to arts and media policy making in the United Kingdom', *International Journal of Cultural Policy*, 11 (1): 15–29.

Garnham, Nicholas (2011) 'The political economy of communication revisited', pp. 41–61 in Janet Wasco, Graham Murdock and Helena Sousa (eds.), *The Handbook of Political Economy of Communications*. Chichester: Wiley.

Gereffi, Gary (1994) 'The organization of buyer-driven global commodity chains: how U.S. retailers shape overseas production networks', in Gary Gereffi and Miguel Korzeniewicz (eds.), *Commodity Chains and Global Capitalism*. Westport: Praeger.

Gereffi, Gary (1995) 'Global production systems and third world development', pp. 100–42 in Barbara Stallings (ed.), *Global Change, Regional Response: The New International Context of Development*. Cambridge: Cambridge University Press.

Gereffi, Gary (1999) 'International trade and industrial upgrading in the apparel commodity chain', *Journal of International Economics*, 48 (1): 37–70.

Gereffi, Gary, John Humphrey and Timothy Sturgeon (2005) 'The govern-ance of global value chains', *Review of International Political Economy*, 12 (1): 78–104.

Gereffi, Gary, Miguel Korzeniewicz and Roberto P. Korzeniewicz (1994) 'Introduction: global commodity chains', pp. 1–14 in Gary Gereffi and Miguel Korzeniewicz (eds.), *Commodity Chains and Global Capitalism*. Westport: Praeger.

Gibbon, Peter and Stefano Ponte (2008) 'Global value chains: from governance to governmentality?', *Economy and Society*, 37 (3): 365–92.

Gibson, Janine (1997) 'Pearson grabs All American', *Broadcast*, 3 October: 1.

Gilbert, Paul (2014) Senior vice president, international formats, CBS Studios International. In panel 'The other format: scripted series going global', NATPE 2014 session, 4 February. https://www.youtube.com/watch?v=MblzLECoxf4&list= PLK7DwLI4AtM2mGuTSQuwh2zN8TxThSk5o&utm.

Gillespie, Marie (1995) *Television, Ethnicity and Cultural Change*. London: Routledge.

Graham, Jefferson (1988) *Come On Down!!! The TV Game Show Book*. New York: Abbeville.

Grasso, Aldo (2004) *Storia della televisione italiana*, new edn. Milan: Garzanti.

Griffen-Foley, Bridget (2009) *Changing Stations: The Story of Australian Commercial Radio*. Sydney: University of New South Wales Press.

Gross, Peter and Karol Jakubowicz (eds.) (2013) *Media Transformations in the Post-Communist World: Eastern Europe's Tortured Path to Change*. Plymouth: Lexington Books.

Guider, Elizabeth (2005) 'Talbot created int'l formats', *Variety*, 18 July: 48.

Guider, Elizabeth (2013) 'L.A. screenings recap', *WorldScreen Weekly*, 23 May: 1–6.

Hallenberger, Gerd (1992) '"Amerikanisierung" versus "Germanisierung": Quizsendungen und Game Shows im deutschen Fernsehen – eine "mittatlantische" Programmform?', pp. 81–93 in Irmela Schneider (ed.), *Amerikanische Einstellung: Deutsches Fernsehen und US-amerikanische Produktionen*. Heidelberg: Universitatsverlag Winter.

Hallenberger, Gerd and Joachim Kaps (1991) *Hätten Sie's Gewusst? Die Quizsendungen und Game Shows des deutschen Fernsehens*. Marburg: Jonas.

Handley, Claire (1998) 'Planet 24 cooks up a Polish breakfast', *Broadcast*, 13 February: 13.

Havens, Timothy (2006) *Global Television Marketplace*. London: BFI.

Hazelton, John (2001) 'Sony's different sides', *Broadcast International*, 5 October: 32–4.

Herman, Edward S. and Robert W. McChesney (1997) *The Global Media: The New Missionaries of Corporate Capitalism*. London: Cassell.

Hesmondhalgh, David (2005) 'Media and cultural policy as public policy: the case of the British Labour government', *International Journal of Cultural Policy*, 11 (1): 95–109.

Hesmondhalgh, David (2013) *The Cultural Industries*, 3rd edn. London: Sage.

Hill, Annette (2002) '*Big Brother*: the real audience', *Television and New Media*, 3 (3): 323–41.

Hill, Annette (2005) *Reality TV: Audiences and Popular Factual Television*. London: Routledge.

Hogan, James (1997) *Let a Thousand Flowers Bloom: Independent Producers and Democratic Representation*. London: Department of Sociology Working Paper Series, LSE.

Hoggart, Richard ([1957] 2009) *The Uses of Literacy: Aspects of Working-Class Life*. London: Penguin.

Holmes, Su and Deborah Jermyn (2004) *Understanding Reality Television*. London: Routledge.

Holt, Jennifer and Alisa Perren (2009) *Media Industries: History, Theory, and Method*. Malden: Wiley-Blackwell.

Hopkins, Terence K. and Immanuel Wallerstein (1986) 'Commodity chains in the world economy prior to 1800', *Review*, 10 (1): 157–70.

Humphreys, Peter J. (1996) *Mass Media and Media Policy in Western Europe*. Manchester: Manchester University Press.

Ishita, Saeko (2000) 'Television genre and audience: quiz shows in Japanese television', *Studies in the Humanities: Bulletin of the Faculty of Literature and Human Sciences*, 52 (5): 25–38.

ITV (2014) *ITV plc Annual Report and Accounts 2013*. London: ITV.

Jeffcutt, Paul and Andy C. Pratt (2002) 'Editorial: managing creativity in the cultural industries', *Creativity and Innovation Management*, 11 (4): 225–33.

Jenkinson, David (2007) 'Armoza backs formats', *c21media.net*, 30 April. http://www.c21media.net/armoza-backs-formats/?ss=Armoza+backs+formats.

Jones, Mike (1995) 'Analysis', *Broadcast – The Indie Survey*, 21 July: 5.

Jost, François (2005) 'La télévision des années 70 existe-t-elle?', pp. 13–32 in François Jost (ed.), *Années 70: la télévision en jeu*. Paris: CNRS.

Kanter, Jake (2011) 'All3 sets challenge to bidders', *Broadcast*, 15 July: 5.

Kanter, Jake (2012) 'Blasts from the past', *Broadcast*, 4 May: 26–7.

Kanter, Jake (2014) 'Pact chief slams BBC and C4 for "peddling terms of trade myth"', *Broadcast*, 19 September: 6.

Kanter, Jake, Andreas Wiseman and Peter White (2014) 'Drama set for digital revolution', *Broadcast*, 30 May: 1.

Kavka, Misha (2012) *Reality TV*. Edinburgh: Edinburgh University Press.

Keane, Michael (2004) 'Asia: new growth areas', in Albert Moran and Michael Keane (eds.), *Television Across Asia: Television Industries, Programme Formats and Globalization*. London: Routledge.

Keane, Michael and Albert Moran (2008) 'Television's new engines', *Television & New Media*, 9 (2): 155–69.

Keighron, Peter (2001) 'Super indies soar to a higher level', *Broadcast*, 14 September: 18–19.

Khalsa, Balihar (2013) 'C5 and cashflow worry indies', *Broadcast*, 31 May: 1.

Kilborn, Richard (1994) '"How real can you get?":' Recent developments in "reality" television', *European Journal of Communication*, 9 (4): 421–39.

Kilborn, Richard (2003) *Staging the Real: Factual TV Programming in the Age of Big Brother*. Manchester: Manchester University Press.

Koranteng, Juliana (2012) 'Say it again', *WorldScreen*, April: 338–44.

Kunz, William M. (2007) *Culture Conglomerates: Consolidation in the Motion Picture and Television Industries*. Lanham: Rowman & Littlefield.

Lacalle, Charo (2001) *El espectador televisivo: los programas de entretenimiento*. Barcelona: Gedisa.

Lacroix, Jean-Guy and Gaetan Tremblay (1997a) 'The emergence of cultural industries into the foreground of industrialization and commodification: elements of context', *Current Sociology*, 45 (4): 11–37.

Lacroix, Jean-Guy and Gaetan Tremblay (1997b) 'The "information society" and cultural industries theory', *Current Sociology*, 45 (4): 1–154.

Lambert, Stephen and Eli Holzman, with Mark Levine (2011) *Undercover Boss: Inside the TV Phenomenon that is Changing Bosses and Employees Everywhere*. San Francisco: Jossey-Bass.

Lampel, Joseph and Jamal Shamsie (2003) 'Capabilities in motion: new organizational forms and the reshaping of the Hollywood movie industry', *Journal of Management Studies*, 40 (8): 2189–210.

Lampel, Joseph and Jamal Shamsie (2006) 'Uncertain globalization: evolutionary scenarios for the future development of cultural industries', pp. 275–86 in Joseph Lampel, Jamal Shamsie and Theresa K. Lant (eds.), *The Business of Culture: Strategic Perspectives on Entertainment and Media*. Mahwah: Lawrence Erlbaum.

Leveneur, Laurence (2005) 'La fabrique du jeu: de l'artisanat à l'âge d'usine', pp. 181–209 in François Jost (ed.), *Années 70: la télévision en jeu*. Paris: CNRS.

Leveneur, Laurence (2009) *Les travestissements du jeu télévisé*. Paris: Sorbonne Nouvelle.

Lévi-Strauss, Claude (1983) *The Raw and the Cooked: Mythologiques, Volume One*. Chicago: University of Chicago Press.

Liebes, Tamar and Elihu Katz (1993) *The Export of Meaning: Cross-Cultural Readings of Dallas*. Cambridge: Polity.

Littlejohn, Sarah (1997) 'Barraclough Carey to merge with Mentorn', *Broadcast*, 10 January: 1.

Longnos, Brice (2014) 'Korean TV formats: a new Korean wave?', *Korea Blog*, 18 July. http://blog.korea.net/?p=20768.

Lotz, Amanda D. (2007) *The Television Will Be Revolutionized*. New York: New York University Press.

M&M Global (2015) *Global Agency Network Map 2015*. London: M&M Global.

Mansfield, Laura (2014) 'US-style pitches bring vitality', *Broadcast*, 5 September: 20.

Marlow, Jane (2014) 'Perfect pitch', *WorldScreen.com*, 7 October.

Mato, Daniel (2005) 'The transnationalization of the *telenovela* industry, territorial references, and the production of markets and representations of transnational identities', *Television & New Media*, 6 (4): 423–44.

Mattelart, Armand (2002) 'An archaeology of the global era: constructing a belief', *Media, Culture & Society*, 24 (5): 591–612.

Mayer, Vicki (2014) 'Cast-aways: the plights and pleasures of reality casting and production studies', pp. 57–73 in Laurie Ouellette (ed.), *A Companion to Reality Television*. Chichester: Wiley-Blackwell.

McCabe, Janet (2013) 'Introduction: "Oh Betty, you really are beautiful"', in Janet McCabe and Kim Akass (eds.), *TV's Betty Goes Global: From Telenovela to International Brand*. London: I.B. Tauris.

McCabe, Janet and Kim Akass (eds.) (2013) *TV's Betty Goes Global: From Telenovela to International Brand*. London: I.B. Tauris.

McCann, Bryan (2004) *Hello, Hello Brazil: Popular Music in the Making of Modern Brazil*. Durham: Duke University Press.

McCarthy, Anna (2004) '"Stanley Milgram, Allen Funt, and me": postwar social science and the "first wave" of reality TV', pp. 19–39 in Susan Murray and Laurie Ouellette (eds.), *Reality TV: Remaking Television Culture*. New York: New York University Press.

McNeil, Alex (1997) *Total Television*, 4th edn with CD-ROM. Harmondsworth: Penguin.

Mediaset (2014) 'Scripted formats'. http://mediasetdistribution.com/scripted/home.

Mediatique (2008) *All Grown Up: Cash, Creativity and the Independent Production Sector*. London: Mediatique.

Merlin, Louis (1966) *C'était formidable!* Paris: Julliard.

Middleton, Richard (2014) 'Latin leanings', *c21media.net*, 4 June. http://www.c21media.net/latin-leanings.

Middleton, Richard (2015) 'Adapting to Asia', *c21media.net*, 20 January. http://www.c21media.net/adapting-to-asia.

Miller, Jade L. (2010) 'Ugly Betty goes global: global networks of localized content in the telenovela industry', *Global Media and Communication*, 6 (2): 198–217.

Miller, Stephen (2005) 'Paul Talbot, 86, sold American television fare to the world', *New York Sun*, 12 July: 6.

Miller, Toby, Govil Nitin, John McMurria, Richard Maxwell and Ting Wang (2011) *Global Hollywood 2*. London: BFI.

Moran, Albert (1985) *Image and Industry: Australian Television Drama Production*. Sydney: Currency.

Moran, Albert (1998) *Copycat Television: Globalisation, Program Formats and Culture Identity*. Luton: University of Luton Press.

Moran, Albert (2006) *Understanding the Global TV Format*. Bristol: Intellect.

Moran, Albert (2013a) 'Global television formats: genesis and growth', *Critical Studies in Television*, 8 (2): 1–19.

Moran, Albert (2013b) *TV Format Mogul: Reg Grundy's Transnational Career*. Bristol: Intellect.

Moran, Albert and Michael Keane (2004) *Television Across Asia: Television Industries, Programme Formats and Globalization*. London: Routledge.

Mosco, Vincent (2009) *The Political Economy of Communication*, 2nd edn. London: Sage.

Navarro, Vinicius (2012) 'More than copycat television: format adaptation as performance', pp. 23–36 in Tasha Oren and Sharon Shahaf (eds.), *Global Television Formats: Understanding Television Across Borders*. London: Routledge.

Nededog, Jethro (2014) 'Inside Fox's war over $50 million reality gamble "Utopia"', *Wrap*, 29 April. http://www.thewrap.com/fox-utopia-simon-andreae-david-hill-john-de-mol-clash.

Nederveen Pieterse, Jan (2004) *Globalization and Culture: Global Mélange*. Lanham: Rowman & Littlefield.

Negrine, Ralph (1988) 'Introduction', pp. 1–21 in Ralph Negrine (ed.), *Satellite Broadcasting: The Politics and Implications of the New Media*. London: Routledge.

Nordenstreng, Kaarle and Herbert I. Schiller (1979) *National Sovereignty and International Communication*. Norwood: Ablex.

Ofcom (2006) *Review of the Television Production Sector: Consultation Document*. London: Ofcom.

Ofcom (2014) *The Communications Market Report*. London: Ofcom.

Oliver & Ohlbaum (2014) *Channel 4: Taking Risks, Challenging the Mainstream*. London: Channel 4 and Oliver & Ohlbaum.

Oren, Tasha (2013) 'On the line: format, cooking and competition as television values', *Critical Studies in Television*, 8 (2): 20–35.

Ouellette, Laurie (2014) 'Introduction', pp. 1–8 in Laurie Ouellette (ed.), *A Companion to Reality Television*. Chichester: Wiley-Blackwell.

Ouellette, Laurie and Susan Murray (2004) 'Introduction', pp. 1–15 in Susan Murray and Laurie Ouellette (eds.), *Reality TV: Remaking Television Culture*. New York: New York University Press.

Pact (2002) *Pact Submission to ITC Programme Supply Review*. London: Pact.

Pact (2008) *Response to Ofcom PSB Review: Phase 1*. London: Pact.

Page, David and William Crawley (2001) *Satellites over South Asia: Broadcasting, Culture and the Public Interest*. New Delhi: Sage.

Paulu, Burton (1961) *British Broadcasting in Transition*. London: Macmillan.

Peyrefitte, Alain (1994) *C'était de Gaulle. Tome 1*. Paris: de Fallois and Fayard.

Phillips, William (1995) 'Financially dependent', *Broadcast in Production*, 5 May: 4–6.

Picard, Robert (2005) 'Unique characteristics and business dynamics of media products', *Journal of Media Business Studies*, 2 (2): 61–9.

Pickard, Michael (2011) 'Laughing all the way to the bank', *c21media.net*, 29 July. http://www.c21media.net/laughing-all-the-way-to-the-bank/?ss=Laughing+all+the+way+to+the+bank.

Pietschmann, Horst (2002) 'Introduction: Atlantic history – history between European history and global history', pp. 11–54 in Horst Pietschmann (ed.), *Atlantic History: History of the Atlantic System, 1580–1830*. Göttingen: Vandenhoeck & Ruprecht.

Porter, Michael E. (1998) *The Competitive Advantage of Nations*. Basingstoke: Palgrave.

Porter, Michael E. (2004) *Competitive Advantage: Creating and Sustaining Superior Performance*. New York: Free Press.

Potter, Ian (2008) *The Rise and Rise of the Independents*. Isleworth: Guerilla.

Pratt, Andy C. and Galina Gornostaeva (2009) 'The governance of innovation in the film and television industry: a case study of London, UK', pp. 119–36 in Andy C. Pratt and Paul Jeffcut (eds.), *Creativity, Innovation and the Cultural Economy*. London: Routledge.

Pratt, Andy C. and Paul Jeffcut (2009) 'Conclusion', pp. 265–76 in Andy C. Pratt and Paul Jeffcut (eds.), *Creativity, Innovation and the Cultural Economy*. London: Routledge.

Raikes, Philip, Michael Friis Jensen and Stefano Ponte (2000) 'Global commodity chain analysis and the French filière approach: comparison and critique', *Economy and Society*, 29 (3): 390–417.

RDF Media Group (2008) *Annual Report and Accounts 2008*. London: RDF.

Reevel, Philip (2014) '*Bake Off* final takes bronze', *Broadcast*, 24 October: 42.

Ritchie, Jean (2000) *Big Brother: The Official Unseen Story*. London: Channel 4 Books.

Rivero, Yeidy M. (2009) 'Havana as a 1940s–1950s Latin American media capital', *Critical Studies in Media Communication*, 26 (3): 275–93.

Robertson, Colin (2000) 'Woman of the people', *Broadcast*, 7 July: 20.

Robins, Kevin and Asu Aksoy (2005) 'Whoever looks always finds: transnational viewing and knowledge-experience', pp. 14–42 in Jean K. Chalaby (ed.), *Transnational Television Worldwide: Towards a New Media Order*. London: I.B. Tauris.

Rohter, Larry (2006) 'How do you say "desperate" in Spanish?', *www.nytimes. com*, 13 August. http://www.nytimes.com/2006/08/13/arts/television/13roht. html?pagewanted=all&_r=0.

Rosser, Michael (2009) 'Ukraine makes its own version of *Yes Minister*', *Broadcast*, 20 November. http://www.broadcastnow.co.uk/news/international/ ukraine-makes-its-own-version-of-yes-minister/5008309.article.

Rosser, Michael (2011) 'India to remake *Money Drop*', *Broadcast*, 20 September. http://www.broadcastnow.co.uk/india-to-remake-money-drop/5032294.article.

Roudometof, Victor (2005) 'Transnationalism, cosmopolitanism and glocalization', *Current Sociology*, 53 (1): 114–35.

Rouse, Lucy (1999) 'Studio deal opens up US for Hat Trick', *Broadcast*, 23 July: 1.

Rouse, Lucy (2001) 'Are imports on the slide?', *Broadcast – International Supplement*, 5 October: 38–9.

Rushfield, Richard (2011) *American Idol: The Untold Story*. New York: Hyperion.

Rushton, Kathrine (2009) 'Snap buy boosts Endemol UK', *Broadcast*, 27 November: 1.

Rushton, Kathrine (2010) 'Shine rises to top of indie pile', *Broadcast*, 19 March: 1.

Sakr, Naomi (2007) *Arab Television Today*. London: I.B. Tauris.

Schiller, Herbert I. (1992) *Mass Communications and American Empire*. New York: Augustus M. Kelley.

Schmitt, Marie-Paule (2005) *Les jeux radiophoniques en France, 1944–1974: étude comparative des radios publiques françaises et de deux stations privées, Radio-Luxembourg et Europe N°1. Tome Premier*. Paris: Ecole Nationale des Chartes.

Schwartz, David, Steve Ryan and Fred Wostbrock (1999) *The Encyclopedia of TV Game Shows*, 3rd edn. New York: Checkmark Books.

Screen Digest (2005) *The Global Trade in Television Formats*. Cologne and London: FRAPA and Screen Digest.

Sendall, Bernard (1982) *Independent Television in Britain. Vol. 1: Origin and Foundation, 1946–1972*. London: Macmillan.

Shahar, Keren (2014) Head of distribution and acquisitions, Keshet International. In panel 'Focus on Israel: how to create successful scripted formats/dramas?', MipTV session, 9 April. https://www.youtube.com/watch?v=Oleo-vJZHGk.

Shed Media (2009) *Annual Report and Accounts 2008*. London: Shed Media.

Sinclair, John (1999) *Latin American Television*. Oxford: Oxford University Press.

Sinclair, John and Graeme Turner (eds.) (2004) *Contemporary World Television*. London: BFI.

Sinclair, John, Elizabeth Jacka and Stuart Cunningham (eds.) (1996) *New Patterns in Global Television: Peripheral Vision*. Oxford: Oxford University Press.

Singh, Sukhpreet (2010) *The Protection of Television Formats: Intellectual Property and Market Based Strategies*. Bournemouth University: PhD thesis.

Smith, Quentin and Richard Life (1993) 'Dutch indies merge into world force', *Broadcast*, 17 December: 4.

Smitherman, Gary (2013) 'The feelgood factor', *c21media.net*, 12 June. http://www.c21media.net/the-feelgood-factor/?ss=%22The+feelgood+factor%22.

Sparks, Colin (2007) 'What's wrong with globalization?', *Global Media and Communication*, 3 (2): 133–55.

Sparks, Colin (2008) *Globalization, Development and the Mass Media*. London: Sage.

Starkey, Ken, Christopher Barnatt and Sue Tempest (2000) 'Beyond networks and hierarchies: latent organizations in the U.K. television industry', *Organization Science*, 11 (3), May–June: 299–305.

Starks, Michael (2013) *The Digital Television: Origins to Outcomes*. Basingstoke: Palgrave Macmillan.

Steemers, Jeanette (2004) *Selling Television: British Television in the Global Marketplace*. London: BFI.

Stephens, Joanna (2013) 'Mega hits', *World Screen – TV Formats*, April: 202–6.

Stephens, Joanna (2014a) 'Return to forever', *WorldScreen.com*, 7 October.

Stephens, Joanna (2014b) 'Twice as nice: the business of adapting scripted dramas and comedies across borders is picking up steam', *WorldScreen*, April: 292–300.

Stevenson, Robert L. (1984) 'Pseudo debate', *Journal of Communication*, 34 (1): 134–42.

Straubhaar, Joseph (2007) *World Television: From Global to Local*. London: Sage.

Straubhaar, Joseph (2012) 'Telenovelas in Brazil: from traveling scripts to a genre and proto-format both national and transnational', pp. 148–77 in Tasha Oren and Sharon Shahaf (eds.), *Global Television Formats: Understanding Television Across Borders*. London: Routledge.

Strauss, Will (2002) 'Death by a 1,000 cuts', *Broadcast*, 11 October: 16.

Stuart, Jay (2012) 'The super indies', *WorldScreen*, April: 152–8.

Sturgeon, Timothy (2009) 'From commodity chains to value chains: inter-disciplinary theory building in an age of globalization', pp. 110–35 in Jennifer Bair (ed.), *Frontiers of Commodity Chain Research*. Stanford: Stanford University Press.

Tartaglione, Nancy (2014) 'MIPTV: is Turkey as hot as it's cracked up to be? Can formats really go west?', *deadline.com*, 9 April. http://deadline.com/2014/04/turkey-television-industry-formats-on-rise-miptv-711365.

TBI Formats (2013) 'Reality round the clock', *TBI Formats*, October/November: 23–5.

TBI Formats (2014a) 'Europe's most valuable formats', *TBI Formats*, April/May: 22–5.

TBI Formats (2014b) 'Format focus: *Dropped* into reality', *TBI Formats*, April/May: 16.

Thussu, Daya K. (2007) *Media on the Move: Global Flow and Contra-Flow*. London: Routledge.

Thussu, Daya K. (2013) *Communicating India's Soft Power: Buddha to Bollywood*. Basingstoke: Palgrave Macmillan.

Tomlinson, John (1991) *Cultural Imperialism: A Critical Introduction*. London: Continuum.

Tomlinson, John (1999) *Globalization and Culture*. Cambridge: Polity.

Torre, Paul (2012) 'Reversal of fortune? Hollywood faces new competition in global media trade', pp. 178–200 in Tasha Oren and Sharon Shahaf (eds.), *Global Television Formats: Understanding Television Across Borders*. London: Routledge.

Tracey, Michael (1985) 'The poisoned chalice? International television and the idea of dominance', *Daedalus*, 114 (4): 17–56.

Tunstall, Jeremy (1977) *The Media Are American: Anglo-American Media in the World*. London: Constable.

Tunstall, Jeremy (2008) *The Media Were American: U.S. Mass Media in Decline*. Oxford: Oxford University Press.

Tunstall, Jeremy and David Machin (1999) *The Anglo-American Media Connection*. Oxford: Oxford University Press.

Waisbord, Silvio (2004) 'McTV: understanding the global popularity of television formats', *Television & New Media*, 5 (4): 359–83.

Waller, Ed (2005) 'FRAPA unravels €2.4bn global format industry', *c21media.net*, 12 April. http://www.c21media.net/?s=FRAPA+unravels+%E2%82%AC2.4bn+global+format+industry.

Waller, Ed (2006) 'EBU to launch pubcaster format exchange', *c21media.net*, 10 April. http://www.c21media.net/ebu-to-launch-pubcaster-format-exchange.

Waller, Ed (2007) 'Reality rules the fall', *c21media.net*, 23 May. http://www.c21media.net/reality-rules-the-fall/?ss=%22Reality+rules+the+fall%22.

Waller, Ed (2010a) 'Israeli format wave arrives', *c21media.net*, 20 April. http://www.c21media.net/israeli-format-wave-arrives.

Waller, Ed (2010b) 'Love in a cold climate', *c21media.net*, 1 February. http://www.c21media.net/love-in-a-cold-climate/?ss=%22Love+in+a+cold+climate%22.

Waller, Ed (2010c) 'Playing the long game', *c21media.net*, 26 January. http://www.c21media.net/playing-the-long-game/?ss=%22playing+the+long+game%22.

Waller, Ed (2011a) 'The idea of selling ideas', *c21media.net*, 2 October. http://www.c21media.net/the-idea-of-selling-ideas.

Waller, Ed (2011b) 'Upskilling by adapting formats', *c21media.net*, 19 December. http://www.c21media.net/perspectives/upskilling-by-adapting-formats.

Waller, Ed (2012) 'The format factor', *c21media.net*, 22 May. http://www.c21media.net/remakes-take-over-from-reboots/?ss=%22The+format+factor%22.

Waller, Ed (2013a) 'Brazilian boom', *c21media.net*, 18 February. http://www.c21media.net/archives/101652.

Waller, Ed (2013b) 'Chinese whispers', *c21media.net*, 2 December. http://www.c21media.net/chinese-whispers.

Waller, Ed (2013c) 'De-risking pilot season', *c21media.net*, 14 May. http://www.c21media.net/the-globalisation-of-pilot-season/?ss=%22De-risking+pilot+season%22.

Waller, Ed (2014a) 'Korean wave crosses the Pacific', *c21media.net*, 7 September. http://www.c21media.net/korean-wave-crosses-the-pacific.

Waller, Ed (2014b) 'Risk management', *c21media.net*, 23 May. http://www.c21media.net/perspective/risk-management-2.

Waller, Ed (2014c) 'Think local, act local', *c21media.net*, 6 February. http://www.c21media.net/perspective/think-local-act-local.

Wallerstein, Immanuel (1983) *Historical Capitalism*. London: Verso.

Webdale, Jonathan (2005) 'Working Title returns to UK television', *c21media.net*, 27 July. http://www.c21media.net/working-title-returns-to-uk-television.

White, Peter (2013) 'UK indies storm US upfronts', *Broadcast*, 5 April: 1.

White, Peter (2014a) 'ABC eyes UK for "risky" series', *Broadcast*, 28 November: 10.

White, Peter (2014b) 'DNI replaces Julian Bellamy', *Broadcast*, 7 November: 2.

White, Peter (2014c) 'First-look deals double in 2014', *Broadcast*, 21 November: 1.

White, Peter (2014d) 'UK shows primed for the US', *Broadcast*, 18 April: 8.

Whittingham, Clive (2014) 'War of independents', *c21media.net*, 20 September. http://www.c21media.net/war-of-independents.

Whittingham, Clive (2015) 'Playing catch-up', *c21media.net*, 9 January. http://www.c21media.net/playing-catch-up.

Whittock, Jess (2011a) 'Dancing on air', *c21media.net*, 6 June. http://www.c21media.net/dancing-on-air/?ss=%22Dancing+on+air%22.

Whittock, Jess (2011b) 'India scores Hat Trick improv format', *c21media. net*, 16 November. http://www.c21media.net/india-scores-hat-trick-improv-format/?ss=India+scores.

Winseck, Dwayne (2012) 'The political economies of media and the transformation of the global media industries', pp. 3–48 in Dwayne Winseck and Dal Yong Jin (eds.), *The Political Economies of Media: The Transformation of the Global Media Industries*. London: Bloomsbury.

Wood, David (2010a) 'How to make it in the US', *Broadcast*, 25 June: 26–8.

Wood, David (2010b) 'The new British invasion', *Broadcast*, 21 May: 25.

Woods, Faye (2014) 'Classed femininity, performativity, and camp in British structured reality programming', *Television & New Media*, 15 (3): 197–214.

Woodward, John (1998) 'Our time has come', *Broadcast*, 30 January: 18.

World Screen (2011) Interview with Jeffrey Schlesinger, president, Warner Bros. International Television, *World Screen*, May: 22.

WTO (2009) *International Trade Statistics 2009*. Geneva: WTO.

WTO (2013) *International Trade Statistics 2013*. Geneva: WTO.

Yorke, John (2013) *Into the Woods: A Five-Act Journey into Story*. London: Penguin.

Zein, Andrew (2014) Senior vice president, creative format development and sales, Warner Bros. International Television Production. In panel 'The other format: scripted series going global', NATPE 2014 session, 4 February. https://www.youtube.com/watch?v=MblzLECoxf4&list=PLK7DwLI4AtM2mGuTSQuwh2zN8TxThSk5o&utm.

Zhao, Yuezhi (2008) *Communication in China*. Lanham: Rowman & Littlefield.

Index